LUTHER'S THEOLOGICAL TESTAMENT

O dear Lord Jesus Christ, . . . help us who are poor and miserable, who sigh to you and earnestly seek you, according to the grace you have given us through your Holy Spirit, who with you and the Father lives and reigns, forever praised. Amen.

MARTIN LUTHER, PREFACE, THE SCHMALKALD ARTICLES

LUTHER'S THEOLOGICAL TESTAMENT

The Schmalkald Articles

William R. Russell

Fortress Press   **Minneapolis**

To my dear wife, Ann, with loving gratitude

LUTHER'S THEOLOGICAL TESTAMENT
The Schmalkald Articles

Text design: Joseph Bonyata
Cover design: Terry Bentley

Library of Congress Cataloging-in-Publication Data

Russell, William R., 1954-
    Luther's theological testament : the Schmalkald articles / William R. Russell.
      p.   cm.
    Includes bibliographical reference (p.) and index.
    ISBN 0-8006-2660-5 (alk. paper) :
      1. Luther, Martin, 1483–1546. Schmalkaldischen Artikel.
  I. Luther, Martin, 1483–1546. Schmalkaldischen Artikel. English.
  II. Title.
  BX8070.S4R87   1994
  238'.41—dc20   94-33437
                                                            CIP

Manufactured in the U.S.A.   AF 1–2660
99   98   97   96   95   1   2   3   4   5   6   7   8   9   10

Contents

Foreword
by George W. Forell

IT HAS BEEN FREQUENTLY NOTED THAT THE CONSCIOUSNESS OF THE IMMEDI-
ate approach of death has the tendency to focus the mind on essentials. Samuel
Johnson once observed, "When a man knows he is to be hanged in a fortnight,
it concentrates his mind wonderfully." It is William Russell's point that Martin
Luther, at the time he was asked to prepare the *Schmalkald Articles*, was convinced that the end of his life was very near. This perception made it urgent
for him to express those thoughts that seemed most important to him, to state
only the bare essentials of the Christian faith. Russell suggests that we should
read and study these articles as Luther's Last Will and Testament, and he wants
to assist us in this investigation.

In view of the fact that Luther wrote so much and that even in English we
have a fifty-five volume translation of his works and in addition a multitude of
other sermons, letters, and commentaries—not to mention the vast secondary
literature that has been produced in this century alone—we may be well advised to follow Russell's recommendation. Not all theologians are interesting
people. The conventional wisdom has it that they are rather boring. Be that as
it may, Luther was never dull, but a very fascinating human being. The result
has been that every aspect of his life has been investigated from all possible
points of view. Not only historians and students of religion, but sociologists,
educators, linguists, psychologists, and psychiatrists have tried to understand
and interpret him. The result has been that Luther's own concern has sometimes been lost in the multitude of studies that his fascinating personality has
evoked.

This book claims that Luther wanted only to be a teacher of God's Word.
The *Schmalkald Articles* furnished a key to Luther's understanding of God's
plan for humanity as revealed in His Word. The document eventually became
part of *The Book of Concord*, the collection of confessions that guides the Lutheran movement in its reading of the Scriptures, the only writing of Luther
besides his Large and Small Catechism so honored. It may help us understand
him as he wanted to be understood. At the Diet of Worms Luther may not
have said, "Here I stand," but he wrote about the document here presented:

"These are the articles on which I must stand and on which I intend to stand, God willing, until my death." We owe William R. Russell a debt of gratitude for introducing us to them.

GEORGE WOLFGANG FORELL
CARVER PROFESSOR EMERITUS
THE UNIVERSITY OF IOWA

Preface

THE FIRST BOOK-LENGTH INVESTIGATION INTO THE HISTORY AND THEOLOGY of Martin Luther's Schmalkald Articles in English—this fact continues to surprise me. For nearly five hundred years these articles have, in a concise and accessible manner, pointed to Luther's highest theological priorities. Indeed, because this writing is part of Lutheranism's confessional heritage and thus also officially bears witness to the theological priority of Lutherans as well as Luther himself, one would expect that any number of books through the centuries would have attempted to explicate such an important document. Unfortunately such is not the case. This book therefore is an effort to help fill a gap in the understanding of Luther and the Reformation.

This book, based on the Schmalkald Articles, is more than mere commentary on the text. This testamentary document, written rather late in Luther's career, refers to so many of the major controversies and personalities of the Reformation period that a complete investigation would lead to a work far exceeding the confines of a volume this size.[1] In order to point to these matters—without wanting to distract—a rather large number of annotations have been included, indicating some of the issues that stand behind Luther's text as well as where the curious can go to find more information. The goal of this work is thus kept in focus, namely, to provide an accurate and readable introduction to the theology of Martin Luther and the Lutheran confessional writings from the perspective of the Schmalkald Articles.

There is a small but real controversy regarding the document that is the object of this investigation: English-speaking scholars disagree about whether we have before us the "Smalcald" Articles or the "Schmalkald" Articles.[2]

---

1. An example of how a book like this might grow in to a work of great magnitude is Albrecht Peters, *Kommentar zu Luthers Katechismen*, 5 vols. (Göttingen: Vandenhoeck & Ruprecht, 1990–).

2. The disagreement of scholars became evident when, in 1991, *LQ* published two of my articles: "Luther's Theological Testament, the Smalcald Articles" (Autumn) and "A Theological Guide to Luther's Smalcald Articles" (Winter). Both articles had been submitted using "Schmalkald" in the title. The spelling "Smalcald," however, was mandated by the editorial board. Moreover, my doctoral dissertation, which also dealt with this document, even goes so far as to argue for the opposite position of the one that will be advocated here (see *The Smalcald Articles as a Confessional Document in the Context of Luther's Life and Thought* [Ann Arbor: UMI, 1990], xiii).

"Smalcald" made its way into English through the Latin and has been, until rather recently, the more popular spelling. "Schmalkald," however, is to be preferred. This spelling more closely resembles the German original (*Die Schmalkaldischen Artikel*). This is helpful because most of the secondary literature related to Luther's articles is in German. Also, "Schmalkald" makes a more obvious connection with the historical circumstances surrounding the document's inception and the town of Schmalkalden, Germany, which has lent its name to these articles. Furthermore, "Schmalkald" has become increasingly more popular among historians and theologians.[3]

A new translation of the Schmalkald Articles is included in this volume. Quotations from the articles throughout the text of this volume use this new translation and follow the customary practice of citing the Lutheran confessional writings by means of Parts, Articles, and Verses, rather than by the page numbers, either of the translation included in this present work or the current critical English edition of *The Book of Concord*.[4] For example, "The first and chief article . . ." is referred to as SA II, 1, 1; not "below, page 121" or "*BC*, page 292" or "*BSLK*, page 415."

This project has benefited greatly from the supportive and generous efforts of many persons. My thanks go out first and foremost to my dear wife and friend, to whom this work is dedicated. This small expression of public thanks can only begin to convey my profound gratitude to Ann. A word of thanks is due also to our children, Sarah, John, and Mary, who continue to find such creative ways to give us great joy.

I am also grateful to those who have read and commented on this work at various stages along the way. In particular, my *Doktor-Vater*, George W. Forell, deserves special thanks. Dr. Forell has been a source of theological and academic inspiration to me since my freshman year in college. He proves the veracity of Luther's words, "It takes persons of exceptional ability to teach."

Robert Kolb has been a consistent source of encouragement and practical

---

3. Here is a small sampling of recent significant works that refer to the Schmalkald(ic) Articles: Mark U. Edwards, Jr., *Luther's Last Battles* (Ithaca, N.Y.: Cornell University Press, 1983); Heiko Oberman, *Luther: Man between God and the Devil* (New Haven: Yale University Press, 1989); and James M. Kittelson, *Luther the Reformer* (Minneapolis: Augsburg Publishing House, 1986). *Religion Index One: Periodicals* (Evanston, Ill.: American Theological Library Association, 1949–) uses "Schmalkald" as the preferred spelling of the name of this document (if one seeks entries related to the "Smalcald" Articles, one finds "See the Schmalkald Articles"). The *Encyclopedia of the Reformation* (New York: Oxford University Press, forthcoming) uses "Schmalkald" as its preferred spelling. "Schmalkald," therefore, represents a growing consensus in current scholarship.

4. Theodore Tappert, ed., *The Book of Concord* (Philadelphia: Fortress Press, 1959), is the current critical English edition of the Lutheran confessional writings.

guidance to my work on these articles. His gracious help, with respect to both the translation and its interpretation, went far beyond the call of duty.

Charles Anderson, Robert Brusic, Frederick Gaiser, Eric Gritsch, Robert Jenson, Carter Lindberg, Heiko Oberman, Michael Rogness, Eugene Skibbe, Thomas Trapp, and Richard Walker all gave me many helpful suggestions. I am honored by the care with which they read these pages and most appreciative of their wise advice. I have, and this work has, benefited from the insights they were willing to share with me.

The last person to be thanked by name is certainly not the least. Timothy Staveteig, my editor, deserves special thanks. He has been able to take the naive proposal of a first-time, would-be author and turn it into a book.

The schools where I have taught have provided much-needed institutional and collegial support as I worked on this project. If any of the Friday afternoon "Friends of the Lutheran Confessions" at Luther Northwestern Seminary perchance read this book, they will recognize that much of it was presented to them in rather rough form in the last few years. Also, the reference and inter-library loan librarians at Augsburg College, Luther College, and Luther Northwestern Seminary have my gratitude for their patient and competent fulfillment of my many requests and renewals. I also wish to thank Alicia Allen, Zane Peaslee, and Stephanie Lourey, students at Waldorf College, for their assistance in preparing the index. The bulk of the manuscript was completed at Duke University, under the auspices of a National Endowment for the Humanities grant.

Abbreviations

AC   The Augsburg Confession.

ACAp   The Apology to the Augsburg Confession.

BC   Theodore Tappert, ed. *The Book of Concord*. Philadelphia: Fortress Press, 1959.

BSLK   *Die Bekenntnisschriften der evangelisch-lutherischen Kirche*. 10th edition. Göttingen: Vandenhoeck & Ruprecht, 1986.

CC   Johann Cochläus. *Ein nötig und christlich bedenck auff des Luther artickeln, die man gemeinem concilio fürtragen sol*, ed. Hans Volz, in *Corpus Catholicorum. Werke Katholischer Schriftsteller im Zeitalter der Glaubensspaltung*. Vol. 18, 1–64. Münster: Verlag der Aschendorffschen Verlagsbuchhandlung, 1932.

CR   *Corpus Reformatorum*. 99 vols. Halle, Berlin, and Leipzig, 1834–.

FCEp   Epitome, Rule and Norm, of the Formula of Concord.

FCSD   Solid Declaration of the Formula of Concord.

LC   The Large Catechism.

LQ   *Lutheran Quarterly,* New Series.

LW   *Luther's Works*. Vols. 1–30, ed. Jaroslav Pelikan. St. Louis: Concordia Publishing House, 1955–86; vols. 31–55, ed. Helmut Lehmann. Philadelphia: Fortress Press, 1955–86.

MSG   Jacques Paul Migne, ed. *Patrologiae Series Graecae*. Paris, 1866–.

MSL   Jacques Paul Minge, ed. *Patrologiae Series Latinae*. Paris, 1844–80.

SA   The Schmalkald Articles.

SC   The Small Catechism.

SCJ   *The Sixteenth Century Journal*.

TCS   The Three Chief Symbols.

Tr   Treatise on the Power and Primacy of the Pope.

UuA   *Urkunden und Aktenstücke zur Geschichte von Martin Luthers Schmalkaldischen Artikeln*. Ed. Hans Volz and Heinrich Ulbrich. Berlin: De Gruyter, 1957.

WA   *D. Martin Luthers Werke. Kritische Gesamtausgabe,* 58 vols. Weimar, 1883–.

WABr   *D. Martin Luthers Werke. Briefwechsel*. 15 vols. Weimar, 1930–.

WADB   *D. Martin Luthers Werke. Deutsche Bibel.* 12 vols. Weimar, 1906–61.

WATR   *D. Martin Luthers Werke. Tischreden.* 6 vols. Weimar, 1912–21.

Walch   Johan G. Walch, ed. *D. Martin Luthers sämmtliche Schriften.* 23 vols. in 25. St. Louis, 1880–1910.

WC   The Wittenberg Concord of 1536. In *The Book of Concord,* vol. 2, 253–56. Philadelphia: General Council Publication Board, 1883.

ZKG   *Zeitschrift für Kirchengeschichte.*

ZST   *Zeitschrift für Systematische Theologie.*

ZTK   *Zeitschrift für Theologie und Kirche, neue Folge.*

Introduction

MARTIN LUTHER, AS ONE OF THE MAIN CHARACTERS IN ONE OF THE MOST TU-
multuous and important periods in the history of Western civilization, had
only one real weapon: the power of persuasion. Luther was no general. He was
not a head of state. He was not wealthy. Luther was a teacher and a preacher.
So he taught and preached, spoke and wrote, debated and disputed. His output
was so prodigious that he became one of the most important and prolific theological writers in the history of the Christian church.[1]

This, however, creates an immediate problem for anyone—particularly the
nonspecialist—who wishes to learn more about Luther and the Reformation.
If it is true that "in most big libraries, books by and about Martin Luther
occupy more shelf room than those concerned with any other human being
except Jesus of Nazareth,"[2] then where does one begin to study Luther? Which
of the reformer's hundreds, even thousands, of works, which together take
up so much space in all those "big libraries," gives a good, or even the best,
representation of the reformer's life and work? Is there any place where Luther
lays out, in an orderly and accessible way, what he deemed most central to his
life and career?

These are not idle questions for inquirers. What we need is a document
that can serve as a sort of blueprint or schematic that allows us to see the bases
on which Luther built his theology. It would be best if this document was
written by Luther himself, so that we could read what the reformer himself saw
to be the center of his theological program. We need a document, written late in
the reformer's career, so it might summarize what the mature Luther deemed
most important in his theology. We need a document that is readable. All of
these things we find in the little document known as the Schmalkald Articles.

The Schmalkald Articles can indeed be seen as a schematic of Luther's theology. They are more than an arid piece of esoteric theology, for the reformer

---

1. Gerhard Ebeling takes note of Luther's large literary production when he describes *WA* by
saying that, after some 112 folio volumes, "with certain qualifications, the time has come that
the work on this critical edition can be declared to be at an end" ("Hundert Jahre Weimarer
Lutherausgabe," in *Lutherjahrbuch* 52 [1985]: 239). One qualification that Ebeling makes is that
the projected critical apparatus to *WA* will not be completed "until the year 2003" (p. 240).

2. John M. Todd, *Luther: A Life* (New York: Crossroad, 1982), xvi.

1

has written much of himself into these articles. One has the sense that, in SA, one encounters something of the man behind the words on the page. Luther's style in SA is polemical and pithy, profound and personal. He summarily calls the pope the "antichrist,"[3] lampoons the medieval mass as a "dragon's tail . . . [that] has produced many noxious pests and the excrement of numerous idolatries,"[4] and identifies his opponents as "enthusiasts," who have "the old devil and old snake."[5] Luther is famous for this kind of colorful language and he uses it in SA to draw a vibrant, vital picture of the Christian faith.

In the articles, Luther also makes numerous references to his own experience. When these references are recognized as such, they can bring both his life and his work into sharp focus. A couple of examples can be easily cited. First, Luther alludes to the famous thunderstorm on the outskirts of Stotternheim in 1505 that prompted him to enter the Augustinian monastery at Erfurt.[6] This event nudged Luther down the path to reformation. Second, Luther the man comes through in SA when he mentions something we would ordinarily not even talk about in polite company, let alone in an official statement of faith written for the church. The reformer mentions his nocturnal emissions, which occurred in spite of his best efforts, as an example of how futile it is to try to use the monastic life to become what one is not and thereby improve one's self and earn God's favor.[7]

When we read SA, we read the "real" Luther. This encounter with Luther is underscored when we take into account the specific factors in his life that influenced the form and content of SA. When Luther wrote SA, he (and those around him) thought he was about to die. The specter of death influenced SA from beginning to end, causing the reformer to express himself in a particularly clear and pointed manner. The existential urgency with which Luther wrote SA underscores the importance of this document in the context of the reformer's life and theology. For Luther, SA was indeed a sort of "last, theological will and testament" and, as such, is one of his most carefully formulated works, written as if it were to contain the final words of a dying man. If we miss the personal energy with which Luther wrote SA, we miss a critical dimension to the importance of this document for the reformer himself.

Fundamentally, SA is a summary statement of faith, an expression of Luther's mature theological priorities. These priorities fall into two basic catego-

3. SA II, 4, 10.
4. SA II, 2, 11.
5. SA III, 8, 3–5.
6. SA III, 3, 2.
7. SA III, 3, 28.

ries. These categories serve as poles or pillars that are grounded deep in the
bedrock of the reformer's fundamental view of the Christian faith. The first
theological pillar of SA is Luther's commitment to the trinitarian, creedal tradition of the church. The reformer begins SA with a short compendium of
classical trinitarian theology. Luther provides a creedal starting point for all
that is to follow. He expresses his convictions in SA as a self-conscious member
of the Western Christian church. This is the "catholic" pole of the theological
edifice that Luther builds in SA.

The use of the word *catholic* here is not to be identified solely with Roman
Catholic. The church catholic (lowercase *c*) is the universal church (whether
Protestant or Roman Catholic) that confesses the authority of the Scriptures,
trinitarian theology, the efficacy of the sacraments, both the divinity and the
humanity of Christ, and salvation as God's gift to humankind.[8] The term *catholic* is used to indicate the basic, ecumenical concerns of Luther as a representative member of the Western Christian theological tradition.

The other theological pillar in SA is what I term Luther's *evangelicalism.*
Justification by faith, apart from works of the law, is put forth as the distinctively Lutheran theological emphasis. For Luther, the gospel, not the law, saves
humankind. With particular clarity in SA, Luther emphasizes God's grace and
the promise of the forgiveness of sin (which is the gospel). This understanding
of the Scriptures is expressed by Luther by means of his famous distinction
between law and gospel. Luther interpreted the Scriptures evangelically, that
is, with a clear focus on what he thought was central: the gospel (i.e., the promise, given in the Old Testament, fulfilled by Jesus Christ in the New Testament),
and not the law, is what saves humankind. For Luther, this was the great hope
of the Christian life.

Evangelicalism, then, is not to be confused with modern notions of American evangelicalism, which are generally related too closely to fundamentalism.
Used with respect to SA, this term in the sense used in this book grows out of
its specifically biblical (*euangelion*, Greek for "gospel" or "good news") and
Reformation (*evangelisch[e]* or *Evangelisten*) contexts. Evangelicalism, as eluci-
dated in SA, emphasizes the action of God (i.e., the good news of God's grace)
that gives the gift of salvation through the gospel of the forgiveness of sin
in Christ.

It is, strictly speaking, inaccurate to call this aspect of the reformer's theology "the distinctively *Lutheran* theological emphasis." Luther did not set out
to start a denomination, nor did he want a bailiwick of the Christian church

---

8. Cf. Eric W. Gritsch and Robert W. Jenson, *Lutheranism: The Theological Movement and Its
Confessional Writings* (Philadelphia: Fortress Press, 1976), 5.

named after him. He wanted primarily to reform the church. Luther straight-forwardly expressed his opinion about such matters in 1522:

> I ask that no one make reference to my name and call themselves not Lutherans but Christians. What is Luther? After all, the doctrine is not mine, nor have I been crucified for anyone. St. Paul in I Corinthians Three would not allow Christians to call themselves Pauline or Petrine, but Christian. How then, should I, a poor evil-smelling maggot sack, have people give to the children of Christ my worthless name? Not so, dear friends. Let us cast out party names and be called Christians after him whose doctrine we have.[9]

As dismayed as Luther might have been, however, "Lutheran" stuck. Tradition has named the German "evangelicals" of the sixteenth century and the distinctive theological emphases of this continuing movement after their founder. Tradition, with occasional impetus from Luther himself,[10] wins out over the reformer's own wishes, and therefore the theology confessed in SA is indeed "Lutheran." However anachronistic it might be, at this point, the present work submits to the conventions of this tradition.

When we bring together the theological poles of the Lutheran understanding of the Christian faith as expressed in SA, we find that these priorities can be succinctly summarized with the phrase "catholic evangelicalism."[11] The specifically theological meaning of SA's "catholic evangelicalism" will be discussed at length in due course. First, however, we shall focus on the role and function of SA in the context of Luther's life and career. This attention to the historical circumstances that gave rise to SA will put us in a position to analyze its theological and confessional content.

At various other points in his career, Luther indicates the catholic-evangelical pillars of his theology, but rarely are they so clearly evident and closely connected as in the pages of SA.[12] The theological significance of SA

---

9. *A Sincere Admonition to All Christians to Guard against Insurrection and Rebellion* (1522) (*WA* 8:685; *LW* 45:16).

10. Cf. *The Private Mass and the Consecration of Priests* (1533) *WA* 38:237,; *LW* 38:196).

11. This phrase also expresses the basic, foundational commitments of *The Book of Concord,* with its catholic starting point (the catholic creeds are given a position of priority at the beginning of *The Book of Concord* and each of the confessional symbols [save Tr] expresses adherence to the trinitarian creeds) and evangelical ("by faith alone") emphasis.

12. Documents that emphasize the general, catholic side of the reformer's theology are *Confession concerning Christ's Supper,* Part III (*WA* 26:499ff.; *LW* 37:360ff.), and SC (1529). The bulk of Luther's literary production, however, stemmed from polemical encounters with opponents. Therefore the distinctive, evangelical aspect of his program was more often emphasized. E.g., the "three Reformation treatises" of 1520 (*The Babylonian Captivity of the Church* [*WA* 6:497–574; *LW* 36:3–126], *On the Freedom of the Christian* [*WA* 7:1–73; *LW* 31:327–77], and *To the Christian Nobility of the German Nation concerning the Reform of the Christian Estate* [*WA* 6:404–69; *LW* 44:115–217])

lies in the exactness with which Luther shows his traditionalist or catholic commitments as well as his distinctively Lutheran or evangelical emphases. It is, then, a summary document designed to explicate, seemingly for the last time, the reformer's central theological concerns. The fact that Luther's catholic evangelicalism shows up so clearly in his theological testament indicates that his basic theological priorities can be found in the theological structure that is built on these foundational pillars.

The Significance of the Schmalkald Articles

The reformer wrote SA in the last decade of his life, between 1536 and 1538. As a mature thinker, with some twenty years of reforming activity behind him, he wrote the articles as a public confession of faith—the only such writing penned by him.[13] The reformer's own positive regard for SA is evident in explicit statements within the document as well as in sources outside it. In a January 1537 letter from Philip Melanchthon[14] to Veit Dietrich,[15] we read a secondhand reference to Luther's opinion of SA. Melanchthon told Dietrich: "Luther has written his articles, which he intends to defend to the utmost."[16] Some years later, Luther revealed the same type of approving attitude toward SA when he corresponded with Chancellor Gregor Brück[17] in April of 1541. Luther mentions in this letter the value of SA as it relates to some questions raised by Brück (about a current series of theological dialogues with the Ro-

emphasize the distinctive theological proposal of the Lutheran Reformation. SA brings together these two fundamental emphases in one short, accessible document.

13. SC and LC are certainly "public" documents, but they were not originally written as confessions. They were designed by Luther as teaching aids. Only later were they pressed into service as confessional writings. Cf. Hans Volz, "Zur Entstehungsgeschichte von Luthers Schmalkaldischen Artikeln," *ZKG* 73, no. 3–4 (1963): 316.

14. Melanchthon (d. 1560) was an influential and important coworker with Luther in the Reformation. Master Philip (he never attained the doctorate) came to the University of Wittenberg in 1518 as an instructor in Greek. He wrote the first Lutheran dogmatics, the *Loci communes*, in 1521, which was revised and reprinted some eighty times in his lifetime. Melanchthon's participation in the establishment or reorganization of the Universities of Marburg, Königsberg, Jena, and Leipzig earned him the title *Praeceptor Germaniae* ("The Teacher of Germany").

15. Dietrich (d. 1549) was converted to Lutheranism in the early 1520s and became Luther's private secretary in 1527, accompanying the reformer to Marburg in 1529 and to the Coburg castle in 1530. Dietrich was a pastor in Nürnberg from 1535 until his death.

16. *CR* 3:238.

17. Brück (d. 1557) was a jurist and the chancellor of Electoral Saxony during the electorates of Fredrick the Wise, John the Constant, and John Fredrick. He presented AC to the Diet of Augsburg in 1530 and presented the Latin copy to the emperor. Highly regarded for his eloquence and negotiating skill, he was a consistent representative of the Lutherans at important religious colloquies.

man Catholics): "In the second place, I leave the matter as it is found in the articles adopted at Schmalkalden; I shall not be able to improve on them; nor do I know how to yield anything further."[18]

Luther was not alone in considering SA a significant work. A number of his contemporaries also judged it representative not only of his individual theological concerns but of their own as well. The earliest recorded evaluation of SA was by a small gathering of theologians that discussed Luther's work at Wittenberg in December of 1536. Luther, Melanchthon, John Agricola,[19] Justus Jonas,[20] Nicolaus von Amsdorf,[21] John Bugenhagen,[22] Caspar Cruciger,[23] and George Spalatin[24] all demonstrated their acceptance of the faith confessed in SA by signing the articles.[25] Spalatin later wrote a sort of "History of the Refor-

---

18. Letter dated April 4, 1541 (WABr 9:355). Translated in Friedrich Bente, *Historical Introductions to the Book of Concord* (St. Louis: Concordia Publishing House, 1965), 58.

19. Agricola (d. 1566) began teaching at the University of Wittenberg in 1519 (the same year he served as Luther's secretary at the Leipzig debate with John Eck). He began to speak publicly against the use of law in the church in the late 1520s. Agricola became a chief protagonist in the "antinomian controversy" at Wittenberg in the mid-1530s. He fell out of favor with both Melanchthon and Luther and went to Berlin as court preacher for the Elector of Brandenburg. He was the main Protestant architect of the Augsburg Interim.

20. Jonas (d. 1555) was an intimate friend and close collaborator with Luther. He was with Luther at Worms (1521); attended the wedding of Luther and Katie and bore witness to the subsequent consummation of the marriage (1525); he was at Marburg (1529) and at Luther's death (1546), and he preached Luther's first funeral sermon at Eisleben. Jonas had considerable humanistic training, which he used to translate important Reformation works (e.g., Luther's *Bondage of the Will* and Melanchthon's *Loci*) from Latin into German. Jonas was dean of the theological faculty at Wittenberg for a decade (1523–33), lecturing on both the Old and the New Testament. As a church visitor in Saxony, he wrote the new church ordinances enacted there as a result of the Reformation.

21. Von Amsdorf (d. 1565) was a student and, later, a professor at the University of Wittenberg. A close friend of Luther, he was with the reformer at Leipzig in 1519 and at Worms in 1521. Luther ordained him Bishop of Naumburg in 1543. After Luther's death, von Amsdorf saw himself as a defender of orthodox Lutheran teaching, most notably against George Major's assertion that "good works are necessary for salvation."

22. Bugenhagen (d. 1558) was born in Pomerania and was sometimes referred to as Pomeranus or Pomer. He was pastor of the City Church of Wittenberg from 1522 until his death. He contributed to Luther's translations of the Bible and occasionally lectured at the university.

23. Cruciger (d. 1548) was professor of theology and pastor of the castle church at Wittenberg from 1525 until his death. Cruciger assisted Luther in his translation of the Bible and participated in important theological debates and conferences. He was instrumental in reforming Leipzig in 1539.

24. Spalatin (d. 1545) was Elector John Fredrick's boyhood tutor. In 1514, Spalatin became private secretary to Fredrick the Wise. A friend of Luther, Spalatin exercised great influence on behalf of the Reformation in the Saxon court.

25. *UuA*, 75.

mation,"[26] which included an account of the December 1536 meeting. Spalatin called SA "the most important articles of Christian doctrine which the honorable, learned Dr. Martin Luther formed in a most pure and Christian way."[27] In addition, Elector John Fredrick declared in early January of 1537 that Luther's articles were "Christian, pure, and clear."[28] The Elector remained so convinced by the profundity of SA that some years later he even commended SA to his heirs in his will.[29]

Ratifications of SA continued to grow in number throughout the sixteenth century. During the February 10 to March 6, 1537, Protestant meeting at Schmalkalden, SA was subscribed as a semiconfessional declaration of faith by most of the theologians in attendance (although they did so more as individuals than as official representatives of their princes or territories).[30] A further endorsement, also from Schmalkalden in 1537, is this sentence regarding SA from a report of Andreas Osiander to his pastoral colleagues at Nürnberg: "Luther had written previously at Wittenberg some articles in German. They are brief, to be sure, but clear and penetrating in all these things, regarding what we cannot concede at the council without great sacrilege."[31]

---

26. *UuA*, 69 n. 1.

27. *UuA*, 70.

28. Walch, 21b, 2143; Theodor Kolde, ed., *Analecta Lutherana* (Gotha: Friedrich Andreas Perthes, 1883), 285; and *UuA*, 84. Prince John Fredrick (1503–54), nephew of Fredrick the Wise and son of John the Constant, became Elector of Saxony upon his father's death in 1532. He was a pupil of Spalatin and an ardent follower of Luther. In 1547 he was defeated and imprisoned by Charles V, gave up his electoral position, and was released two years prior to his death.

29. *UuA*, 209. The Elector's will was recorded on December 9, 1553, and he died on March 3, 1554. Cf. also *CR* 4:292 and *CR* 7:1109.

30. At least some of the persons who signed SA in 1537 already saw the document as a confessional writing. E.g., the subscription of Urban Rhegius reads like this: "I, Dr. Urban Rhegius, superintendent of the churches in the Duchy of Lüneburg, subscribe for myself and in the name of my brothers and in the name of the church of Hanover." Also, when Brixius Northanus signed SA, he described himself as a "minister of the church of Christ which is at Soest, [and I] subscribe the articles of the Reverend Father Martin Luther and acknowledge that I have believed and taught likewise and, by the Spirit of Christ, will likewise believe and teach."

Those who declined to afix their signatures to SA at Schmalkalden were Paul Fagius from Strassburg, Boniface Wolfhart from Augsburg, John Fontanus from Lower Hesse, Ambrose Blauer from Constance, and Martin Bucer from Strassburg. Those theologians who were at Wittenberg in December 1536 had already subscribed SA and did not sign again at Schmalkalden (*UuA*, 120–26). Bucer (and some of the others who did not subscribe SA at Schmalkalden in 1537) apparently stopped short of rejecting Luther's articles altogether, as Veit Dietrich writes (to Johanni Forstero of Augsburg): "Bucer said, although he could find nothing wrong with [the articles], he did not have a mandate to subscribe them. Likewise [Ambrose] Blauer, Dionysius Melander [but Melander did in fact sign SA, albeit with a qualification], and our Boniface said the same"(*CR* 3:371).

31. *CR* 3:268.

After Luther's death, SA's significance was underscored by its being included in various Lutheran "bodies of doctrine," which appeared in the middle years of the sixteenth century.[32] Eventually its status as a confessional document of Lutheranism was acknowledged when it became part of *The Book of Concord* of 1580.[33] All of these "bodies of doctrine" were supplanted by the *The Book of Concord*, which was subscribed originally by some eighty-five signatories (including electors, princes, counts, and representatives of imperial cities).[34]

Therefore SA is more than a witness to the theological priorities of a great thinker and reformer of church and society. It is a confessional writing, officially subscribed by a significant portion of the church catholic. For over four hundred and fifty years SA, along with the other documents of *The Book of Concord,* has pointed to the central theological concerns of Lutheranism.[35]

The evaluations of twentieth-century historians and theologians further indicate the importance of SA. Two quotations suggest its broad twentieth-century scholarly evaluation. First, pointing to its internal theological consistency, Erdmann Schott wrote, "More clearly than any other confessional writing, the Schmalkald Articles keep Christ and justification in the center."[36] Second, Robert W. Jenson notes the significance of SA in relationship to Luther himself with these words: "The Smalcald Articles are Luther at his most char-

---

32. These *corpora doctrinae* were collections of documents intended to express Lutheran theological commitments. They grew out of the efforts of Lutherans to define themselves theologically following the death of Luther. The first Lutheran collection of doctrinal writings was the *Corpus doctrinae philippicum* or *misnicum* or *wittenbergense,* published in 1560 (Bente, *Introductions,* 7). As its name suggests, this *corpus* was edited by Melanchthon and, except for the three ecumenical creeds, contained works only by this "quiet reformer" (cf. Clyde Manschreck, *Melanchthon: The Quiet Reformer* [Westport, Conn.: Greenwood Press, 1975]). Between the publication of this collection and *The Book of Concord* in 1580, some twenty different Lutheran *corpora* appeared, from different cities, regions, or principalities (Bente, *Introductions,* 6). The *Corpus doctrinae* of Brunswick (the *Brunsvicense*) of 1563 was the first to include SA. Cf. Henry E. Jacobs, ed., *The Book of Concord* (Philadelphia: United Lutheran Publication House, 1888), 2:44; and Jürgen L. Neve, *Introduction to the Symbolical Books of the Lutheran Church,* 2nd rev. ed. (Columbus, Ohio: Lutheran Book Concern, 1926), 364.

33. *The Book of Concord* is the definitive collection of Lutheran confessional symbols.

34. These signatures are listed at the end of the Preface to *The Book of Concord.*

35. Among Lutherans, however, SA has not been uniformly endorsed as a confessional document. E.g., the Lutheran churches of Denmark, Norway, and Sweden were founded on a confessional basis that excluded SA. Cf. Helmut Zeddies, "The Confession of the Church," in *The Lutheran Church Past and Present,* ed. Vilmos Vajta (Minneapolis: Augsburg Publishing House, 1977), 105–6.

36. Erdmann Schott, "Christus und die Rechtfertigung allein durch den Glauben in Luthers Schmalkaldischen Artikeln," *ZST* 22 (1953): 192f.

acteristic."[37] In fact, virtually all twentieth-century scholars who recognize the significance of SA have in common an appreciation of its historical and theological importance as a witness to the basic affirmations of Luther (as well as Lutheranism).[38]

The Scholarly Neglect of the Schmalkald Articles

Among scholars and specialists there is consensus about the significance of SA as a clear witness to the center of Luther's (and Lutheranism's) theological priorities. However, there is no such unanimity about whether the articles have been studied sufficiently. Two respected Reformation scholars, James Schaaf from the United States and Hans Volz from Germany, seem to have come to opposite conclusions based on the same data. Schaaf has written, "Perhaps the least known of all the documents contained in *The Book of Concord* is the Smalcald Articles. It is unfortunate that this writing has been so neglected by students of the Reformation."[39] This statement points in a direction different from that of Volz, who wrote, "*The Schmalkald Articles*, as one of the confessional writings of the Evangelical Lutheran Church written by Luther, have received a privileged position. They have continually attracted the interest of scholarly research."[40]

How can one make sense of these different interpretations of the same data? A reasonable starting point is the numbers of works related to SA. The numbers show that, except in the anniversary years of 1737, 1837, and 1937, significant investigations of SA, in either German or English, have occurred at a rate of approximately one every five years.[41]

Furthermore, among these, no single work devoted solely to SA represents

---

37. Gritsch and Jenson, *Lutheranism,* 2.

38. Among other examples of twentieth-century evaluations of SA are James Schaaf: "[SA is a] remarkable writing which . . . clearly sets forth what the Reformation was really all about" ("The Smalcald Articles and Their Significance," in *Interpreting Luther's Legacy,* ed. Fredrick Meuser [Minneapolis: Augsburg Publishing House 1969], 68); H. G. Haile: "[SA] is a confession of faith most revealing of Luther's very simple theology" (*Luther: An Experiment in Biography* [Princeton: Princeton University Press, 1980], 209); and Klaus Schwartzwäller: "[SA] is the most 'reformational' of the confessional writings" ("Rechtfertigung und Ekklesiologie in den Schmalkaldischen Artikeln," *Kerygma und Dogma* 35 [April-June 1989]: 84). Attitudes such as these are typical of the positive regard expressed by most all modern scholarship concerned with SA.

39. Schaaf, "The Smalcald Articles," 69.

40. Hans Volz, "Luthers Schmalkaldische Artikel," *ZKG* 68 (1957): 259.

41. A "significant treatment" is an investigation of sufficient length and depth to be published in a scholarly journal.

even a reasonably complete synthesis of the history and content of the document. Despite the Lutheran propensity to study the confessional symbols of *The Book of Concord*, no book-length treatment of SA, prior to this present study, has been published in English.

With these data in mind, it is possible to evaluate the disparate statements of Schaaf and Volz. Schaaf's comment would appear to be more accurate than Volz's—SA indeed "has been . . . neglected by students of the Reformation." However, when we recall that Volz wrote, "*The Schmalkald Articles*, as one of the confessional writings . . . have continually attracted the interest of scholarly research," we can affirm that Volz is, in one sense, also right. He underscores the fact that SA has been discussed in the context of the broad attention focused on the Lutheran confessional writings. But this attention has mainly been in the form of short, prefatory "Historical Introductions" to *The Book of Concord* or general surveys of all the confessional documents of Lutheranism. The Schmalkald Articles could not easily be left out of such works. Nor does such a setting lend itself to a full explication of any of the documents.[42]

But this leaves open some obvious questions: Whatever happened to SA? What explains the scholarly neglect of these articles? If SA is really such a significant document in the life and thought of Luther (and subsequent Lutheranism), why has this confessional symbol of the Lutheran church received such insufficient attention?

The reasons for this situation are not self-evident, although some plausible explanations can be offered. First, the fact that SA was written relatively late in Luther's career has tended to keep scholarly attention from it. The sights of church historians and theologians traditionally have been focused on Luther's early theological development. Most biographies of Luther, for example, chart carefully the dramatic events that led up to the Diet of Worms in 1521 and, in some cases, to the Diet of Augsburg in 1530.[43] Few investigations of Luther

---

42. Cf., eg., Willard D. Allbeck, *Studies in the Lutheran Confessions* (Philadelphia: Muhlenberg Press, 1952); Bente, *Introductions;* Theodor Kolde, *Historische Einleitung in die symbolischen Bücher der evangelisch-lutherischen Kirche* (Gütersloh: C. Bertelsmann Verlag, 1907); and Richard Schmauck, *The Confessional Principle and the Confessions of the Lutheran Church* (Philadelphia: General Council Publication Board, 1911).

43. A helpful discussion of this phenomenon can be found in Kittelson, *Luther the Reformer,* 14–16. Luther biographies perhaps provide the best evidence for this traditional preoccupation with the "young Luther" (none of these listed has much, if any, information about Luther after 1530): Roland H. Bainton, *Here I Stand: A Life of Martin Luther* (Nashville: Abingdon-Cokesbury Press, 1950); Heinrich Boehmer, *Martin Luther: Road to Reformation* (Cleveland, Ohio: World Publishing Co., 1967); Martin Brecht, *Martin Luther: His Road to Reformation, 1483–1521* (Philadelphia: Fortress Press, 1985); Carter Lindberg, *Martin Luther: Justified by Grace* (Nashville: Graded Press, 1988); and Gordon E. Rupp, *Luther's Progress to the Diet of Worms* (New York: Harper & Row, 1964).

give much attention to the last fifteen years of the reformer's life.[44] Apparently, the period of the "older" Luther has been either too problematic or simply uninteresting to scholars.[45]

A second factor has curiously contributed to the neglect of SA: it is included among the confessional writings in *The Book of Concord*. This has come about because the individual confessional writings tend to be subordinated in "Theologies of the Lutheran Confessions" to the larger concerns of systematic theologians.[46] In such analyses, the role of SA has tended to be one of supporting the main argument of the author by means of proof texts.

Where attention has been given to particular documents within *The Book of Concord*, it has primarily focused on the Creeds, the Augsburg Confession, the Catechisms, and the Formula of Concord.[47] Thus, while SA's inclusion in *The Book of Concord* underscores its authority, it has also led ironically to its being overshadowed by the attention given to the other documents in *The Book of Concord*.[48] There is a sense in which SA has been "buried" in the tome of the collected Lutheran confessional symbols.

This can be illustrated by a quick look at the 1988 "Bibliography of the

44. Three biographies that give significant attention to Luther's later life are Kittelson, *Luther the Reformer;* Julius T. Köstlin and Gustav Kawerau, *Martin Luther: Sein Leben und seine Schriften,* 2 vols. (Berlin: Verlag von Alexander Duncker, 1903); and Walther von Loewenich, *Martin Luther: The Man and His Work* (Minneapolis: Augsburg Publishing House, 1986).

45. Edwards, *Battles,* 2. Regarding the advisability (or lack of it) of such periodization of Luther's life, see Heiko Oberman, "*Teufelsdreck:* Eschatology and Scatology in the 'Old' Luther," *SCJ* 19, no. 3 (Fall 1988): 435–39.

46. E.g., Friedrich Brunstäd, *Theologie der Lutherischen Bekenntnisschriften* (Gütersloh: C. Bertelsmann Verlag, 1951); Holsten Fagerberg, *A New Look at the Lutheran Confessions* (St. Louis: Concordia Publishing House, 1972); Friedrich Mildenberger, *The Theology of the Lutheran Confessions* (Philadelphia: Fortress Press, 1986); and Edmund Schlink *Theology of the Lutheran Confessions* (Philadelphia: Muhlenberg Press, 1961).

47. These writings have been closer to the center of research for various reasons: the ecumenical creeds are the common property of the church catholic and play an unparalleled role in the history of dogma, AC marks the beginning of a new theological and ecclesiological epoch in Western Christianity, the catechism(s) has been in constant catechetical use since its publication in 1529, and FC has been controversial from the beginning and is not accepted as confessional by all Lutherans.

48. The following is a select list of exemplary works that discuss the individual documents of *The Book of Concord* (this kind of literature is generally lacking for SA): Re the Creeds: Francis J. Badcock, *The History of the Creeds,* 2nd ed. (London: SPCK, 1938); and J. N. D. Kelly, *Early Christian Creeds* (New York: David McKay Co., 1972).
Re AC and ACAp: Wolfgang Bartholomae, *Einführung in das Augsburger Bekenntnis* (Göttingen: Vandenhoeck & Ruprecht, 1980); George Forell and James McCue, eds., *Confessing One Faith* (Minneapolis: Augsburg Publishing House, 1981); Günther Gassmann, *Das Augsburger Bekenntnis deutsch 1530–1980* (Göttingen: Vandenhoeck & Ruprecht, 1981); Jürgen Lorz, *Das Augsburgische Bekenntnis* (Göttingen: Theologische Lehrbücher, 1980); Wilhelm Maurer, *Historical Commentary*

Lutheran Confessions."[49] This reference tool needs but six pages to list the works devoted to both SA and Tr. (The tradition of identifying Tr as an appendix to SA is without warrant.) By comparison, 104 pages are needed to list the works related to AC and AP. Twenty-five pages are required for SC and LC; thirty-four pages for FC.[50]

A third factor has also contributed to the scholarly neglect of SA. The writing of it and the subsequent rise to confessional status occurred without a specific, easily identifiable public event. For example, unlike the other confessional documents of Lutheranism, SA has no formal, generally recognized date for its composition, presentation, or adoption.[51] If such a fixed date existed, it would have lent itself to the types of anniversary recognitions by which chroniclers have traditionally marked significant events in history.

A summary of the circumstances of SA's origin will bear this out. The original draft of SA was written by Luther in mid-December of 1536.[52] It was then

on the *Augsburg Confession* (Philadelphia: Fortress Press, 1986); Lutz Mohaupt, *Wir glauben und bekennen: Zugänge zum Augsburger Bekenntnis* (Göttingen: Vandenhoeck & Ruprecht, 1980); and Michael Reu, *The Augsburg Confession* (Chicago: Wartburg Publishing House, 1930).

Re SC and LC: Kurt Aland and Hermann Kunst, eds., *Martin Luther: Der Grosse und der Kleine Katechismus* (Göttingen: Vandenhoeck & Ruprecht, 1980); Peters, *Kommentar zu Luthers Katechismen;* Michael Reu, *Luther's Small Catechism* (Chicago: Wartburg Publishing House, 1929); plus dozens, if not hundreds, of commentaries for parish educational purposes.

Re FC: Lewis W. Spitz and Wenzel Lohff, eds., *Discord, Dialogue, and Concord* (Philadelphia: Fortress Press, 1977); Wenzel Lohff and Lewis W. Spitz, eds., *Widerspruch, Dialog und Einigung* (Stuttgart: Calwer Verlag, 1977); and "The Formula of Concord: Quadricentennial Essays," *SCJ* 8, no. 4 (1977).

Re *BC* in general: Martin Brecht and Reinhard Schwarz, eds., *Bekenntnis und Einheit der Kirche* (Stuttgart: Calwer Verlag, 1980); James Nestingen, *Roots of Our Faith* (Minneapolis: Augsburg Publishing House, 1976); Robert Preus, *Getting into the Theology of Concord* (St. Louis: Concordia Publishing House, 1977); and David Scaer, *Getting into the Story of Concord* (St. Louis: Concordia Publishing House, 1977).

49. "Bibliography of the Lutheran Confessions," ed. David Daniel and Charles Arand, *Sixteenth Century Bibliography* 28 (St. Louis: Center for Reformation Research, 1988).

50. Furthermore, SA has evidently been edited and published only twice in English separately from *The Book of Concord.* A reprint of SA from the Tappert edition of *BC* is included in Timothy Lull, ed., *Martin Luther's Basic Theological Writings* (Minneapolis: Augsburg Fortress, 1989). Also, there was an offprint of SA from the *Concordia Triglotta,* edited by Friedrich Bente: *The Smalcald Articles: A Reprint from the "Concordia Triglotta" in Commemoration of the Four-Hundredth Anniversary of the Presentation of This Confession of the Lutheran Church at Schmalkalden, Germany, in 1537* (St. Louis: Concordia Publishing House, 1937). The mistake regarding "the presentation of this confession" in the title of this publication is puzzling. This is in contrast, e.g., to the numerous separately published edition of AC and SC. The American Edition of Luther's Works does not include a translation of SA.

51. F. Sander, "Geschichtliche Einleitung zu den Schmalkaldischen Artikeln," *Jahrbücher für deutsche Theologie* 20 (1875), 475.

52. *UuA,* 26–35.

revised and subscribed at a small meeting of leading Lutheran theologians at Wittenberg, between Christmas 1536 and January 1, 1537.[53] At Schmalkalden, in February 1537, SA never made it to the floor of the convention, although it was signed by most of the theologians in attendance.[54] It was not until the spring and summer of 1538 that Luther made some further changes, added his extended preface, and published SA.[55] It was this edition that was first included in the 1563 Brunswick "Body of Doctrine," the *Corpus Brunsvicense,* and then began its journey to full confessional status in earnest.[56] In 1580, this 1538 *editio princeps* was accepted into *The Book of Concord.*

This rather uneventful evolution has helped keep SA in its lower profile compared to the other confessional symbols, because anniversary observances have traditionally focused the attention of scholars on significant Reformation events and doctrines.

For example, the celebrations connected with the tercentenary of Luther's Ninety-five Theses[57] played an important role in the confessional struggles of nineteenth-century Lutheranism in both Europe and America. In Europe, this particular anniversary was the occasion that prompted the king of Prussia to initiate a Union Church, which would bring Lutheran and Reformed Germans together into one ecclesiastical body.[58] His initiative prompted a sharply negative reaction among many Lutherans. Part of the movement against the Union Church can be seen as a result of the increased attention given Luther and historical Lutheranism leading up to the anniversary year of 1817.[59]

On the other side of the Atlantic, nineteenth-century American Lutheranism began a struggle over confessional issues that was similarly influenced by such anniversary celebrations and the attention they directed to Luther and the Reformation.[60]

Still another example of the energy that anniversary celebrations have tra-

---

53. *UuA,* 69–77.

54. *UuA,* 102–28.

55. *UuA,* 178–84.

56. Jacobs, *The Book of Concord,* 2:44; and Theodor Kolde, "Schmalkald Articles," in *The New Schaff-Herzog Encyclopedia of Religious Knowledge,* ed. Samuel M. Jackson (Grand Rapids, Mich.: Baker Book House, 1950), 10:249.

57. Historians have generally seen Luther's famous call to an academic debate, his *Disputation on the Power and Efficacy of Indulgences,* as the "beginning" of the Protestant Reformation.

58. Theodore Tappert, ed., *Lutheran Confessional Theology in America 1840–1880* (New York: Oxford University Press, 1972), 5f.

59. Ibid., 9.

60. Sydney Ahlstrom, *A Religious History of the American People* (Garden City, N.Y.: Image Books, 1975); 1:624, 627.

ditionally given scholarly pursuits is the existence of the modern critical edition of the Lutheran confessional writings. The 1930 edition of *BSLK* was "published on the anniversary of the Augsburg Confession."[61] In fact, the official publication date of the original *Book of Concord* itself was June 25, 1580—chosen to coincide with the fiftieth anniversary of the presentation of the Augsburg Confession before Emperor Charles V at Augsburg.

The Schmalkald Articles have no specific, easily identifiable adoption, presentation, or publication date so that they too could enjoy the same kind of impetus such anniversaries have given to the study of so many other important aspects of the Reformation.[62]

A fourth factor also helps explain the ongoing neglect of SA, when compared to the other confessional symbols of Lutheranism: SA is, one might say, "too Lutheran." The reformer writes with a personal urgency and particularly in SA that has been out of vogue in the West since the Enlightenment.[63] Luther's polemics in SA, which actually point negatively to his central theological convictions, can be seen as indications of this particularity.[64]

These four factors, however, cannot completely explain the neglect of such a profound document as SA. Be that as it may, whatever the reasons are for the neglect of SA, we now have an opportunity to take a look at the theological priorities of Martin Luther and Lutheranism through one of the clearest theological windows left by Luther. The Schmalkald Articles are his testament of faith, the theological legacy the reformer wished to bequeath to posterity. They deserve the attention of thoughtful people everywhere.

61. "Herausgegeben im Gedenkjahr der Augsburgischen Konfession 1930," *BSLK*, title page.

62. Such anniversaries have indeed been generally lacking, but not completely so. For the purposes of the argument presented here, however, these exceptions tend to prove the rule. First, there was a formal recognition of the 450th anniversary of the Bundestag at Schmalkalden in 1537: "Smalcalden Revisited, Lutheran–Catholic Relations, 1573–1987, Smalcald Articles Then and Now," at Martin Luther College, New Ulm, Minnesota (October 1, 1987). However, it should be noted that, whereas this was apparently the only such commemoration of SA in 1987, there were numerous commemorations, meetings, and ceremonies relating to the other Reformation anniversaries, from 1977 to 1983. Second, it should be noted that some recognition by scholars of SA's "anniversary" has been made over the years: e.g., one 1737 publication, two publications in 1837 and *Festschrift zur 300-Jahrfeier der Schmalkaldischen Artikel* (Schmalkalden, 1937), along with a handful of other monographs published in 1937.

63. "The Enlightenment" refers to a dominant Western intellectual movement of the eighteenth century. Theologically, the Enlightenment stressed the use of reason and a rather detached, irenic acceptance of various theological and ecclesiastical differences. Religious distinctiveness was downplayed and commonalities were stressed.

64. Luther calls the pope "the antichrist" twice in SA II, 4, and this epithet has been an explicit subject of discussion in the U.S. "Lutheran–Roman Catholic Dialogue" (cf. Paul C. Empie and T. Austin Murphy, eds., *Papal Primacy and the Universal Church* [Minneapolis: Augsburg Publishing House, 1974], 6f.).

1

Indications of History in the Schmalkald Articles

THE SCHMALKALD ARTICLES NOT ONLY SKETCH LUTHER'S BASIC THEOLOGICAL commitments but also outline important aspects of the surrounding historical factors that gave rise to the document. In this way, SA highlights the most influential features of late medieval and early modern Europe for the theology of Luther.

The Protestant Appeal for a General Council

In November 1518, Luther made his first public appeal for a general council to discuss the reform of the church.[1] Luther and his followers then renewed this call periodically during the formative years of the Reformation. Twelve years later, these appeals even made it into AC: "We offer . . . to participate in such a general, free, and Christian council."[2]

Prior to the Diet of Augsburg, the need for a general council had even been recognized and advocated by high-ranking supporters of the Roman Catholic Church. The Recess of Regensburg (1527) and the two diets of Speyer (1526 and 1529) all refer to the need for a general council.[3] Charles V himself, in response to the Protestant request at Augsburg, promised to encourage the pope to convoke a council within a year of the close of the Reichstag.[4] The attempts to secure a council continued into the early 1530s, as the 1532 Peace of Nürnberg, which makes a similar appeal to a general council, shows.[5]

Throughout the 1520s and early 1530s, the popes were reticent to fulfill

---

1. *Appellatio F. Martini Luther ad Concilium,* November 28, 1518 (*WA* 2:36–40), was written shortly after Luther's October 1518 hearing with Cardinal Cajetan at Augsburg. Such a council would have brought together the bishops of the world into one assembly, where they would adjudicate church policy and adopt canon law.

2. AC, Preface, 21.

3. Reu, *Augsburg Confession,* Part II, 32, 33.

4. The Recess of Augsburg, September 22, 1530, is in *Urkundenbuch zu der Geschichte des Reichstages zu Augsburg im Jahre 1530,* ed. Karl E. Förstemann (Halle: Buchhandlung des Waisenhauses, 1833–35), 2:474. For an English translation, see Reu, *Augsburg Confession,* Part I, 390–92.

5. *CR* 3:102.

these requests.[6] Still, the emperor sought to keep his promise made at Augsburg, and there was documented progress on this point toward the end of Clement VII's tenure as bishop of Rome. Both the emperor and the pope issued proclamations in early 1533, which indicated that discussions regarding a possible council of the church had taken place.[7]

It was not until the pontificate of Paul III, however, that these kinds of conversations began to translate into concrete action. In the late fall of 1535, papal legate Paul Vergerio went to Germany in order to access Lutheran attitudes regarding a council—particularly if the council was not to be held on German soil (which had been an oft-cited precondition of the Protestants). During this trip, Vergerio visited separately with both Luther (at Wittenberg) and Elector John Fredrick (at Vienna) about the possibility of a general council. Therefore, when the council was finally called a few months later, the news did not completely surprise the Lutherans.

The reactions of the Protestants were guarded. The Protestants had made many appeals to a general council and they had heard many promises from Roman Catholic rulers to work toward one. But a council had yet to occur. This state of affairs is reflected in Vergerio's remarks, who in his audience with John Fredrick in November 1535 contrasted the previous Roman Catholic policy of making insincere promises about such councils with the true intentions of Paul III. This tact of Vergerio actually validates the healthy skepticism of the Protestants.[8]

As it turned out, this proposed council did not in fact meet at Mantua as originally announced in 1537, but after numerous delays it finally met at Trent (1545–64).[9] Luther summarizes general Protestant attitudes toward the council in the preface to SA (which was written two years after the papal bull convoking the council had been published and one year after the council was to have started):

> Pope Paul III called a council to meet at Mantua last year during Pentecost. Afterward he moved it from Mantua, so that we still do not know where he intends to hold it, or whether he can hold it. . . .

6. In order, these popes were Leo X (1513–21), Adrian VI (1522–23), Clement VII (1523–34), and Paul III (1534–49).

7. The emperor issued his statement on January 8 and the pope issued his statement on January 10 (Bente, *Introductions,* 47; and Allbeck, *Studies,* 187).

8. Haile, *Luther,* 13.

9. The Council of Trent set the official theological agenda for the Roman Catholic Church until at least 1963 and drew the battle lines with Protestantism that have only recently begun to break down.

> So I collected these articles and presented them to our side, . . . and
> it was resolved that we should publicly present the articles as our confes-
> sion of faith—If the pope and his adherents should ever become so bold
> as seriously, genuinely, and without deception or treachery to convene a
> truly free council, as would be his duty.[10]

Nevertheless, in spite of their doubts as to the commitment of the Roman
pontiff, the Lutherans did not completely disregard the possibility that this
council might actually take place. Preparations were thus deemed necessary
and they decided to meet at Schmalkalden, Hesse, in February 1537. At least
two realities made it prudent to take the papal offer seriously. First, the Protestants' consistent requests for such a council would have appeared to be little
more than a propaganda ploy if they failed to be adequately prepared for such
a possibility.[11] Second, the coming council was probably the only alternative
to armed conflict or complete schism. Rome's earlier efforts to deal with Luther had failed. The Lutheran Reformation had been under way for some
twenty years, and the defensive alliance of the Schmalkald League made the
evangelical cause viable even apart from the Roman church.[12] Therefore, as
H. G. Haile puts it, "a general council of the church became inevitable."[13]

The Protestants participated in numerous discussions and exchanged a
number of communications (both formal and informal) about the proposed
council throughout the summer, fall, and winter leading up to the meeting at
Schmalkalden (which had as its primary agendum the formulation of a collec-
tive response to the papal summons).[14] At the outset of these discussions, in
the summer of 1536, the Wittenberg theologians advised their elector that,
although the probability of specific issues being resolved in their favor was
extremely small, they should nevertheless attend the council.

Since 1518, Luther had consistently made appeals to a council and he remained an advocate of such a council throughout his career. Julius Köstlin

---

10. SA, Preface, 1–3.

11. Schaaf, "The Smalcald Articles," 70.

12. The Schmalkald League was a federation of German Protestant princes and cities headed by
the Landgrave of Hesse and the Elector of Saxony, formed to secure their realms against attack
from papal or imperial forces. Taking its name from the town where the alliance was formalized,
the Schmalkald League was formed after the 1530 Diet of Augsburg, in response to the threat of
armed conflict over Reformation issues. The League was defeated in the "Schmalkald War" (1546–
47), but was later able to negotiate the 1555 Peace of Augsburg, which gave legal sanction to
German Protestantism.

13. Haile, *Luther*, 7.

14. Hans Virck, "Zu den Beratungen der Protestanten über die Konzilsbulle vom 4. Juni 1536,"
ZKG 13 (1892): 487–512.

relates this telling story about Luther's parting repartee with the papal nuncio Vergerio in November of 1535: The legate, mounted on his horse: "See that you are prepared for the council." Luther: "Certainly, my lord, with my head and neck."[15] Luther here expresses his virtual unconditional willingness to attend a council—an attitude he held from the very outset of the negotiations. Over a year after Vergerio's visit, when Luther wrote SA, the reformer expressed his opinion in such a way that it appears that he assumes the council, in some form, will in fact happen:

> These four articles will furnish them with enough to condemn at the council. They neither can nor will allow us the smallest little portion of these articles. Of this we may be certain.[16]

John Fredrick, however, was inclined not to participate in the council. He had asked for advice from the theologians and jurists of the University at Wittenberg in July 1536 regarding the proposed Mantua council.[17] In doing so, he placed before his scholars a number of basic issues. First, there was the question of whether or not the papal legate should even be received, especially if there was no imperial envoy with him. Second, the Elector wondered whether reception of the legate would mean automatic subjection to papal authority or whether perhaps a protest should be registered regarding the pope's unilateral calling of the council. Third, the issue was raised regarding the evangelical response if the Elector was cited as a party to stand trial and not as a full participant along with the other estates.

A few days later, John Fredrick issued a statement of his own concerning these issues in an apparent attempt to influence his scholarly advisers with his own negative opinion in regard to the advisability of attending the council.[18] Therefore, when the Elector received his scholars' opinion recommending a Protestant presence at Mantua, he requested that they reexamine the issue with even more "diligence."[19]

These kinds of discussions, beginning in the summer of 1536, continued off and on throughout the remainder of the year.[20] The Elector himself came to Wittenberg in early December and delivered a memorandum with specific

---

15. Köstlin and Kawerau, *Martin Luther,* 2:375.

16. SA II, 4, 15.

17. *CR* 3:119ff.

18. *CR* 3:99ff.

19. Bente, *Introductions,* 51.

20. *CR* 3:119.

instructions about the development of a set of articles by Luther.[21] This request or commission came to Luther because John Fredrick wanted specific advice from the reformer regarding these issues. SA is a means by which to view these larger developments inasmuch as Luther wrote his articles, at least in part, in response to the papal call to a council of the church.[22]

Late Medieval Conciliarism versus Curialism Debate

The process that led to the convoking of the general council just described can be seen as an analogue to the debates in the late medieval church that grew out of the Great Schism. The Great Schism resulted from the transfer of the papal residence from Rome to Avignon, France, from 1309 to 1376 (the so-called Babylonian captivity) and the struggle to move it back to Italy. During the decades when this multifaceted dispute was raging, there were at one point three competing popes—each with a more or less legitimate claim to the see of Peter. Luther in SA refers openly to these events when he makes this observation about the dismal circumstances of the church and the papacy in the fourteenth and fifteenth centuries:

> And I assert that the pope should want to renounce his claim so that he would not be supreme in the church "by divine right" or by God's command. However, in order that the unity of Christendom might be preserved against the sects and heretics, we might accept a head in which all others are held together. Such a head would now be elected by the people and it would remain in their power and by their choice whether to change or depose this head. This is virtually the way the council at Constance handled the popes, deposing the three and electing the fourth.[23]

Luther, by mentioning the Council of Constance, which officially brought the medieval controversy to an end, [24] indicates that a "general, free, and Christian council" (as the Preface to AC put it) would stand above the pope as the arbiter of the ecclesiastical controversies. Luther underscores the ongoing Protestant plea for a general council, with an implicit appeal to the conciliarist theories of at least the preceding one hundred and fifty years.[25]

---

21. *UuA*, 22.

22. Finally, at the February 1537 meeting of the Schmalkald League, the invitation to attend the proposed council was officially rejected by the Protestants.

23. SA II, 4, 7.

24. At Constance, John XXII, Benedict XIV, and Gregory XII all either abdicated or were deposed and Martin V was elected as the single reigning pontiff.

25. Luther's notion of a general council does not, however, simply accept earlier conciliarist theory. A general council was a means to an end for Luther. Such a council, if it were to be free and Christian, would look to the Word of God as the ultimate authority. Even a reform council could err. Yet it was the only conceivable way to further the reformation of the church from within.

Indeed, this appeal to the higher authority of a council encouraged the bishops of Rome and their curialist supporters to maintain their unresponsive and negative attitude toward these requests throughout the 1520s and early 1530s. Bernhard Lohse aptly summarized this phenomenon when he wrote: "The popes' experiences with the councils of the fifteenth century partially explain why they were reluctant to call a council in the sixteenth century. The popes' drive for power and their unwillingness to reform the church were major reasons that led them to reject the councils."[26]

The Schmalkald Articles and Papal Authority

In SA, while rejecting the most extreme papal claims for authority, Luther writes:

> All [the pope's] bulls and books, in which he roars like a lion, ... state that no Christians can be saved unless they are obedient and submit to him in all things—what he wills, what he says, what he does.[27]

Luther rejects here sentiments similar to those expressed by Pope Boniface VIII in the 1302 bull *Unam Sanctam*: "Further, We declare, say, define, and pronounce that it is absolutely necessary for the salvation of every human creature to be subject to the Roman pontiff."[28] Luther's reference points to the ever-widening influence of the medieval papacy "from the middle years of the thirteenth century, [when] the papacy was involved at the highest level in European politics: not—as Innocent III had striven to be—as a disinterested arbiter, but as an interested party."[29]

Such papal claims contributed to "the crisis of the medieval papacy" and eventually to the Babylonian captivity and the Great Schism.[30]

Luther is indicating here that both canon law and church history had set precedent for viewing such a council as above the pope. Cf. "The Leipzig Debate" of 1519 (*WA* 2:158–61; *LW* 31:313–25); and "On the Councils and the Church" (*WA* 50:509–653; *LW* 41:3–178).

26. Bernhard Lohse, *Martin Luther: An Introduction to His Life and Work,* trans. Robert C. Schultz (Philadelphia: Fortress Press, 1986), 9. Geoffrey Barraclough arrived at a conclusion similar to Lohse's: "[The failure of conciliar reform in the late Middle Ages] was the tragedy of the medieval papacy. The conciliar movement gave it its last opportunity. The trouble with the popes was that they were too clever to take it, but not clever enough to see the consequences of not taking it" (*The Medieval Papacy* [New York: W. W. Norton, 1968], 172).

27. SA II, 4, 4.

28. John Clarkson et al., eds., *The Church Teaches* (St. Louis: Herder Book Co., 1955), 75.

29. Barraclough, *Papacy,* 118.

30. Ibid.

The Schmalkald Articles and Enthusiasm

In SA III, 8, "On Confession," Luther indicates that the Roman church was not the only threat to the evangelical witness. The reformer mentions five times in the thirteen paragraphs of this article that the left wing of the Reformation is also an adversary. In other contexts, Luther refers to the adherents of this movement as *Schwärmer* or *Schwärmerei*,[31] but here he uses the term *Enthusiasmus* or *Enthusiasten*.

The Schmalkald Articles provide this view of their surrounding historical context, alluding to both the career of Thomas Münzer and the happenings at Münster in 1535:

> In these things, which concern the spoken, external word, it is certain to stay with this: God gives no one his Spirit or grace apart from the external word which goes before. We are thus protected from the enthusiasts, that is, the spirits who boast that they have the Spirit apart from and before contact with the word. They judge the Scriptures or the word accordingly, interpreting and stretching them however it pleases them. Münzer did this, and there are still many who do this today.[32]

When Luther writes, "Münzer did this, and there are still many who do this today" (i.e., "boast that they have the Spirit"), he indicates something significant about his context and his methodology: Luther was a theologian who sought to relate the teachings of the church to the concrete concerns of everyday life. Thus, because the recent events at Münster had caused such a stir, it was natural for the reformer to illustrate the dangers of the "enthusiasts" by referring to the infamous Münzer as well as the erstwhile "Kingdom of God."[33]

This reference takes on even more meaning when Luther goes on to draw this conclusion: "The papacy is also pure enthusiasm."[34] As Luther interprets

---

31. *Against the Heavenly Prophets* . . . , 1525 (*WA* 18:62–125, 134–214; *LW* 40:73–223).

32. SA III, 8, 3.

33. Münzer (1489–1525) was a fiery fanatic who felt that he received direct revelations from the Holy Spirit. He sought to extirpate the ungodly from towns where he held influence (Zwickau, Allstedt, Mühlhausen, and, finally, Frankenhausen). He was executed after the fall of Frankenhausen in May of 1525. He remained for Luther the symbol of the evils of the left wing of the Reformation. "The Kingdom of God" at Münster, established in 1535 on principles similar to Münzer's, was subsequently overthrown only a year before Luther wrote SA.

34. SA III, 8, 4. Thomas McDonough has written: " 'Enthusiasten' is employed by the Reformer to designate all groups claiming a spiritual superiority with regard to the Reformation movement" (*The Law and the Gospel in Luther* [London: Oxford University Press, 1963], 133 n. 5). McDonough's definition needs qualification. This issue for Luther was not "superiority" but God's theology (i.e., when Luther thought that the revelation of God's word was replaced by special illumination or human authority, he called it "enthusiasm").

the fundamental issue at stake in the Reformation, the "left wing" and the papacy, at their roots, look basically the same.[35] Luther could make this claim, based on his well-known distinction between law and gospel. Both the papists and the enthusiasts had, according to Luther, confused the law with the gospel.[36] On one hand, Thomas Münzer demanded from his followers obedience to himself and a subsequent life-style enforced by the various city laws enacted wherever he held power.[37] On the other hand, the pope presided over a complex, hierarchical system of masses, pilgrimages, penance, and so forth.[38] In both instances, Luther saw an explicit emphasis on human works as the means for obtaining salvation, thus negating the grace of God that comes through the word alone.[39] In Luther's estimation, both systems attempted to offer justification by works, and both were to be rejected.

The specific references that Luther makes to the particular historical circumstances surrounding SA show that it was written in the context of events that mark the end the medieval period and beginning of the modern era. The Reformation represents an epochal turning point of history, and, as we shall see in the next chapter, SA is close to the heart of one of the leading protagonists of this epoch.

---

35. Here is a basis for accepting Heinold Fast's designation of *Der linke Flügel der Reformation* (Bremen: C. Schünemann, 1962) over George H. Williams's *The Radical Reformation* (Philadelphia: Westminister Press, 1962). The word "radical" comes from the Latin *radix*, which means "root." Here Luther indicates that the gospel is actually more "radical" than either the papal church or the enthusiasts recognize. The metaphor "left wing" does not necessarily equal "radical," in its root sense. For a short summary of the issues at stake in this terminological debate, cf. Adolf Laube, "Radicalism as a Research Problem in the History of the Early Reformation," in *Radical Tendencies in the Reformation: Divergent Perspectives*, ed. Hans J. Hillerbrand, Sixteenth Century Essays and Studies, vol. 9 (Kirksville, Mo.: Sixteenth Century Journal Publications, 1986).

36. SA III, 8, 3a.

37. SA III, 8, 3b.

38. SA III, 8, 4.

39. SA III, 8, 6–8.

2

Luther's Theological Testament

FOR ALMOST THREE HUNDRED YEARS, THE COMPOSITE PICTURE OF THE ORIgins of the Schmalkald Articles has been rather consistently described in a manner not unlike what follows: In 1536, Luther's Elector, Prince John Fredrick of Saxony, instructed the reformer to write a statement of Christian doctrine that could be presented as a confession of faith at the recently called council of the church (which was to meet at Mantua, Italy, in the spring of 1537). This document, which Luther wrote to clarify the doctrinal issues the reformer deemed nonnegotiable and those issues still open for discussion and perhaps even compromise, was finished in December of 1536. It was discussed, revised somewhat, and subscribed by a small group of theologians at Wittenberg.[1] The Elector had the document brought to a meeting of the Protestant estates at the town of Schmalkalden in February of 1537, so that it might be endorsed as a common evangelical confession of faith. However, the articles were not officially approved by the Schmalkald League, although they were subscribed by the majority of theologians present. After Luther privately published SA in 1538, the authority of the document as a witness to authentic Lutheranism began to grow. These articles were incorporated into various Lutheran *corpora doctrinae* ("bodies of doctrine") of mid-sixteenth-century Lutheranism.[2] They reached authoritative confessional status as part of the 1580 *Book of Concord.*[3]

This traditional picture of the origins of SA sees the recently called council

---

1. *UuA*, 75.

2. For a general account of how these *corpora* evolved into and were superseded by the 1580 *Book of Concord,* see Robert Kolb, *Confessing the Faith: Reformers Define the Church 1530–1580* (St. Louis: Concordia Publishing House, 1990), 119ff.; and Wolf-Dieter Hauschild, "Corpus Doctrinae und Bekenntnisschriften: Zur Vorgeschichte des Konkordienbuches," in *Bekenntnis und Einheit der Kirche,* ed. Brecht and Schwarz, 235–52.

3. Insofar as the periodically revised historical introductions to *The Book of Concord* can serve as guides to the history of the interpretation of SA, this description of the origins of SA represents a rather broad historical consensus. This account of the origins of SA is, on the whole, affirmed by these eight interpreters of *The Book of Concord:* (1) Heinrich Pipping, *Historisch-theologische Einleitung zu denen sämtlichen gewöhnlichsten symbolischen Schrifften der Evangelisch-Lutherischen*

of the church as the primary factor that determined the shape and character of the articles. This significant component, however, is not the only major piece in the historical puzzle of SA's origins. A second and even more important factor gives SA its distinctive place in the context of Luther's life and thought: the reformer wrote SA under the pressure of his supposed pending death.

The decisive factor in shaping SA is the acute illness that befell Luther before, during, and after the text of SA was written. These bouts with ill health caused Luther and his contemporaries to conclude that the reformer was about to die. The specter of death pervades SA and makes this document Luther's testament of faith, designed to express clearly the heart of the reformer's theology for seemingly the last time. This document, then, contains what Luther wished to bequeath theologically to posterity.

Luther's Health in Later Life

By late medieval and early modern standards, when the average life expectancy was perhaps as low as twenty to thirty-five years of age, Luther lived to be a relatively old man.[4] The reformer, however, did not reach such an advanced age (just over sixty-two, when he died) with ease.[5] Because "Luther spoke and wrote freely about his infirmities, often embarrassingly so,"[6] we can determine rather specifically the character of the reformer's various maladies in the formative period of SA.

Throughout the 1530s, Luther was beleaguered with illness. He suffered from "ringing in the ears," which he said already in 1530 "roars like wind and

Kirchen (Leipzig, 1703); (2) Johann Georg Walch, *Christliches Concordienbuch* (Jena, 1750); (3) Jacobs, *The Book of Concord;* (4) Johann Tobias Müller, *Die symbolischen Bücher der evangelisch-lutherischen Kirche* (Gütersloh: C. Bertelsmann Verlag, 1907); (5) Friedrich Bente, ed., *Concordia Triglotta* (St. Louis: Concordia Publishing House, 1921); (6) *BSLK*; (7), *BC*, 59; and (8) the 1986 (10th) edition of *BSLK*.

4. Creighton Gilbert, "When Did Renaissance Man Grow Old?" *Studies in the Renaissance* 14 (1967): 12. The twenty to thirty-five-year figure is cited by Gilbert from a study by Carlo M. Cipolla, *The Economic History of World Population* (Baltimore: Penguin Books, 1962). Gilbert himself concludes: "Between forty and sixty, the Renaissance noticed that people stopped work and died" (p. 13).

5. A number of secondary sources have noted the generally poor status of Luther's health in his adult years. E.g., Georg Buchwald, editor of Luther's sermons of 1535–36, *WA* 41:xii; Edwards, *Battles*, 9; and Andrea van Dülmen, *Luther-Chronik* (Munich: DTV, 1983), 220. For general descriptions of Luther's health history, see Friedrich Küchenmeister, *Dr. Martin Luthers Krankengeschichte* (Leipzig, 1881); and Paul J. Reiter, *Martin Luthers Umwelt, Charakter und Psychose* (Copenhagen: Ejnar Munksgaard, 1941), vol. 2.

6. Haile, *Luther*, 33. A few lines later, Haile also points out that Luther was "childishly open about his characteristic, often violent oscillations in mood, especially during attacks of depression."

flood."[7] Paul Reiter notes that these episodes were of a recurring and, from time to time, disabling nature: "Still in the years 1532–33, we hear in letters and at table his complaints about the ringing in his ears, which would cause him to pass out."[8] Moreover, in 1532, an ulcer on his leg, about which he had first complained a few years earlier,[9] apparently began "to plague him again."[10]

In the summer and fall of 1535, when Pope Paul III was considering whether or not to send his nuncio to Germany in order to explore the possibility of a general council of the church,[11] Luther was suffering from various sorts of sickness. Three specific references from Luther's correspondence during this time indicate the variety of ills that were nagging him. First, in an August 23 letter to Jacob Probst, the reformer mentions, "I have become a decrepit man. To work before noon is impossible, because of the pain."[12]

A second reference to Luther's health was written a few days later, on August 29, when he wrote to Philip Melanchthon:

> Today Dr. Brück arrived. I shall visit him tomorrow if I am able. Yesterday and today I have been suffering from diarrhea, and my body has been weakened so that I cannot sleep and have no appetite, and we have nothing to drink. I hope to feel better tomorrow. In the last two days I have had fifteen bowel movements.[13]

A third specific reference to Luther's health is found in an October 28 letter to Justus Jonas: "I am suffering from a salty catarrhal cold, and sometimes from a slight cough."[14]

Illnesses in 1536

By modern standards, these three illnesses are not extraordinary, but they occurred at a time when medical practices probably killed more people than they

---

7. *WABr* 5:380 (letter to Conrad Cordatus, June 19, 1530).

8. Reiter, *Luthers Umwelt*, 2:37. Reiter cites as his sources for these observations the *Sächsisches Kirchen- und Schulblatt* (1876), 355; and Küchenmeister, *Luthers Krankengeschichte*, 74–75. It should be noted that Reiter's work has not been given unanimous endorsement by historians. E.g., Walther von Loewenich writes: "The work of Paul J. Reiter, despite its wealth of material, is . . . one-sided . . . [in its] judgment of phenomena" (*Luther*, 375).

9. Edwards, *Battles*, 9.

10. Reiter, *Luthers Umwelt*, 2:37. Reiter relates this comment to Luther's bleeding leg. However, his reference, which points to Köstlin and Kawerau, *Martin Luther*, 2:272, does not correlate with this statement concerning Luther's injured leg.

11. For an account of Nuncio Vergerio's visit (which was accepted explicitly by Kittelson [*Luther the Reformer*, 264 n. 10]), see Haile, *Luther*, 7–31.

12. *WABr*, 7:239$_{10}$.

13. *WABr*, 7:245; *LW*, 50:87.

14. *WABr*, 7:316; *LW* 50:108.

healed. Without analgesics and antibiotics and a germ theory of disease, each illness could seem terminal. Moreover, Luther's bouts with such physical ills began to intensify in early 1536, the year the text of SA was written. Luther mentions three times in a January 19 letter to Caspar Müller[15] that he is suffering the adverse effects of "coughing and sneezing."[16] This particular virus lasted at least until February 1, when Luther wrote to the Elector: "I have had a cold and sinus drainage, along with accompanied unpleasantness."[17]

A few weeks later, in a letter to Martin Bucer, Luther reports a different sort of malady: "I must write briefly, my dear Bucer, because I have been on my back for two weeks with pains in the left hip which cannot be endured; I am just now regaining some life."[18]

Both the severity of Luther's illness in these weeks and the concern others had about the reformer's health are underscored by the letters of his contemporaries. Philip Melanchthon mentions in a March 19 letter that Luther's hip is causing the reformer "very severe pains."[19] In addition, a letter of sympathy and concern from Margrave George of Brandenburg-Ansbach[20] to Luther on May 21 points to both the high regard this prince had for Luther and the perceived seriousness of the reformer's physical health:

> Worthy and learned, especially beloved [Martin]: Recently it has been reported to us how you have been gripped by a physical ailment from our Lord God. While you suffered this illness, we suffered as Christians with you. When we heard, in answer to our earnest inquiries, that you had again received health from our Lord God, undoubtedly from God's almighty power, . . . we were extremely happy. We hope that God's almighty power will linger with you for a long time and you continue to receive health.[21]

Yet a third interested observer of Luther's condition at this time was Prince George of Anhalt,[22] who mentioned in a March 30 letter Luther's "adverse

15. Caspar Müller (d. ?) was chancellor of the Counts of Mansfeld and corresponded with Luther on a number of occasions. Luther had dedicated *An Open Letter on the Harsh Book against the Peasants* (1525) to Müller (*WA* 18:384; *LW* 46:63) and Müller had visited Luther at Coburg during the Diet of Augsburg.

16. The letter is dated January 19, 1536 (*WABr* 7:348 and 349; *LW* 50:128–29).

17. *WABr* 7:356₆ (letter dated February 1, 1536).

18. *WABr* 7:379₃.

19. Friedrich Wilhelm Schirrmacher, *Briefe und Acten zu der Geschichte des Religionsgespräches zu Marburg 1529 und des Reichstages zu Augsburg 1530* (Amsterdam: Verlag B. R. Grüner, 1968), 375.

20. George of Brandenburg-Ansbach (d. 1543), known as George the Pious, was an ardent proponent of the Reformation.

21. *WABr* 7:416.

22. Prince George of Anhalt (d. 1553) began reading the works of Luther and Melanchthon in the early 1530s and through his studies was won for the Reformation.

health, by which he was detained and though this was not commonly known, it was reported to us." [23]

The acute nature of the sufferings Luther endured during the spring of 1536 is made strikingly clear by Luther himself, who wrote these words to John Briessmann on May 1:

> I have been raised with Christ from the dead this Easter. I had been so sick that I was persuaded that I was about to die and go to Christ our Lord, which I expected and eagerly awaited. But there was another will in heaven to be sure, so I can see more evil things even into the pit. [24]

In fact, it was just a few lines earlier in this letter that Luther referred to himself for the first time, at least in writing, as an "old man," [25] a reference that is best understood in the light of the painful infirmity the reformer suffered in these weeks.

A week and a half later, on May 12, Luther was suffering an attack of kidney stones, to which he refers in a letter to Wolfgang Capito, a member of the delegation making its way toward Wittenberg for the talks that would eventually yield the Wittenberg Concord. [26] Luther had agreed to meet the South Germans at Eisenach, but here he requests a meeting place close to home:

> Deign to approach more closely, that is to Grimma, which is located three miles past Leipzig. Either I myself will be there on the fifth Lord's day, or, if my health impedes me, I will be able to exchange letters within a day's time. [27]

This note does not identify the specific malady that prompted Luther's request, but in a letter to George of Brandenburg at the end of May, Luther discloses the nature of the illness that hindered him from keeping the prearranged appointment: "Because of my new guest, the stone, I was not able to go to Eisenach, as agreed." [28]

During the negotiations that produced WC, Luther was once again ailing. Wolfgang Musculus, [29] a member of the South German delegation from Augs-

23. *UuA*, 19 n. 7 (Otto C. Clemen, *Georg Helts Briefwechsel* [Leipzig, 1907], 102).

24. *WABr* 7:405$_{17}$.

25. *Senex* (*WA* 7:405$_8$).

26. These discussions were held from May 21 to 29, 1536 (Georg Buchwald, "Luther-kalendarium," *Schriften des Vereins für Reformationsgeschichte* 47, Heft 2 [Nr. 147], 1929, 106f.). An English translation of the text of WC can be found in Jacobs, *The Book of Concord*, 2:253–60. Cf. also *WABr* 12:200ff. and *CR* 3:75ff.

27. *WABr* 7:410$_9$.

28. The letter is dated May 30 (*WABr* 7:425).

29. Wolfgang Musculus (d. 1563) had helped to establish the Reformation in Strassburg, after which he served as a pastor in Augsburg from 1531 to 1547. He participated in a number of religious colloquies in the middle years of the sixteenth century.

burg who wrote a firsthand account of the proceedings, made this telling notation about Luther's insomnia on May 22:

> At the appointed time of eight o'clock, we went to Dr. Luther. However,
> when we had entered the house, Pomeranus[30] with some others prevented
> us [from seeing Luther] by explaining that Luther could not meet now
> because he had not slept the preceding night. We were asked to come back
> at three.[31]

Luther's physical difficulties continued in these days. At the festive worship
service on the Sunday after the negotiations had come to an amicable conclusion, Musculus made this observation: "Luther himself was attacked by vertigo
after communion. He was compelled to leave with Philip." [32]

In June 1536, the month that the papal summons to the proposed council
at Mantua was published, Luther continued to have trouble with kidney
stones, as his letter to Justus Jonas indicates:

> I am writing only a little because yesterday all day I suffered with the
> passage of a stone, which you Bavarians call "lead." But there came out,
> through strong wine, a number of granules. I was revived.[33]

Evidently the fall of 1536 was a welcome respite from these types of physical disorders, as there are no extant references to Luther's ailments in these
months. In December, however, this changed dramatically. On the tenth he
preached his last sermon of the year, after which he began diligently to work
on SA in accordance with the Elector's request of December 11 (the bulk of
SA was written in the next seven days).[34] Luther became seriously ill around
the middle of the month, and the length of his recovery kept him out of the
pulpit until January 14, 1537.[35] This hiatus from preaching is significant because it covered the Christmas season of the liturgical calendar. This was the
only occasion, from 1519 to 1542, that Luther did not preach on the festival

---

30. John Bugenhagen (1485–1558), who came to Wittenberg from Pomerania, was pastor of the
City Church from 1522 to 1558 and a close collaborator with Luther.

31. Kolde, *Lutherana*, 218.

32. Ibid., 228.

33. *WABr* 7:428₁₂.

34. Luther had been at work already by December 12 (*UuA*, 29f.; cf. also *WATR* 3:361f.).

35. There is a mistake in the table of Luther's sermons in *WA* 41:xiv–xvii, which indicates that
Luther preached in Lichtenberg on December 21. This could not have happened, because Luther
was clearly too ill. Cf. Hans Volz, *Luthers Schmalkaldische Artikel und Melanchthons Tractatus de
potestate papae* (Gotha: Leopold Klotz Verlag, 1931), 7 n. 4.

of Christmas.[36] All of this points to the debilitating nature of this affliction because, in spite of his recurring ill health over the years, Luther's prodigious capacity to work was rarely impeded sufficiently to keep him out of the pulpit for such a period of time,[37] let alone during such an important season of the church year.

An abundance of sources allows for a fairly precise reconstruction of events. On December 18, when Luther was not quite finished writing SA, he was stricken by an apparent heart attack. Anton Lauterbach noted in his "diary" at this time: "Luther, on the evening of December 18, had a great pain in his chest and was quite pale in the face. But soon, by God's grace, he regained his strength in the presence of the barber."[38] On the next day, however, Luther had a relapse. Lauterbach penned this note: "Year '36, 19 December: around three today, Martin Luther was seized by a great convulsion focused on the chest and he was laid low by it."[39] Then on the following day (December 20), this telling reference to Luther's illness was included in a letter of one Dorothea Kersten[40] to her brother-in-law, Stephen Roth of Zwickau: "You should also know that on the Tuesday before Saint Thomas, around 3:00 pm, something happened: Dr. Martin fell into a death-like illness. What sort of sickness he has, I have no way of knowing."[41] Still another reference to the severity of Luther's illness is an interesting entry in the ledger of Electoral Saxony that notes an emergency call for a physician to come from Torgau to Wittenberg in order to tend to Luther, "who was at the time very weak."[42]

Luther himself refers to the lingering effects of this illness. In a cover letter sent with SA to the Elector after a small gathering of theologians had discussed the articles (between Christmas 1536 and January 3, 1537),[43] Luther mentions that his continuing ill health was the cause of the unexpected length of the discussions concerning his articles at Wittenberg (the meeting lasted two days):

---

36. Luther's published sermons are listed in Kurt Aland, *Hilfsbuch zum Lutherstudium* (Witten: Luther-Verlag, 1970), 205–62; Buchwald's *Kalendarium* lists the occasions of Luther's sermons, even if they were not transcribed and published.

37. Cf. Haile, *Luther,* 34.

38. *WATR* 3:369 n. 3 (*UuA,* 33). Concerning these notes of Lauterbach as "diaries," cf. *WATR* 3:xii.

39. *WATR* 5, no. 6079 (*UuA,* 34).

40. Kersten was a sister-in-law to the Wittenberg printer George Rhau (1488–1548). She was a widow who was apparently living with the Luthers at the time. She died in 1538. Cf. *UuA,* 34 n. 11.

41. *UuA,* 34f.

42. *UuA,* 34.

43. *WA* 50:173.

To these [gathered theologians] I presented the articles, as I formulated them myself. We dealt with them a few days, because of my weakness, which befell me on account of Satan. Otherwise, I had hoped that the discussions would not have lasted more than a day.[44]

This catalog of Luther's health history has spanned the months leading up to Luther's completion of the text of SA and has brought us to early 1537 and the eve of the reformer's most serious bout with illness prior to his death. This episode with the "stone" came close to claiming Luther's life and provides further evidence that while writing SA, the reformer was wrestling with his mortality.

Kidney Stones at Schmalkalden

The influence of Luther's health on SA is evident beyond the effect it had on the mere completion of the text. Luther fell critically ill at the meeting of the Schmalkald League in February of 1537 and was unable personally to attend any official proceedings. If the reformer had been able to participate in the meetings at Schmalkalden, there is no telling what would have happened to SA and, perhaps, to the Schmalkald League as well. Presenting SA to a full gathering of the assembly would probably have reopened old questions for fresh debate and it is doubtful whether SA could have produced the needed unity, as is evident in the lack of unanimity regarding SA among the theologians.[45] Certainly Luther's strong presence would have been difficult to contradict and would have altered the course of events significantly.

Luther arrived in Schmalkalden on Wednesday, February 7, and then took off the next day.[46] February 8, however, was hardly an ordinary day of rest, as is evident from Luther's letter to Justus Jonas, penned after the reformer had preached on Friday morning, in the City Church of Schmalkalden.[47] He writes:

Yesterday I suffered a stone, but without pain—it passed out through black urine so that it was unnoticeable. I did not take notice of the stone (to be sure, it was broken into pieces in the liquid itself), nor did I sense

---

44. *WABr* 8:3₁₁ (January 3, 1537). Gregor Brück likewise mentions Luther's illness at this time in a letter to John Fredrick, dated January 6: "I look forward to seeing Martin tomorrow . . . he should be up to it" (*UuA*, 79).

45. Philip Melanchthon apparently expressed this type of concern to Philip of Hesse in Schmalkalden on the eve of the Bundestag. Cf. Volz, *Luthers Schmalkaldische Artikel und Melanchthons Tractatus*, 17–19.

46. Buchwald, "Luther-kalendarium," 111.

47. Kolde, *Lutherana*, 269.

this secret before it went out. . . . If your stone were as secret as these, we would congratulate you and you would rejoice.[48]

Prior to this paragraph, Luther had mentioned to Jonas something that is perhaps indicative of the physical trials to come. Luther noticed that, while preaching in the "vast and lofty" City Church of Schmalkalden, his voice sounded as weak as a "shrew mouse."[49]

This letter ends with a request for Jonas, along with Caspar Cruciger,[50] to pray for the Schmalkalden gathering of the German estates. Luther himself, as it turned out, needed those prayers even more than he realized, because the apparent passage of blood in his urine anticipated the onset of a severe attack of kidney stones.[51] This extremely painful and protracted episode nearly killed the reformer.

On Sunday, February 11, after preaching that morning at his quarters, Luther again had a bout with the stone.[52] In fact, by that evening it was said that Luther was "drowning in his own water."[53] This episode also passed, and Luther preached again in the City Church on the next Sunday.[54]

However, by Saturday, February 17, Luther's malady was intensifying, as this sentence in a letter written that day shows: "I am not able to write everything, because all day I am, on account of the painful stone, a useless person."[55] Useless or not, Luther summoned enough strength to preach the next morning.[56] By the afternoon of February 18, Luther's suffering began to intensify, as this notation from an eyewitness indicates: "He became very ill in the after-

---

48. *WABr* 8:40.

49. Ibid. (cf. also *WA* 54:xvi).

50. Caspar Cruciger (d. 1548) studied at the University of Wittenberg in the early 1520s and became preacher at the castle church and professor in Wittenberg in 1528.

51. Wilhelm Ebstein, *Dr. Martin Luthers Krankheiten* (Stuttgart: Verlag von Ferdinand Enke, 1908), 20f. Ebstein explains Luther's lack of suffering at this time as related to an earlier episode, being much worse, that had stretched the ureter so that the passage of a smaller stone would not necessarily be accompanied with great pain.

52. *CR* 3:268; *UuA*, 114.

53. *WATR* 3:587$_{31}$. Haile (*Luther*, 214) connects this quotation with the most severe struggle Luther had with kidney stones at Schmalkalden, which began the next Sunday, but Lauterbach's report is from February 13.

54. Haile, *Luther*, 214; *WA* 45:25ff.

55. *WABr* 8:45$_{32}$ (letter to Jacob Meyer of Basel).

56. *WA* 45:25. Haile mentions that on this occasion Luther "marveled at how small his voice sounded [in the City Church]," but he seems to be confusing this description with the reformer's earlier comment about sounding like a "shrew mouse" (*Luther*, 214).

noon, with the stone."[57] Luther's condition developed into a very critical situation, as he became completely unable to urinate. He later reported to his wife Katherine:[58] "No little drop of water would come from me, I could not rest or sleep, drink or eat."[59]

As physicians were called to tend to Luther, he was compelled to suffer not only from the illness but from the indignities and ministrations of his medieval medicos as well. The notes of one of the attending physicians at Schmalkalden, Mathias Ratzeberger (the Elector's personal physician), provide a firsthand account.[60] An attempt was made to insert a catheter, but to no avail. Apparently even a potion that contained a mixture of garlic and horse manure was administered.[61] The reformer could neither eat nor sleep. His entire body became bloated with edema as he followed the recommendation to force liquids in an effort to push the stone through the bladder and out the urethra. Luther summarized the indignities of the experience: "They gave me as much to drink as if I were a huge ox and treated all my limbs, even sucking my private parts."[62] Finally Luther had had enough and commanded the physicians: "Do not come again!"[63] He then quickly added, "I would rather die!"[64] The attending physician complied because he "could do nothing for him but wait until the end."[65]

Ratzeberger's report continues: "On account of that, Dr. Luther placed himself in God's hand and blessed his brothers who were gathered with him. He then expressed his wish not to die in Schmalkalden, but rather in Gotha, in Saxony." Therefore, on February 26, the Elector of Saxony sent his personal coach to transport the patient to Gotha.

That day the entourage made it only as far as Tambach, about ten miles away. There, perhaps from the jostling experienced while en route, "Luther had a great desire to urinate." And urinate he did (over a gallon!). Luther was

---

57. *WATR* 6:301$_{28}$.

58. Katherine von Bora (d. 1552) married Luther on June 13, 1525. She was a former nun who had left her Cistercian convent in 1523 and come to Wittenberg. Her strong personality was a good match for Luther's.

59. *WABr* 8:51$_6$.

60. Ratzeberger's report is quoted at length in Reiter, *Luthers Umwelt*, 2:38f.; cf. also von Loewenich, *Luther*, 377.

61. Both von Loewenich (*Luther*, 377) and Haile (*Luther*, 214) report this, but neither offers a primary reference for it.

62. *WATR* 3:578$_{10}$. Translation from Oberman, *Luther: Man between God and the Devil*, 330.

63. *WATR* 5:96$_{12}$.

64. Ibid.

65. Reiter, *Luthers Umwelt*, 2:39.

so relieved that he happily wrote to Melanchthon in the predawn hours of February 27:

> To my dear Philip: blessed be the God and Father of our Lord Jesus Christ, Father of mercies and all comfort who in this second hour of the night opened urethra and bladder unexpectedly when I arose to urinate (as you have seen me do, but fail). In scarcely a quarter of an hour, I urinated more than seven times, so that I voided more than a pot. Thus happiness compels me to measure this liquid, so vile to others, but most precious to me.[66]

Luther immediately sent the letter to Schmalkalden with a horseman, who rode into the sleeping town shouting, "Luther lives! Luther lives!"[67] Although the stone returned the next day in Gotha, this episode lasted but two days and Luther returned to Wittenberg in order to recuperate.

This episode provides a fitting climax to the argument that SA was formulated under the pressure of the reformer's supposed pending death: The composition of SA was surrounded and interpenetrated by Luther's ongoing confrontation with his finitude. Before, during, and after Luther wrote SA, he (and those around him) thought he was going to die.

The Attitudes of Luther and His Contemporaries

In the middle years of the 1530s, Luther's chronic health problems made death seem imminent. He therefore wanted to leave the world a faith legacy that would be clear and pointed, emphasizing the most significant features of his theology. The pending council and the Elector's commission, coupled with his own health problems, were the motivations that the reformer needed. The professor and the prince were both concerned that future generations have an authentic expression of Lutheran theology. If the council did not happen, or the Protestants did not attend, SA would still remain as a clear confession of evangelical faith.

Because Luther and his coworkers saw SA as perhaps his final theological statement to the world, written as if it were from the author's deathbed, SA should be seen in the context of Renaissance understandings of "the art of dying well."[68] In sixteenth-century Germany this process was, whenever pos-

---

66. *WABr* 8:49₁. This letter was written between 2 and 3 A.M. on February 27.

67. Reiter, *Luthers Umwelt*, 2:39.

68. "The Art of Dying" is a name given to various manuals related to the subject in late medieval Europe (Haile, *Luther*, 215).

sible, an event of solemn dignity. The terminally ill person was not taken to a strange, sterile environment to die under the care of anonymous people, as death so often comes in Western culture today. In the sixteenth century, the dying person, when possible, died at home and "presided" at the occasion of his or her death.[69] H. G. Haile describes it this way:

> Dying was a familiar and important part of Renaissance life. Family and friends gathered at one's bedside and the scene often possessed a rare dignity. The dying endeavored to display exemplary composure and to instill into survivors proper faith in the life of the soul. One's last moments and sayings were noted well and long remembered.[70]

For a Christian thinker like Luther, it was natural that he would want to make in SA a final theological statement that would indeed be "noted well and long remembered."[71] This is precisely what Luther did in SA.

Luther

Luther indicates this perspective within the document itself. The Preface, written a year after the text of SA was completed and while Luther was preparing to publish his work, indicates that the reformer continued to view SA as his faith testament:

> Therefore I wanted to make these articles available through the public press at this time, in case I should die before a council could take place (as I fully expect and hope). I wanted to do this . . . so that those who live and remain after me will have my testament and confession. . . . I have held fast to this confession until now and, by God's grace, I will continue to hold to it. What should I say? Why should I complain? I am still alive— every day I write, preach, and teach. Yet there are such poisonous people. . . . What will happen in the future after my death?
> Should I indeed respond to everything while I am still living?[72]

This quotation from the Preface of SA has much within it that indicates the testamentary character of SA. And there is much additional evidence in this document that indicates that it was intended to preserve Luther's legacy of faith for subsequent generations. At the end of SA, Luther writes:

---

69. Creighton Gilbert makes note of the "farewells to friends" that are described in sixteenth-century sources in "When Did Renaissance Man Grow Old?" 17.

70. Haile, *Luther,* 216.

71. Ibid.

72. SA, Preface, 3–5.

These are the articles on which I must stand and on which I intend to stand, God willing, until my death. I know of nothing in them that can be changed or conceded.[73]

These two quotations, coming at the beginning and end of SA, bracket (as it were) Luther's confession of faith, his theological testament for posterity. Moreover, the testamentary mood found in these sentences pervades all that falls between. Luther is willing to stake his very life on the view of faith presented in SA. This is particularly true with respect to the central, "first and chief article," about which Luther writes: "We cannot yield or concede anything in this article, even if heaven and earth, or whatever, do not remain."[74]

Luther reveals the intensity and sense of personal urgency with which SA was written in yet another way. The reformer seems to forget, from time to time in SA, the larger community he is supposed to represent when he lapses into the first person singular *ich* from the plural *wir*.[75] For example, Luther's grammatical inconsistency serves to emphasize the personal importance with which he viewed this work.

One could expect that a dying person would speak in a familiar, intimate manner and not with detached, academic language. And this is, in a sense, what Luther does. The articles are written in German—a curious language to use for one intent upon having such a document presented to a sixteenth-century council of the church. Latin would have been the expected language of discourse at Mantua, and Luther would have been well aware of that. Nevertheless, the reformer chose to write SA in his native tongue, a fact that lends further credence to the notion that Luther wrote with a personal stake in what he says. Luther intends, by means of SA, to speak a strong (and in a way, even intimate) word to his followers.

Yet another piece of evidence points to the testamentary character of SA: the mere existence of Part I. This short section, which asserts the main features of trinitarian theology, ends with these words: "These articles are not matters of dispute or conflict, for both sides confess them. Therefore it is not necessary to deal with them at greater length."[76] If Luther really felt that this is the case, then a question regarding his motivation in including these articles at all might legitimately be raised: Why spend the time asserting the veracity of topics that everyone agrees are true?

Because SA was to contain Luther's theological legacy to the world, he

---

73. SA III, 15, 3.

74. SA II, 1, 5.

75. E.g., SA II, 4, 14; III, 13, 1, 2; III, 28, 42.

76. SA I, 4.

could not pass over in silence what he saw as vital, even though his opponents would not argue with him at this point. The catholic, trinitarian basis of Lutheran theology had to be made explicit.[77]

In summary, then, SA is Luther's supposed last formal theological statement to the world. SA was, in Martin Luther's mind, his "last theological will and testament."

Elector John Fredrick

Early in the summer of 1536, when the papal bull summoning the long-hoped-for general council reached Germany, the Saxon Prince took the initiative to encourage the formulation of a cogent evangelical response to the proposed council.[78] The Elector's interest in a brief statement from Luther regarding his theological priorities was motivated not only by an earnest desire for advice about the council from his university's most famous professor but also by the fear that Luther was soon to die (as reports of Luther's serious health problems during the previous weeks and even months had indicated to him).[79]

While Luther lived, he could obviously serve as the authoritative interpreter of his view of the Christian faith. But now that his death was seemingly approaching, John Fredrick feared the possibility for increased misunderstanding or misrepresentation of evangelical faith.[80]

When, therefore, a general council of the church became, for the first time, a real possibility, a summary statement from Luther that could also serve as his theological testament seemed imperative. The Elector's interest in such a definitive document is revealed in the communications the Saxon Prince had with Luther as well as in correspondence he had with the other Wittenberg scholars. For example, in his memorandum of early December 1536, John Fredrick writes:

> It will be highly necessary for Dr. Martin to prepare his basis and opinion with the divine scriptures, indicating all the articles upon which he has written, preached, and taught. He should do so for the sake of the council, but also in view of his final departure from this world to the almighty judgment of God. He should indicate what he thinks, maintains, and where he remains in order not to offend the divine majesty—the points

---

77. The same sort of testamentary motivation had prompted Luther to write his *Confession concerning Christ's Supper* in 1528, as he himself makes clear while citing his reasons for publishing SA (SA, Preface, 3). WA 26:261–509; LW 37:161–372.

78. For the date of the papal bull, cf. *UuA*, 15. Concerning the Elector's relevant activities in the summer of 1536, cf. *UuA*, 18 n. 1.

79. Hans Volz, "Luthers Schmalkaldische Artikel," *ZKG* 68 (1957): 260f.

80. *UuA*, 91; Luther himself shared this concern (cf. SA, Preface, 4–9).

we must maintain without regard to body or possessions, peace or conflict.[81]

Such language about Luther's "final departure from this world to God's almighty judgment" indicates that the nature of this document as Luther's theological testament played a significant role in the Elector's request for the formulation of SA.

Furthermore, after the Elector received and read what was to become SA, in early January of 1537, he wrote an enthusiastic note of approval to Luther that reveals John Fredrick's ongoing concern that Luther's health might not allow him to finish SA:

> We have received your note from Master Spalatin, together with the articles which through God's grace you discussed with the other theologians, your brothers. We give thanks to God the Almighty Father and to our Lord Christ, that he allowed you health and strength to finish such Christian, pure, and clear articles.[82]

Three days later, on January 9, John Fredrick expressed his desire to have these articles subscribed by Saxon clergy prior to the upcoming meeting at Schmalkalden. Although only one such subscription was obtained (from Gabriel Didymus of Torgau),[83] the Elector's note to Brück regarding subscription to SA contains yet another reference to the testamentary character of SA:

> In particular, we also think that subscription to the articles by the pastors and preachers would be serviceable. Because, *when God almighty takes Doctor Martin from this world* (which will happen according to the divine will), these same pastors and preachers will have to remain true to the articles and no special or individual opinions and ideas will arise.[84]

A final datum indicates John Fredrick's attitude toward SA: the Elector was an early and convinced opponent of sending an evangelical delegation to Mantua and yet commissioned Luther to write SA. Although there is some disagreement in the secondary literature regarding the Elector's attitude toward the proposed council,[85] it is clear that already in the summer of 1536,

---

81. *UuA*, 23.

82. *UuA*, 84.

83. Didymus (1487–1558) had been pastor at Torgau since 1523.

84. *UuA*, 91, emphasis added.

85. This small sampling gives a taste of the differing conclusions drawn by scholars: Allbeck, *Studies*, 188: the Elector was "originally positive" and therefore preparations were necessary. Ernest G. Schwiebert, *Luther and His Times* (St. Louis: Concordia Publishing House, 1950), 740: when Vergerio met with the Elector, he "found him in agreement with the theologians." Bente, *Introductions*, 48: "From the very beginning, Elector John Fredrick was opposed to a council." Ernst Bizer, "Zum geschichtlichen Verständnis von Luthers Schmalkaldischen Artikeln," *ZKG* 67 (1955–56):

when his professorial advisers at Wittenberg had returned to him an opinion endorsing a Protestant presence at the council, John Fredrick declared his opposition by returning the scholars' opinion with a request that they reconsider what they had proposed.[86]

The Elector's firm refusal to attend the council (which is a conclusion the Prince had drawn, by all accounts, before the time he approached Luther about SA) raises this question: If John Fredrick was against attending the proposed council, then why would he ask his foremost theologian to prepare so diligently for something that was not to happen? Apparently the Elector wanted a testamentary theological document from Luther and found in the papal council a convenient occasion for commissioning Luther to write it.

Electoral Chancellor Gregor Brück

In the summer of 1536, Chancellor Gregor Brück mediated a number of council-related communications between the Elector and his scholarly advisers at the University of Wittenberg.[87] This continued into the fall, and in a report to the Elector on September 3, 1536, Brück penned a few lines that have proved controversial to historians. The Chancellor writes first of fulfilling "the command of your Electoral Grace," and second, Brück mentions a conversation with Luther:

> I delivered the note to Doctor Martin which your Electoral Grace gave to me, and I was able to speak with him about it, your Electoral Grace. He promises to be obedient in everything and I think, also, that he is already hard at work, your Electoral Grace, to open his heart on the matter of religion as if it were his testament.[88]

In the 1950s, Hans Volz and Ernst Bizer debated in the pages of *Die Zeitschrift für Kirchengeschichte* whether or not Brück's reference to a "testament" referred to the specific document that actually became SA.[89] Does Brück's note lend further evidence to the claim that SA was a theological "testament" of Luther, or was SA really more of a public document, designed for use as a confession of faith at a general council of the church? The problems here involve the date and the nature of the Elector's request for Luther to prepare

---

62: "The Elector declared already on July 26, 1536, that, for many reasons, the papal summons would not be accepted."

86. *CR* 3:99ff.

87. Virck, "Zu den Beratungen der Protestanten über die Konzilsbulle vom 4. Juni 1536," 487–512.

88. *UuA*, 19.

89. Bizer, "Zum geschichtlichen Verständnis," 64; Volz, "Luthers Schalkaldische Artikel," 261; and Ernst Bizer, "Noch einmal: Die Schmalkaldischen Artikel," *ZKG* 68 (1957): 287–94.

articles of faith as well as the lack of a specific, extant document—outside of SA—penned by Luther that could reasonably play the role of the "testament" indicated by Brück's report. Had the Elector, already in late summer of 1536, specifically asked Luther to prepare a document that could serve as the reformer's theological "testament"?

At stake in the controversy is how one understands the origin and intended purpose of SA. On the basis of the surrounding context (the papal summons to Mantua and the upcoming meeting at Schmalkalden), Bizer argued for the received interpretation: the pending council was the primary factor that gave rise to SA. Volz argued on the basis of the above-quoted paragraph in Brück's letter and the internal evidence provided by SA itself (SA, Preface, 3, and SA III, 15, 3) that SA had its origins as Luther's personal "testament."

The debate went like this: Volz had concluded in 1931 that Brück's reference in September to Luther's "testament" related specifically to the document that was eventually to become SA.[90] Bizer took issue with this some years later: "It does not appear to me evident that Luther [in September of 1536] had already a special commission in this regard, because the Wittenbergers were hardly in general agreement about it."[91] Volz countered that SA is "not supposed to be viewed only with reference to the council—as a general confessional writing."[92]

As one reads through the scholarly works that comprise this controversy, there is evidence that the respective conclusions of the two scholars began to converge, perhaps without themselves even realizing the extent of their agreement. In a special *ZKG* edition devoted to the interpretations of Volz and Bizer, Volz wrote: "Luther fulfilled the wish of the Elector that his articles not only be the basis of discussion for the evangelicals relative to the council . . . , but rather that they should also be his personal confession."[93] This sounds actually quite similar to Bizer, who wrote in a response to Volz's article, "The composition of the Articles is indeed more complicated than a testament of Luther. Is not a document specifically for the council also capable of being at the same time a 'testament'?"[94] The original either/or of the discussions apparently gave way to a consensus of both/and.

The Volz-Bizer debate yielded this fruitful conclusion: given the general

90. Volz, *Luthers Schmalkaldische Artikel und Melanchthons Tractatus*, 3f.

91. Bizer, "Zum geschichtlichen Verständnis," 64.

92. Volz, "Luthers Schmalkaldische Artikel," 273.

93. Ibid., 268f.

94. Bizer, "Noch einmal," 289.

state of affairs in Luther's life in 1536–37, and the Elector's interest in having the reformer pen a summary statement of faith, SA's origin and purpose look like this: SA was both a personal, theological testamentary statement of faith and a public, confessional document related to Protestant deliberations about the Mantua council.

This debate and its resulting conclusion are thus quite complementary to the testamentary thesis presented here. However, there are some significant differences.[95] Neither Bizer nor Volz gives due attention to the poor state of Luther's health and the concerns raised by his contemporaries about the reformer's pending death. Volz does mention these factors, but they are relegated to the periphery of his argument, mentioned only in footnotes.[96] Bizer, of course, wanted to play down the influence of these factors. The argument presented in this present study points rather to the centrality of Luther's ill health and impending death as a determining factor, along with the deliberations that related to the Mantua council, in the origins of SA. By emphasizing the health history of Luther during the formative months of SA, the testamentary character of this document comes into sharper focus. In this way, the importance of SA as a witness to the central theological concerns of the reformer is underscored.

The exact nature of the relationship between the "testament" mentioned by Brück and SA has been and will remain "a mystery."[97] The circumstances of Luther's life in these months, and the Elector's desire for some sort of testamentary statement of faith by Luther, do not necessarily mean that Brück is referring specifically to the document that became SA. Nevertheless, the surrounding context does provide circumstantial evidence that Brück could have seen a very early form of what eventually became SA.

In the Elector's December 1536 "memorandum," in which he communicated his desire for Luther to draw up a set of articles that could serve as a summary of Lutheran doctrine, there is no specific mention of an earlier request for such a summary. If John Fredrick had made a specific appeal for a confessional statement of Luther's theology in August, then it is curious that he did not mention it again in December. Although this is an argument from

---

95. Karl Thieme came to a similar, twofold conclusion with respect to the origins of SA, although he also handles the evidence along the lines of Volz and Bizer in *Luthers Testament wider Rom in seinen Schmalkaldischen Artikeln* (Leipzig: A. Deichert, 1900), 10.

96. *UuA*, 19 n. 7, and Volz, "Luthers Schmalkaldische Artikel," 260 n. 5. Volz's work has lent great impetus to the testamentary thesis presented here. However, what is a footnote to Volz's investigation is central to this one.

97. Schaaf, "The Smalcald Articles," 73.

silence, the December note certainly reads as something other than a mere reminder for Luther to finish a previously assigned project.[98]

This memorandum reads as if it is the first such communication that the Elector had sent to Luther in this regard. Perhaps John Fredrick is adding a new emphasis to what he had requested in the late summer of 1536. Where the accent of the Elector's request in August was on a personal theological testament, in December he adds to this the need for a public document suited for use at a council of the church (or at least suitable for Protestant deliberations regarding such a council).

These two emphases and Brück's September 1536 letter are best accounted for if one posits the existence of two separate requests to Luther from John Fredrick. The first would have been that which led to Brück's comment about Luther's "testament." This would mean that the Elector had asked Luther for a personal summary statement of his faith by September 3, 1536. Then, as the Protestant meeting at Schmalkalden was drawing near, John Fredrick made a second request of his famous professor. Luther was now to fashion his statement so that it might be used for public, confessional purposes as well. This emphasis, coupled with the fact that this memorandum was sent to a group of Wittenberg theologians and not just to Luther,[99] made reference to the earlier electoral request unnecessary.

This look at the attitudes of Luther and his contemporaries regarding the role of SA in the context of the reformer's life and thought further underscores the testamentary character of SA. Luther and those around him viewed this document as a most significant witness to the heart of Lutheran theology partly because they understood that it was written as if it contained the final words of a dying man to the world.

The Schmalkald Articles as Luther's Testament of Faith

Scholars of the Lutheran confessional writings, as evident in the historical introductions to critical editions of The Book of Concord, have expressed a rather amazing consensus regarding the origins of SA. Unfortunately this consensus has tended to ignore the most significant aspect of what gave rise to these articles: this document was written and published under the direct influence of Martin Luther's supposed pending death and thus represents the theological

---

98. Allbeck's conclusion seems implausible at this point: "Apparently [Luther] had been assigned the task as early as August 20. But it seems that he did nothing about it until reminded at the beginning of December" (Studies, 188).

99. UuA, 26f.

legacy the reformer wanted to bequeath to posterity. This testamentary document, written some twenty years after the Lutheran Reformation had gotten under way in earnest, ought to command a preeminent place in the interpretation of both the Lutheran confessional writings and Luther's own theological program.

3

Luther's Confessional Testament

CHRISTIAN CONFESSIONAL DOCUMENTS BY NATURE MAKE ASSERTIONS WITH-
out extensive attention to explanation or apologetics. A confession of the
Christian faith is not systematic theology. The important task of systematizing
theology serves the church in a different way from confessions of faith. Indeed,

> dogmatics has not only the right but also the duty to present the church's
> doctrine by means of a more thorough exegetical support and a more
> comprehensive systematic order and development than could be done in
> the Confessions because of their brevity.[1]

The Nature of Confessional Documents

Although a theological system does stand behind, or is implied in, confessions
of faith, one ought not to expect a full-blown discussion of the system within
the confessional document itself.

At least two things are involved in the assertion of a confession of faith: the
Word and a community. Christian confessional documents arise out of the
desire and need of the confessors to bear witness to (i.e., "assert") their interpretation of the Word of God. Regardless of the specific circumstances that
might conceivably give rise to particular confessional documents, the Word
of God is to act as the scriptural and theological basis for such statements.[2]
Confessional writings are meant to express the most important convictions of
the community about God and God's involvement with the world.

After someone formulates a confession of faith, the community somehow
ratifies the assertions of the document.[3] This ratification may reflect a formal,

---

1. Schlink, *Theology of the Lutheran Confessions*, 33.

2. The history of the church provides examples of the various circumstances that can give rise to
confessional writings. For instance, the Nicene-Constantinopolitan creed grew out of the Arian
controversy of the fourth century, whereas the so-called Apostles' Creed has its origins in the
baptismal rite of the early church (Badcock, *The History of the Creeds*, 34, 122ff.); SC was originally,
and still remains, a catechetical tool.

3. Gritsch and Jenson, *Lutheranism*, 2ff.

political process (where a group might vote to embrace a certain kind of statement over another proposal); or it may happen informally (by the mere use of such a statement in worship, for example, it may de facto make it a confession of faith).

In SA, Luther summarized what he thought to be the most important aspects of the Christian faith. This document was designed to say what Luther had, in various ways, said before—only in SA, this was presented in a succinct and orderly manner. It presents to the church and the world a summary of what Luther interpreted as the Word of God. That meant that SA had to be basic, summarizing the fundamental articles of faith. This, in turn, meant that SA was to bring together the main features of Luther's theology that had been worked out over the course of the previous two decades.[4]

Paul Althaus noted a strongly traditional component to Luther's overall theological program when he mentioned rather summarily that "Luther . . . did not intend to say anything particularly original."[5] Luther himself made the same sort of traditionalist claim, at the outset of his famous Lectures on Galatians, published in 1535:

> We have taken it upon ourselves in the Lord's name to lecture on this Epistle of Paul to the Galatians once more. This is not because we want to teach something new or unknown.[6]

With SA in particular, and throughout his career in general, Luther did not intend to be theologically innovative. An analysis of Luther's theology based on SA corroborates the conclusion of Elector John Fredrick as he wrote to Luther on January 7, 1537, complimenting the reformer that SA did indeed reflect the theology "which [Luther] had always taught, preached, and written."[7]

The reformer had had more than twenty years of teaching and preaching, controversy and debate prior to SA in order to work out his theology. The document, written as it was toward the end of Luther's career, clearly reflects what must otherwise be culled from his hundreds of earlier theological works. It is distinctive precisely because it summarizes so clearly the theological priorities of the reformer, while at the same time it applies those priorities in a specific way to the Christian life, as we shall see.

---

4. Martin Willkomm, *Ein Vermächtnis Luthers an die Kirche* (Zwickau: Verlag von Johannes Herrmann, 1936), 28f.

5. Paul Althaus, *The Theology of Martin Luther*, trans. Robert C. Schultz (Philadelphia: Fortress Press, 1966), 3.

6. *WA* 40¹39; *LW* 26:3. This quotation is the opening line of these lectures, on the introductory page.

7. *UuA*, 84.

Luther's lack of innovation in SA is completely in line with the traditional nature of confessional documents. They are ordinarily designed so that their content is in continuity with previous dogmatic expressions. Confessional writings are formulated in order to exemplify the convictions of those who write and subscribe to them at particular moments in history. Such writings intend to synthesize what the confessor(s) "believe, teach, and confess."[8] Therefore they are meant to say something, in an organized and shortened form, that has in various ways already been said. Such summary statements serve as exemplars or witnesses to the core of the theology that underpins them and in this way offer a particular confession of faith to the church and the world.[9]

Luther's Theology in SA

The following explication of the theology of SA revolves around three poles or foci, which correspond to the three major parts of the document. Generally speaking, in Parts I and II, Luther outlines a catholic, trinitarian theology that emphasizes the evangelicalism of the forgiveness of sin (i.e., "law and gospel"). Then the reformer applies these theological priorities to the significant issues of his day as he works out the implications of his understanding of "catholic evangelicalism" in Part III. Thus, SA presents itself as a quintessential Lutheran confessional document.

Throughout this discussion of SA we would do well to keep the testamentary aspect of the document clearly in view. Luther sees himself passing on his theological legacy and thus he writes with an energy that signifies his own sense of personal commitment to the theology described.

An Overview of the Structure

Luther's Original Foreword to the Schmalkald Articles. On the cover page of Luther's original autograph appear a few lines of smudged and faded Latin text, thus making portions difficult to read. They are probably authored by Luther himself, although, given Luther's interest in classical literature, they could be a quotation adapted from one of the ancients. The last line is from Matthew 6:34.

Luther writes:

> In these things, there is sufficient doctrine for the life of the church. For the rest, in the political and economic spheres, the laws are sufficient to

---

8. This formula is used throughout FC.

9. The creeds of the church are classic instances of the summary, exemplary nature of confessional documents.

obligate us. Beyond this, it would not be useful to make burdens as if they were necessary. "Today's trouble is enough for today."[10]

These lines were not included by Spalatin in the copy of SA that he made when the document was discussed and approved at Wittenberg in December of 1536, sent to the Elector in January of 1537, and taken to Schmalkalden in February.[11] Nor were these lines included in the first published edition of 1538.

Although this epigram has no confessional status, it stands as a witness to the attitude and circumstances of Luther as he originally wrote SA. H. G. Haile has noted Luther's concern about "pedanticism and legalism among his older disciples."[12] Haile puts it this way: "Those last words he wrote across the cover of his testament struck a major theme of his career, especially in its last years."[13]

The Preface.

Luther wrote a formal preface in the spring of 1538, while preparing to publish SA the following summer (publication took place in June). The Preface covers some seven pages in *BSLK* and, as we have seen, indicates quite clearly the testamentary as well as the conciliar origins of SA.

Early in the Preface we find this problematic statement:

> So I collected these articles and presented them to our side. They were accepted and unanimously confessed by us, and it was resolved that we should publicly present the articles as our confession of faith—If the pope and his adherents should ever become so bold . . . to convene a . . . council.[14]

Contrary to Luther's apparent assumption here, SA was not officially approved by the gathered estates at Schmalkalden. It did not even come up for discussion in plenary session at the Bundestag. Three reasons help explain this. First, Luther's severe illness kept him from the proceedings and he was thus unable to present the document himself. Had Luther been able to attend the meetings, his presence would have increased the likelihood of the articles' discussion on the convention floor.

Second, Elector John Fredrick apparently viewed SA primarily as a theo-

---

10. Cf. also *UuA,* 35–37; Bente, *Introductions,* 59; *WA* 50:192; and K. Zangemeister, *Die Schmalkaldischen Artikel vom Jahre 1537* (Heidelberg: Carl Winter Universitätsbuchhandlung, 1886), 51. The original is in the Heidelberg University Library (cod. Pal. germ. 423, 40).

11. Spalatin's copy is in the Staatsarchiv in Weimar (Reg H 124, Bl. 1a–38b).

12. Haile, *Luther,* 212.

13. Ibid., 213.

14. SA, Preface, 2.

logical, confessional document. This would be in contrast to a writing such as AC, which was presented to Emperor Charles V in the political context of a German diet and was basic for the unity of the Schmalkald League. Recall that, when the Saxon Prince wrote "that subscription to the articles by the pastors and preachers would be serviceable,"[15] he did not mention the estates or other princes of the Schmalkald League.

Third, the gathering had decided not to attend the proposed council at Mantua. This decision rendered the question of SA's status, at Schmalkalden, moot. SA as a confession of faith for the council simply was not necessary. There was no need to debate a confessional document that was ostensibly written for an event, attendance at which the Protestants had rejected.

Nonetheless, the theologians who accompanied the rulers were not without matters to consider.[16] The recess of Schmalkalden mentions two official items that are of a specifically theological nature.[17] First, when the League reaffirmed AC as a common confessional symbol, the theologians were charged with fortifying it with proof texts from the Scriptures and traditional sources. This task, however, was postponed because of the lack of resource materials at Schmalkalden. Second, a special statement on the papacy was deemed necessary. This was drawn up by Melanchthon at Schmalkalden and approved by the assembly (this was Tr).[18]

The nineteenth-century Reformation historian Theodor Kolde explains Luther's assumption that SA was "presented, . . . accepted, and unanimously confessed" at Schmalkalden in this way: "[Luther], because of his illness in Schmalkalden, was never properly informed about it."[19] Theodore Tappert explains similarly: "Luther was still laboring in 1538 under the misapprehension that these things had happened in Smalcald."[20] These explanations can, however, only account for some of the facts.

Given the time that had elapsed from the recess of Schmalkalden to the publication of SA, it is unlikely that Luther had not been accurately informed about the fate of his articles and simply assumed that they were approved. Still,

---

15. *UuA*, 84.

16. As part of the invitation to this gathering, Elector John Fredrick and Landgrave Philip of Hesse requested that each delegation include some theological scholars to act as advisers to the rulers (*UuA*, 81f.).

17. "Abschied des Bundestages von Schmalkalden," in *UuA*, 139.

18. Cf. Neve, *Introduction to the Symbolical Books of the Lutheran Church*, 358f.

19. Theodor Kolde, "Die Schmalkaldischen Artikel," in A. Hauck, ed., *Realencyklopädie für protestantische Theologie und Kirche* (Leipzig: J. C. Hinrichs'sche Buchhandlung, 1906), 17:644.

20. *BC*, 288 n. 4.

the fact that this explanation is unlikely does not necessarily discredit it. If Luther wrote these words under the influence of a mistaken assumption, then that would explain their place in the first published edition of SA. However, this conclusion does not adequately explain how they came to remain without correction in each succeeding reprint of SA (nor does anyone who was at Schmalkalden seem to have questioned Luther's assertion). Tappert and Kolde assume that Luther was never fully apprised of the fate of SA at Schmalkalden and therefore labored under this misconception throughout his life.

The difficulties raised by this statement in the Preface to SA are best accounted for by Friedrich Bente, who has accumulated data that point toward this conclusion:

> Evidently, then, Luther's statement was generally regarded as being substantially and approximately correct and for all practical purposes in keeping, if not with the exact letter and form, at least with the real spirit of what transpired at Smalcald and before as well as after this convention.[21]

Bente goes on to point out that, broadly speaking, SA was in fact "adopted" at Schmalkalden, although "not officially and by the Schmalkald League as such."[22]

Bente's explanation is credible because, in fact, the vast majority of the theologians did subscribe SA, and thus SA did generally correspond to the views of those assembled. Since, however, the politicians had already decided against attending the council, there was no compelling reason to debate SA as a new confession to be presented at Mantua.

A plenary discussion of SA at Schmalkalden might also have brought to a head the theological differences between the North Germans and the South Germans to such a degree that a rupture in the alliance could have resulted. The officials at Schmalkalden, although generally in agreement with SA, used discretion in choosing not to bring it up for formal discussion.

This explains Luther's ongoing impression of events at Schmalkalden, as evident in the reformer's reference to SA in a 1541 letter to Chancellor Brück, when the reformer mentions "the articles which were accepted at Schmalkalden."[23]

Moreover, Elector John Fredrick, who would surely have known the facts of the Schmalkalden meeting, seems to have adopted a similar opinion of SA, when he wrote to Luther about republishing "the articles of our Christian reli-

---

21. Bente, *Introductions*, 58.
22. Ibid.
23. *WABr* 9:355 (letter dated April 4, 1541).

gion in which you, along with our allies of the Christian religion, were . . . united at Schmalkalden in '37." [24] Indeed, even nine years later the Elector was continuing to refer to SA in a way that indicates that it had received an official recognition that does not, strictly speaking, correspond to the events at Schmalkalden as we know them:

> And we have often desired from the bottom of our hearts that in the churches of our former lands and other lands, no change based on human wisdom would have been introduced in the matters as they were held during the life of the blessed Dr. Martin Luther and accepted by all the pastors and preachers and estates of the Augsburg Confession in '37 at Schmalkalden.[25]

Luther wrote the Preface, made some alterations in the text, and had SA published more or less as a private work over a year after the Schmalkalden meeting had adjourned, in the summer of 1538.[26] Once SA was published, it began its journey to authoritative, confessional status in earnest.

The Three Main Parts.

The structural and textual issues of each of these parts of SA will be dealt with in more detail in connection with their role in the theological explanation that follows. Nevertheless, an overview of the structure of these parts will help set the stage.

Part I is so brief that its four "articles" are little more than a series of sentences covering just nineteen lines in *BSLK*. They provide a short summary of trinitarian theology, referring by name to both the Apostles' Creed and the Athanasian Creed as well as to SC.

Part II contains four articles, each one longer than those of Part I. The first article of Part II is what Luther calls "the first and chief article" and summarizes the reformer's basic theological assertion, his view of "Christ and Faith." [27] It comprises only twenty-one lines, but one should not be misguided by the brevity of this article. Its theological significance for Luther is hard to overesti-

---

24. *UuA*, 188; *WABr* 10:438 (letter dated October 27, 1543).

25. *UuA*, 197.

26. That Luther published SA more or less as a private work leaves open the possibility of a part played by the Elector in having SA published. There is documenting evidence that John Fredrick encouraged a reprint of SA in 1543 (*UuA*, 188f.) and it is possible that he sought SA's original publication in 1538. Cf. Schaaf, "The Smalcald Articles," 80.

27. "Der erste und Häuptartikel" (SA II, 1, 1). This title, as well as the titles of the other articles in SA, Part II, is borrowed from *BC*. The titles were not so designated by Luther, although Luther did provide headings for Part III.

mate. Each of the remaining articles of Part II is explicitly related to this article, as we shall see.[28]

Part III contains fifteen articles. In them, Luther gives particular attention to the relationship between his central theological concerns and the concrete realities of the Christian life. In Part III, Luther shows the practical application of both Parts I and II.

The Subscriptions to the Schmalkald Articles.

Following the text of SA is a list of subscriptions, which were obtained in four stages. First, there are the signatures of the eight theologians who gathered at Wittenberg in December of 1536 to discuss Luther's articles. Their signatures were obtained at that time. Second, Gabriel Didymus (1487–1558), pastor at Torgau (the Electoral residence), signed SA in January 1537 (his signature represents the initial step toward fulfilling the Elector's intention of having the articles subscribed "by the pastors and preachers" of Saxony).[29] Third, another twenty-five signatures were affixed at the conclusion of the Schmalkalden Bundestag in March 1537. Fourth, the last ten signatures were garnered when Luther's entourage stopped in Erfurt on March 4 and 5, 1537.

There are two particularly noteworthy features to this set of subscriptions. First, Melanchthon's signature carries with it this paragraph:

> I, Philip Melanthon,[30] also regard the above articles as true and Christian. About the pope, however, I maintain that if he would allow the gospel, we might allow him his superiority over the bishops which he has *by human right*. We could make this concession for the sake of peace and general unity among those Christians who are now under him and might be in the future.

---

28. Textually, Article 2 of this second part includes some significant additions to Luther's original. The first two such additions were made by Luther himself for the 1538 publication of SA and thus were not a part of the document, either at Wittenberg or at Schmalkalden. These were II, 2, 5 and II, 2, 13–15. The former of these describes the Mass "as a human institution [which] can be omitted without sin" (*UuA*, 39). The latter of these is significant because it includes Luther's strong words, which state that "the Word of God shall establish articles of faith and no one else, not even an angel" (*UuA*, 41f; cf. also Galatians 1:8).

The third interpolation of significance in Part II is a separately titled subsection, "On Prayer to Saints" ("*Von Heiligen-Anrufen*" [SA II, 2, 25–28; *UuA*, 43f.]). This section was the only addition made to SA by the gathered theologians at Wittenberg, in December of 1536. Three other changes were proposed at this gathering but rejected by Luther (perhaps his concern about the proliferation of dogma in the church, expressed in the Latin verse of this cover page, shows itself here). The three unaccepted articles were "*Vom hochwirdigen Sacrament . . .*," "*Von der Ordination und Weihe . . .*," and "*Von den adiaphoris . . .*" (*UuA*, 72f.).

29. *UuA*, 91.

30. Melanchthon began spelling his name "Melanthon" in 1531.

A long tradition of Reformation scholarship has tended to interpret this extended subscription as evidence of significant theological differences between Melanchthon and Luther.[31] The scholars of this tradition, which has driven a wedge between Luther and Melanchthon and between SA and AC, have in this instance tended to make a couple of basic errors. First, they have reflected long-standing "stereotypes"[32] and even "myths"[33] of Luther and Melanchthon. Second, they have tended to neglect the surrounding factors that informed Melanchthon's expression of adherence to SA. When these factors are considered in their proper context, a clearer picture of what the younger reformer's signature means comes into focus. This picture shows that Melanchthon's subscription to SA ought not to be used as evidence for the existence of a substantive theological difference between the two reformers.

Most interpreters of Melanchthon's subscription have seen these words in a rather pejorative way, as an example of Melanchthonian "pussy-footing."[34] For example, already in the second half of the seventeenth century, Johann Benedict Carpzov and Ludwig von Seckendorf accented the differences between Lutheran theology and Melanchthon's subscription to SA. Carpzov declared summarily: "[Melanchthon's subscription] is not a part of the Book of Concord."[35] Von Seckendorf's comment that SA expressed a "completely different opinion than Melanchthon" about the papacy was reprinted in 1755 as part of a compendium of his *Historia Lvtheranismi*.[36]

The majority of modern Reformation scholars have differed little from these types of conclusions. Early in the twentieth century, Otto Reichert, editor of the Weimar Edition, volume 50, wrote:

> The *Schmalkald Articles* are thus Luther's personal statement of freedom over and against Melanchthon's "light-stepping" of 1530—the counter attack of the genuine spirit of Luther against the intentionally compromising *Augustana* of Melanchthon.[37]

---

31. Bengt Hägglund, "Melanchthon versus Luther: The Contemporary Struggle," *Concordia Theological Quarterly* 44, no. 2–3 (July 1980): 123f.

32. Heinz Scheible, "Melanchthon and Luther," *LQ* (Autumn 1990): 317–39.

33. Timothy Wengert, "The Day Philip Melanchthon Got Mad," *LQ* (Winter 1991): 420f.

34. Ibid., 421.

35. Johann Benedict Carpzov, *Isagoge in libros ecclesiarum lutheranarum symbolicos* (Leipzig, 1665), 823.

36. Veit Ludwig von Seckendorf, *Compendium Seckendorfianum oder kurzgefasste Reformations-Geschichte, III. und IV. Theil* (Frankfurt and Leipzig, 1755), vol. 3, 292.

37. WA 50:161. Reichert's reference to Melanchthon's "light-stepping" makes use of Luther's famous remark about AC: "I have read through Master Philip's *Apologia*, which pleases me very

In 1921, Friedrich Bente picked up on this theme as he explained that here Melanchthon "still adhered to the position which he had occupied at Augsburg," thus demonstrating that Melanchthon was "not entirely cured of his utopian dream."[38] Ernest G. Schwiebert, in his 1952 biography of Luther, epitomizes this interpretive school when he emphasizes Luther's dissatisfaction with the Augsburg Confession and describes SA as "a declaration of independence . . . from the compromising *Leisetreterei* of Melanchthon at the Diet of Augsburg."[39]

Such a characterization of Melanchthon's adherence to SA, however, does not adequately account for all of the data. First, Melanchthon's subscription to SA bears a strong resemblance to a number of periodic statements made by Luther himself. For example, in 1530, while sequestered at the Coburg castle during the Diet of Augsburg, Luther made these two relevant comments, which correspond rather closely with how Melanchthon signs SA:

> Certainly, if the Pope would agree to [a diminution of power] . . . , then I maintain that we Lutherans would be more help at guarding and protecting his honor and authority than the Emperor himself and all the world. We could do it with God's Word and power, without the sword, what the Emperor with the fist, without God's power, can never do, etc.[40]

Luther expresses a similar opinion about the practical condition necessary for the evangelical acceptance of the papacy, when he writes these words a month later:

> If the Pope wants to be Lord or overseer, we would gladly allow it. We do not care how much honor or wealth he has; rather we care that he would freely allow us the gospel (this he owes to us).[41]

---

much; I know nothing to improve or change in it; nor would this be appropriate, since I cannot tread so softly and quietly [*leisetreten*]. May Christ, our Lord, help [this *Apologia*] to bear much and great fruit, as we hope and pray" (*WABr* 5:319; *LW* 49:297–98). Luther wrote these words in a May 15, 1530, letter to Prince John. (John "the Steadfast" [d. 1532] was the father of John Fredrick. John became Elector of Saxony following the death of his brother, Fredrick the Wise.) Most interpreters have understood this as a term of derision, even though Luther was apparently complimenting Melanchthon while admitting to a weakness in himself.

38. Bente, *Introductions*, 54.

39. Schwiebert, *Luther*, 741.

40. *WABr* 12:116f. (letter to Melanchthon, June 1530).

41. *WABr* 5:432 (from Coburg, July 1530). There is some doubt as to the authorship of this quotation, although Otto Clemen (the editor of *WABr* 5) concludes that it is Luther's (p. 43). Cf. also another letter that Luther sent to Melanchthon from Coburg in July of 1530 (*WABr* 5:435₅f.).

This understanding of Luther persisted, as a sermon, preached between March and September 1538 (SA was published in the summer of 1538), bears witness:

> I would gladly listen to the pope and bishops, and not destroy their authority but magnify it, if they would accept their offices and preach the gospel of Christ, read the Holy Scriptures, administer the Lord's Supper, baptize, comfort poor troubled consciences among the dying.[42]

By signing SA the way he did, Melanchthon disagrees with Luther over the theoretical possibility of a reformed papacy and does so by using language similar to what Luther used in other contexts. Melanchthon thought there was still a chance that the papacy could see itself in subjection to the gospel. Melanchthon's subscription, then, although theoretically at variance with SA, actually conforms to the elder reformer's own periodic statements about the pope.[43]

In SA, however, Luther does not express even the theoretical possibility that the papacy will ever allow itself to be reformed. In fact, he goes on to state in SA that the pope is both useless and unnecessary.[44]

A second important datum to keep in mind in order to understand Melanchthon's subscription to SA is to recognize that he had been concerned for some time about the possible domination of the church by the princes if episcopal authority (which was derived from the primacy of the bishop of Rome) were completely abandoned. In fact, Melanchthon had originally desired that AC be subscribed only by the theologians and not the princes, so as to underscore the theological (as opposed to the political) nature of the matters involved.[45] This concern is evident when, from Augsburg on August 31, 1530, Melanchthon wrote to Joachim Camerarius:[46]

> Oh would that it would be possible, not indeed to confirm the despotism, but restore the administration of the bishops. For I envision what kind of church we shall have when ecclesiastical polity is dissolved. I see that

---

42. WA 47:436, 36ff. (a sermon on Matthew 23).

43. Cf. the listings under "*Luther und der Papst*" in the *Gesamtregister* in WA 58¹:131f.

44. SA II, 4, 5–6. Cf also Scott Hendrix, *Luther and the Papacy* (Philadelphia: Fortress Press, 1981), 150.

45. Hägglund, "Melanchthon versus Luther," 126.

46. Camerarius (d. 1574) was a Protestant humanist and friend of Melanchthon who shared many educational and theological priorities with Philip. He was present at the Diets of Speyer and Augsburg. Camerarius published a biography of Melanchthon in 1566.

afterwards there will arise a much more intolerable tyranny [of the princes] than there ever was.[47]

This quotation demonstrates Melanchthon's concern over the dangers inherent in the ecclesiastical power vacuum that could result in the absence of the papacy. The younger reformer foresaw the princely domination of the church.[48] This issue, although not specifically mentioned by Melanchthon in his subscription to SA, is nevertheless addressed by the way in which Melanchthon pens his name to Luther's testament of faith.

A third piece of evidence that helps clarify Melanchthon's subscription to SA is that the Elector of Saxony had given quite specific instructions to his theologians as they gathered to discuss Luther's articles.[49] John Fredrick explicitly requested that any unresolved issues be noted and sent on to him with Luther's articles. The Elector said: "If someone still has reservations about an article or two, which cannot be completely resolved, he should write down the basis and reason for his opinion and show it to us along with what is sent." [50]

When Melanchthon penned his subscription along with the others gathered at Wittenberg in late December 1536, he was conforming to the wishes of his prince. Melanchthon wanted to explain his opinion in accord with the stated directions of the meeting.[51]

In addition to these external factors, when one analyzes the actual content of Melanchthon's extended subscription, one finds that it conforms on a practical level with what Luther himself had actually said in the text of SA. They both put forth the same basic, necessary condition for acceptance of the papacy. Luther wrote:

> And I assert that the pope should want to renounce his claim so that he would not be supreme in the church "by divine right" or by God's command. However, in order that the unity of Christendom might be preserved against the sects and heretics, we might accept a head in which all others are

47. *CR* 2:334.

48. Clyde Manschreck points toward the same general conclusion when he writes, "Cognizant also of the increasing control of the evangelical churches by the princes, Melanchthon thought some means should be devised for keeping church polity independent of the state" (*The Quiet Reformer*, 251).

49. On December 11, 1536, the Elector asked Luther to prepare a document that could serve as both the reformer's theological testament and an evangelical confession of faith for use in Protestant deliberations concerning the proposed general council called for Mantua in May 1537. John Fredrick also gathered a small group of evangelical theologians at Wittenberg to discuss Luther's work, prior to the February Bundestag at Schmalkalden. The Wittenberg meeting took place during the last week of December.

50. *UuA*, 28.

51. *UuA*, 86; *WABr* 8:5.

held together. Such a head would now be elected by the people and it would remain in their power and by their choice whether to change or depose this head. . . . Now I assert (says I) that it is impossible for the pope and the chair of Rome to renounce such things and to want to accept this view, because he would have to allow his entire government and order to be overthrown and destroyed with all his laws and books. In summary, he cannot do it.[52]

Luther then goes on to take a rather pragmatic view of a papacy conceived in *"jure humano"* terms. The reformer writes, "Christendom would not be helped in any way. There would be many more sects than before, because . . . the head of this church would rather easily and quickly be despised, until it would finally have not even one member."[53] Luther summarizes his view of the papacy in SA with these strong words:

> This shows authoritatively that he is the true antichrist or contrachrist, who has raised himself over and set himself against Christ because the pope will not let Christians be saved without his authority, which amounts to nothing. It is not ordered or commanded by God.[54]

The positions expressed by the two reformers are not theologically incompatible. There is evident here, to be sure, a characteristic difference of emphasis and style.[55] Luther is apt to be brash and hyperbolic. Melanchthon is more measured and circumspect, displaying his penchant for theological thoroughness and nuance.[56] In the end, however, both reformers put forth the same practical condition for evangelical acceptance of papal authority: Roman submission to the gospel and Roman recognition that any authority the papacy

---

52. SA II, 4, 7.

53. SA II, 4, 8.

54. SA II, 4, 10.

55. In 1531, Luther put his assessment of the differences between Melanchthon and himself in a very positive light, emphasizing God's complementary gifts: "I was born to wage war and take the field against mobs and devils. Therefore, my books are rather stormy and war-like. I pull out the stumps and roots, hack away at the thorns and thistles, drain the swamps. I must be the rough pathfinder, must blaze and prepare a new trail. But Master Philip comes neatly and quietly to it. He cultivates and plants, sows and waters with joy, according to his gifts, which God has richly given" (*WA* 30[II]:68). It should be noted that Melanchthon made a similar characterization of Luther and himself in the summer of 1537 (*CR* 3:383).

56. Note that this characterization of Melanchthon does not accuse the younger reformer of any psychological weakness, as, e.g., Bernhard Lohse appears to in "Philipp Melanchthon in seinen Beziehungen zu Luther," in *Leben und Werk Martin Luthers von 1526–1546,* ed. Helmar Junghans (Berlin and Göttingen, 1983), 403–18 (cf. esp. p. 404, where Lohse writes of Melanchthon's "anxious nature" [*ängstliche Natur*]). The stance of Melanchthon's subscription to SA, on the other hand, displays a rather large amount of personal integrity and assertiveness. Cf. also Scheible, "Luther and Melanchthon," 27.

might have would be derived from human law, not from divine law.[57] Both men agreed regarding the necessary, practical requirement for Lutheran/Roman reconciliation at this point.

The difference lies in Melanchthon's willingness to leave open the theoretical possibility of a reformed papacy, whereas Luther had given up such hope. This theoretical disagreement between the two reformers about the potential (or lack of it) for the papacy to be reformed does not alter the fundamental agreement they shared on a practical level.[58]

This congruence is further evident in the comparison between SA and Melanchthon's Tr, written at Schmalkalden in February of 1537. Here Melanchthon develops an argument that is completely in line with that which is maintained by Luther in SA. As we have seen, Luther flatly calls the pope "the true antichrist." Melanchthon, although a bit more guarded than Luther, comes to the same basic conclusion: "The errors of the Pope's kingdom are manifest, and the Scriptures unanimously declare these errors to be doctrines of demons and of the Antichrist."[59]

From these data, it is apparent that whatever differences existed between Philip Melanchthon and Martin Luther, Melanchthon's subscription to SA cannot be used as evidence to build a case for significant theological divergence between the two reformers. By subscribing SA in the way he does, Melanchthon does not substantively deviate from his elder counterpart but rather shows himself to be in basic agreement with Luther.

When we recognize the practical agreement between the two reformers at this point, a third problem with traditional interpretations of Melanchthon's subscription comes into clearer view. If it were truly an important deviation from Lutheran theology, then Luther's own acceptance of the matter remains unaccounted for. This argument from silence is compelling because Luther was certainly not hesitant to distance himself from others who disagreed with him in substantive theological matters.[60]

Beyond Melanchthon's subscription to SA, there is a second significant problem involving the subscriptions to SA: the problematic ending of Part III, and thus the text of SA itself. If one accepts the present reading of Part III, 15,

---

57. In SA II, 4, 1, Luther writes: "The pope is not the head of all Christendom 'by divine right.'" He then goes on to say that the pope has contributed to the destruction of "the entire holy Christian church . . . and negates the first, chief article on the redemption of Jesus Christ" (SA II, 4, 3).

58. Scheible concludes that Luther did not take issue with Melanchthon's subscription, because Luther knew that they were "in basic agreement" ("Luther and Melanchthon," 337f.).

59. Tr, 42.

60. Scheible, "Luther and Melanchthon," 335.

"On Human Regulations," as the intended ending to SA, then one must account for a number of puzzling factors.[61]

There are five paragraphs in this article. The first paragraph was written at the top of the twenty-second sheet of Luther's original, leaving blank the remaining two-thirds of the page.[62] The second paragraph (III, 15, 3), printed in *BSLK* without distinction from what precedes and follows it, actually stands at the top of the next full page of Luther's autograph and in fact contains nothing related to human regulations.[63] This second paragraph could easily have fit on the same page directly following the opening paragraph of the article, if it was originally supposed to have been a part of III, 15.[64] The final three paragraphs of SA return to specific issues of human regulations and relate more naturally to the opening paragraph of the article.

It is questionable whether Luther intended the second paragraph of SA III, 15 to be where it is. Three factors point in this direction. First, the sentiments expressed in this paragraph are quite personally from Luther and do not follow from what was written before them (i.e., Luther's reference to "human regulations" [SA III, 15, 2]), nor do they connect with what follows (i.e., Luther's reference to "the papal bag of tricks" [SA III, 15, 4]).

Also, this is one of the few instances in which Luther uses the first person singular in SA (outside of the later Preface and III, 13). Part III ordinarily makes use of the royal "we" and then resumes such use following Luther's lapse into the first person singular in the paragraph under consideration.[65]

Furthermore, it appears from the original draft of SA that this second paragraph is actually in the reformer's own hand, as opposed to the rest of III, 4–15, which was dictated by Luther to a secretary.[66]

---

61. There really is no formal "conclusion" to SA, in the sense of a summation or final, general word from Luther.

62. Zangemeister, *Die Schmalkaldischen Artikel*, 70f.; *UuA*, 68.

63. This paragraph is on the back of sheet 22, ibid.

64. The original 1580 Dresden edition of *The Book of Concord* printed this paragraph with an ornamental initial that differentiates it from the preceding. *BC* does something similar when it leaves a blank space between the first and the second paragraphs.

65. Cf. SA III, 15, 5.

66. Concerning Luther's dictation of the end of SA, see *UuA*, 60 n. 80, and *BSLK*, 449. Luther's hand is distinguishable from his secretary's at two points. First, Luther characteristically used the spelling *darinn(e)* as opposed to the *darynn(e)* of his secretary (cf. *WA* 50:191). The word *darinne* occurs in SA III, 15, 3. Second, there is a distinctive form of the captial "D" in both Luther's signature and the paragraph in question. Luther wrote, "Dis sind die Artikel, . . ." and he signed his name, "Martinus LutheR D. subscripsit." The "D" in both cases looks very similar (Zangemeister, *Die Schmalkaldischen Artikel, in loco*). We can see that what stand now as the concluding paragraphs of SA were written by Luther's secretary: III, 15 4 contains the word *Kyrchweyhe*

A tentative explanation for this state of affairs can be posited. Because "On Human Regulations" is the last article of SA, the apparent confusion over the ending of the document led to the insertion of what is now seen as SA III, 15, 3 into its present place. It appears that this paragraph was originally meant to be an extended subscription by Luther (akin to Melanchthon's, as well as other signers of SA).[67] These words begin a new page, perhaps intended to begin the list of subscriptions that were to be added to SA. Luther's signature was to be given preeminence. However, between Luther's writing of these sentences and the actual affixing of his name, what appear now as the final paragraphs of SA III, 15 were added at the bottom of the page (these paragraphs really fit more compatibly with the reformer's initial comments about human regulations). Luther's personal words, intended to underscore the commitment he felt for his articles as he prepared to sign them, were thus inadvertently separated from his signature and the other subscriptions, which begin with Luther's at the top of the next full page. This state of affairs led to the impression that Part III, 15, as disjointed as it now stands, was originally designed to be so by Luther.

This theory of Luther's misplaced, extended subscription further underscores the testamentary aspects of SA. When Luther signed SA, at the conclusion of the December 1536 meeting of theologians at Wittenberg, he had scarcely recovered from a serious heart attack. The prospect of his impending death, which he mentions in his misplaced subscription, was evidently very real.

The Distinctiveness of the Schmalkald Articles

When Luther's Elector asked him to fashion a set of articles that would summarize the most important features of Lutheran theology, the reformer could have directed the Elector's attention to AC. He could have sent the Elector a copy of SC or LC. Obviously, Luther did not think that any existing document captured the essence of his view of the Christian faith as did SA. Therefore Luther wrote SA so that this document, like no other, could serve as a witness to what he saw as theologically central.

Given the mature age of the reformer, the theology asserted in SA is a rather unique summary of Luther's entire theological program, filled throughout with a sense of personal exigency born of the keen awareness of his approaching death.

(Zangemeister, *Die Schmalkaldischen Artikel,* 71). Luther, however, consistently used the spelling *Kirche* (*WA* 50:191).

67. A number of signatories besides Luther and Melanchthon subscribed SA with commentary beyond the mere signing of their names: Urban Rhegius, Conrad Figenbotz, Dionysius Melander, Brixius Northanus, and John Lang.

4

The Catholic Pillar of Luther's Theology

The first part of the articles is about the lofty articles of the divine majesty, namely:

1. That Father, Son, and Holy Spirit, three distinct persons in one divine essence and nature, is one God, who created heaven and earth, etc.

2. That the Father was begotten by no one, the Son was begotten by the Father, the Holy Spirit proceeds from the Father and the Son.

3. That neither the Father nor the Holy Spirit, but the Son became a human being.

4. That the Son became a human being in this way: he was conceived by the Holy Spirit without male participation and was born of the pure, holy Virgin Mary. After that, he suffered, died, was buried, descended to hell, rose from the dead, ascended to heaven, is seated at the right hand of God, in the future will come to judge the living and the dead, etc., as the Apostles' and the Athanasian symbols, and the common children's catechism, teach.

These articles are not matters of dispute or conflict, for both sides confess them. Therefore it is not necessary to deal with them at greater length. (SA, Part I)

Textual Issues

Part I of SA contains two noteworthy textual items. One item involves an addition to the original, the other involves a deletion. Both of these variants are in the fourth "article." First, the Latin translation of SA, made by Nicolaus Selnecker for the Latin *Book of Concord* of 1580, renders "The Son . . . was born of the pure, holy, virgin Mary" as "The Son . . . was born of the pure, holy, *always* virgin Mary."[1] The origin of this innovative translation is not altogether clear, although it has a liturgical sense to it and could have been a formula used in worship and adapted by Selnecker for use in the Latin version of SA.[2]

1. Luther's German reads: "von der reinen, heiligen Jungfrau Maria." Selnecker's Latin reads: "ex Maria pura, sancta, semper virgine."

2. The perpetual virginity of Mary had particular pietistic importance for the Roman Catholic Church of the late Middle Ages. Cf. Thieme, *Luthers Testament*, 13 n. 1.

Regardless of its origin, such a reference to the perpetual virginity of Mary, although not from Luther himself, would be in keeping with the generally conservative nature of the Lutheran Reformation.[3] This is particularly true with respect to such liturgical matters.

The second significant textual issue in Part I has, for Luther, rather profound theological importance. Luther's original draft of SA reveals that the reformer deleted a particularly telling phrase from his original draft. Luther had first written: "These Articles are not matters of dispute or contention, for both parties believe and confess them." Luther, however, reconsidered the use of such language with respect to his opponents, and so he crossed out the words "believe and."[4]

Obviously Luther is making a distinction here between merely "confessing" and "believing and confessing." The implications of this deletion will be explored in the context of Luther's notion of belief, which the reformer summarizes in Part II, 1.

Trinitarian Theology

In Part I of SA, Luther refers openly and most approvingly to the trinitarian confession of faith in the three ecumenical or catholic creeds of the church. It was evidently important for Luther to begin his theological testament with reference to the Trinity and the catholic faith expressed in the creeds. This is indicated by the numerous ways the reformer underscores his adherence to classical trinitarian theology.

For example, the first two articles borrow language from the Nicene Creed and Article 4 mentions by name the other two ecumenical creeds: the Apostles' and the Athanasian. The operative Nicene word employed in Article 1 is "essence" (in German, *Wesen*), a translation of the Greek *ousias* (Latin: *substantia* or *essentia*). This language is designed to indicate the essential or substantive trinitarian unity of the Father and Son and Holy Spirit.[5]

In Article 2, the linguistic key is the word "proceeds" (in German, *ausgehend*), which is a translation of the Greek *ekporeuomenon* of the Nicene Creed.[6]

---

3. Cf. FCSD 8, 24. Cf. also C. P. Krauth, *The Conservative Reformation and Its Theology* (reprint, Minneapolis: Augsburg Publishing House, 1963).

4. *BSLK*, 415 n. 1. This deletion is evident in the original autograph as well (Zangemeister, *Die Schmalkaldischen Artikel*, 2, 52.

5. A Greek edition of the Nicene Creed is found in Badcock, *The History of the Creeds*, 211f. A Latin version of the creed is included as one of the confessional symbols in *BSLK*.

6. The Latin *procedens* is used in section 22 of the Athanasian Creed, which refers to the same phenomenon (this latter creed is of course mentioned explicitly in SA I, 4).

That Luther has in mind the Western creedal tradition is evident from his conviction that "the Holy Spirit proceeds from both the Father *and the Son*."[7]

Luther's summary synthesis of the creedal tradition incorporates elements from the Athanasian and Apostles' Creeds, beyond the mere mention of their names in Article 4: SA I, 3 borrows language from section 27 of the Athanasian Creed; and SA I, 4 is closely related to the second article of the Apostles' Creed. By beginning the text of SA is this way, the reformer seeks to demonstrate his commitment to the catholic understanding of the Holy Trinity.

Luther's theological priorities as expressed in SA would clearly seem to reveal at the outset a commitment to the classical creedal and theological traditions of the church catholic. However, interpreters of Luther have not always agreed about the genuineness of this commitment.

Some scholars have concluded that Luther understood the Trinity in a way that was not really in keeping with the classical Christian tradition. Adolf von Harnack, for example, saw "no bridge" from Luther's interpretation of justification by faith to the Trinity and in the end, Luther's interpretation of the Trinity was an "unspeakable confusion," with modalistic tendencies.[8] Karl Thieme argued with von Harnack but then discovered a "naive Ditheism" and "Tritheism" in Luther's writings—or at least Thieme expressed a concern that the reformer's doctrine inferred such polytheism.[9]

Other researchers have concluded that Luther was not fully convinced of the veracity of the statements of faith in the creeds. Albrecht Ritschl, for instance, asserted that Luther (and Melanchthon too, for that matter) adhered to the doctrine of the Trinity as a matter of strategic convenience, because it was required by the Justinian Code of the empire,[10] and thereby "made it possible for the rulers and governments to tolerate and protect them and make common cause with them."[11]

---

7. The *filioque* clause is still an issue in the separation of Eastern and Western Christianity, with the East maintaining that the Spirit "proceeded" only from the Father, not from both the Father and the Son (*filioque*). This use is attributed first to Tertullian and then to Augustine.

8. Schlink, *Theology of the Lutheran Confessions*, 62 n. 16. Cf. Adolf Harnack, *Dogmengeschichte* (5th ed.), 3:874. Schlink also mentions a conclusion of "neo-Protestantism" that the Trinity was relegated "to the periphery of [Luther's] theological thinking that was concentrated in the Gospel of justification by grace."

9. Schlink, *Theology of the Lutheran Confessions*. Cf. Karl Thieme, *Die Augsburger Konfession* (Giessen: A. Töpelmann, 1930), 144ff.

10. The Justinian Code was published by Emperor Justinian I (d. A.D. 565) in 529. It was a legal code that articulated Byzantine theory concerning the relationship between church and state. The code made trinitarian orthodoxy mandatory in the empire.

11. Schlink, *Theology of the Lutheran Confessions*, 62 n. 16. Cf. Albrecht Ritschl, *A Critical History of the Christian Doctrine of Justification and Reconciliation* (Edinburgh: Edmonston and Douglas, 1874), 127.

Still other scholars have tended to attribute the traditionalist tendencies among the Lutherans more to Melanchthon than to Luther. Speaking broadly about the Lutheran confessional symbols, Otto Ritschl has proposed that the attention paid to the creeds of the ancient church by sixteenth-century Lutherans "can be traced in great part to Melanchthonian Traditionalism." [12]

Martin Willkomm, for example, draws a rather sharp distinction in this regard, noting the differences between the concerns expressed by Melanchthon in AC and those expressed by Luther in SA. According to Willkomm, at Augsburg

> it was most important to show that the evangelical doctrine was not a new doctrine and no deviation from the universal Christian church and her faith, as well as seek for the rectification of certain abuses. Now at Schmalkalden, the situation was completely different. [13]

There is some truth to Willkomm's claim. The situations were different. At Augsburg one could with some realism hope for consensus and perhaps even reconciliation. Therefore the irenics of AC were appropriate to that event. In 1530, the Lutherans were, so to speak, "in the dock." The Protestant task at Augsburg was to present a confession of faith that was to be evaluated by the political and ecclesiastical authorities.

By 1536–37, the theological battle lines had been even more sharply drawn and the Protestants no longer had hopes of receiving a fair hearing from the papal party. Therefore Luther wrote SA in a straightforward and sharp manner, designed to show clearly a distinctively evangelical interpretation of what it means to be catholic. Luther writes SA as if the Roman Catholic Church, its teaching, and its practice are now on trial. Luther in SA evaluates the sixteenth-century church of Rome against the standard of the gospel and finds it wanting.

Willkomm, however, has overstated his case—the situations were not "*completely* different." Although, as we shall see, the reformer certainly emphasizes the evangelical pillar of his theology in SA, he does so firmly within the context of his commitment to, in Willkomm's words, "the universal Christian church and her faith." This is why Luther begins his theological testament with a compendium of catholic trinitarianism.

The Schmalkald Articles show the continuity of Melanchthon and Luther

12. Gottfried Seebass, "The Importance of Luther's Writings in the Formation of Protestant Confessions of Faith in the Sixteenth Century," in *Luther's Ecumenical Significance*, ed. Peter Manns and Harding Meyer (Philadelphia: Fortress Press, 1984), 72.

13. Willkomm, *Ein Vermächtnis Luthers an die Kirche*, 25f.

with respect to their shared trinitarian emphasis. Gottfried Seebass interprets Luther in this way:

> Luther always started from church tradition when he consciously wanted to express his faith in a festive manner. . . . Indeed it must be said that Luther was not interested in having his own creed, but in accepting faithfully the confession of the whole church.[14]

By explicitly "accepting faithfully the confession of the whole church," Luther in Part I of SA evidently has two factors in mind. First, the reformer wants to demonstrate that the Lutheran theological movement is not heretical. There is no heresy at this point that could be condemned by the proposed council, by the pope, or by any Christian. Luther's theology is clearly based on the received creedal tradition of the church. The unity of God, as well as the diversity of the three "persons," is unflinchingly upheld and summarized in SA, Part I.[15] It simply was not Luther's purpose here to assert anything theologically new.

In fact, one could say that it is the very presence of the authentic trinitarian tradition of the church in Luther's theology which explains the paradoxical fact that Luther has been accused of both modalism and tritheism by later interpreters. As Edmund Schlink puts it, "The ancient doctrine of the Trinity will always produce these two misconceptions among its opponents."[16]

The second factor that Luther apparently had in mind in asserting his adherence to the Trinity was his understanding of SA as his theological testament. The reformer here bequeaths to posterity the legacy that the trinitarian foundation of Christian dogmatics is to be accepted by all those who would confess the Christian faith in a "Lutheran" way. Put simply, the doctrine of the Trinity as expressed in the ecumenical creeds is the catholic basis upon which Luther's theology is built and he thus points out that those who would be heirs to his theological legacy are to build their theology upon the same foundational pillar.

Because Luther wrote SA as if it were his last theological word for the ages, he felt compelled to include an overt reference to the ecumenical doctrine of the Trinity.

It is perhaps curious that Luther would underscore this basic doctrine in the way he does. There are no Bible passages quoted, no appeals to Holy Writ

---

14. Seebass, "The Importance of Luther's Writings," 72. Seebass then goes on to mention SA as a document that does indeed express Luther's faith in a "festive manner."

15. Schlink, *Theology of the Lutheran Confessions*, 63.

16. Ibid., 65.

that reinforce his statements. One might raise the question, "Where is 'sola scriptura' here?"[17] How does Part I of SA relate to the reformer's strong words in Part II that "God's word should establish articles of faith and no one else, not even an angel"?[18]

This question requires a manifold response. The first reason why Luther could begin his testamentary statement of faith in this way is that, for Luther, the doctrine of the Trinity is axiomatic. In spite of the fact that there are very few summarily trinitarian passages in the Bible (Matthew 28:19 is the best example), Luther identified in the Scriptures a threefold activity and self-revelation of the one God. According to Luther, the Scriptures speak of God as three in one. The divine revelation in the Scriptures is trinitarian and the creeds accurately reflect this self-disclosure of God. Because the creeds were seen as such accurate witnesses to the overall message of the Word of God, Luther saw no need here for an appeal to texts from the Bible.[19] In 1535, the reformer described the Apostles' Creed with language that also describes his general understanding of trinitarian dogma:

> Like a bee gathers honey from many beautiful and happy flowers, this creed gathers from the dear prophets and books of the apostles—that is, from all the Holy Scriptures. It is a fine, short summary for children and naive Christians.[20]

The Bible is the basic source of Luther's theology. To use later language, the Bible is "the norming norm" (*norma normans*) and the confessional symbol (creeds, catechisms, or confessions, etc.) is "the normed norm" (*norma normata*). Luther put it this way in 1544:

> Scripture thus cleverly proves that there are three persons and one God. For I would believe neither the writings of Augustine nor the teachers of

---

17. One simple way of answering the question is by asserting that *sola scriptura* is implicit on every page of SA and *The Book of Concord* generally. Schlink took notice of "the absence of a special article on Scripture" in the Lutheran Confessions but concluded that "the very silence of the Confessions on this point amounts to a doctrinal declaration" (*Theology of the Lutheran Confessions*, 1 n. 1).

18. SA II, 2, 15.

19. In his discussion in *The Three Symbols or Creeds of the Christian Faith* (1538), Luther cites some half dozen "trinitarian" texts from the Old Testament (WA 50:280–81; LW 34:225–26) and ends this treatise with these words: "I shall at this time cite nothing from the New Testament, for in it everything about the divine Trinity or Threefoldness is clearly and powerfully attested to. In the Old Testament this is not so clearly underlined, but is nevertheless powerfully indicated" (WA 50:283; LW 34:229).

20. *Predigten des Jahres 1535*, Nr. 27, May 23 (WA 41:275₃₀ff). Cf. also Werner Elert, *The Structure of Lutheranism* (St. Louis: Concordia Publishing House, 1962), 1:205.

the church unless the New and the Old Testaments would clearly show
this doctrine of the Trinity.[20a]

The revelation of the triune God is foundational to Luther's theological
testament because this doctrine represents for him a faithful summary of the
Word of God. Luther thought that this Word is what encounters humankind
in and through the Scriptures. He had the occasion to explicate his view of
what one might call the "trinitarian encounter" with God in 1528.[21] In particular, Luther brings together the "threeness" and "oneness" of God as essential
to understanding God's relationship to the world:[22]

> These are the three persons and one God, who has given himself to us all
> wholly and completely, with all that he is and has. The Father gives himself
> to us, with heaven and earth and all the creatures, in order that they may
> serve us and benefit us. But this gift has become obscured and useless
> through Adam's fall. Therefore the Son himself subsequently gave himself
> and bestowed all his works, sufferings, wisdom, and righteousness, and
> reconciled us to the Father, in order that restored to life and righteousness,
> we might also know and have the Father and his gifts.
>
> But because this grace would benefit no one if it remained so pro-
> foundly hidden and could not come to us, the Holy Spirit comes and gives
> himself to us also, wholly and completely. He teaches us to understand
> this deed of Christ which has been manifested to us.[23]

This statement corresponds dramatically with SA I. The point of the Word
of God as summarized in Luther's understanding of the doctrine of the Trinity
is to proclaim the reestablishment of the saving relationship between God and
humankind. In 1528, Luther notes that the same God who created the world
also came to the world in Christ and continues to come in the Spirit—so that
God's children might be "restored to life and righteousness." In 1536, the
weight of SA I also rests precisely on the salvific deed of Christ on behalf of
humankind, as SA I, 4 shows. All of this creative, redeeming, and sanctifying
activity is performed by the one and the same God. There is one God, not
three gods, says Luther along with the Athanasian Creed. For Luther, trinitarian dogma summarizes the story or history of salvation, and thus the Scriptures themselves.[24]

20a. *"Promotions disputation von Georg Major und Joh. Faber, 12. Dez. 1544"* (WA 39[II]:305). Trans.
from Althaus, *Theology of Luther*, 199, n. 1.

21. *Confession Concerning Christ's Supper*, 1528 (*WA* 26:261ff.; *LW* 37:360. Luther refers to Part
III of this confession in SA, Preface, 3.

22. Althaus, *Theology of Luther*, 199. Cf. *WA* 39[II]:287.

23. *WA* 26:505f.; *LW* 37:366.

24. Schlink, *Theology of the Lutheran Confessions*, 6.

"Three in one and one in three" is obviously not a philosophically reasonable expression. However, this contradiction to human reason is not a hindrance for Luther. In matters of faith, reason is not paramount. Luther's goal is to stay true to the scriptural witness about God, even if that means asserting something that does not appeal to reason. Luther's words of 1522 are still valid for him in 1538:

> If natural reason does not comprehend this, it is proper that faith alone should comprehend it; natural reason produces heresy and error but faith teaches and holds the truth for it sticks to the Scripture which does not lie or deceive.[25]

The trinitarian language of the church as inherited and passed on by Luther had been carefully worked out in the early centuries of Christianity. Luther accepted the church's creedal statements as a faithful effort to give expression to both the revelation of God in the Word and the experience of God in the context of the life of faith.

A second reason why Luther does not base Part I of SA on an obvious appeal to biblical texts is that, as has been noted, Luther is concerned to show that the accusations of heretical innovation or revolution made against him are unfounded.[26] These references to the creeds establish a point of contact between Luther's theology and the shared creedal tradition of the Roman church. Such a move is entirely in keeping with Luther's general theological and reformation principles.[27]

At the same time, Luther's views expressed here effactually exclude various historical theological movements that had been recognized as heretical by the church. In 1528, Luther named some of the antitrinitarian groups with whom he did not want to be associated: "the Arians, Macedonians, Sabellians, and similar heretics."[28] The theological movements these groups represent, along

---

25. *Wider den falsch genannten geistlichen Stand des Papst und der Bischöfe*, 1552 (*WA* 10[II]:152, 186). Translated in Althaus, *Theology of Luther*, 199 n. 5. This is one more piece of evidence that points to the continuity of Luther's theology throughout his career.

26. SA, Preface, 8, 9.

27. Thieme, *Luthers Testament*, 13.

28. *Confession concerning Christ's Supper*, 1528 (*WA* 26:499ff.; *LW* 37:261ff.). Robert Fischer outlined the views Luther sought to distinguish from his own when he wrote the following (*LW* 37:361 n. 272): "Of the heresies listed here only Arianism is mentioned by name in the *Book of Concord*, e.g., Augsburg Confession, Art. I. . . . Macedonianism, named after Macedonius, a fourth-century archbishop of Constantinople, affirmed that the Holy Spirit is less than divine, not one of the divine persons; this view was condemned at a council at Alexandria in 362 and subsequently. Sabellianism, a third-century form of Modal Monarchianism, treated the terms Father, Son, and Holy Spirit not as distinct divine persons but simply as different modes or even successive phases of the one God. It was Arius' accusation of Sabellianism against his bishop which opened the controversy leading to the Council of Nicaea, 325, where both Arianism and Sabellianism were excluded."

with the church of Rome, are a large part of "the false teaching against which [SA] is directed."[29] Luther's task in SA, however, is to present evangelical theology primarily in relationship to the Roman Catholic position. Therefore, although his affirmations are basically the same as those made in 1528, Luther does not explicitly mention the heresies he listed and rejected almost a decade earlier.

This concern to show continuity with the traditions of the church reveals itself not only with respect to the Trinity but also in another way. Luther makes explicit reference in Article 4 to Christ's incarnation as occurring "without male participation."[30] The emphasis of this comment is apparently to counter the charge, made already in 1522 (by the Elector of Brandenburg, at the Diet of Nürnberg), that Luther supposedly taught a doctrine of the incarnation that asserted that "Jesus was conceived from the seed of Joseph and Mary did not remain virginal, but had many sons after Jesus."[31]

This emphasis on the virgin birth fits together with the assertion of classical trinitarian theology at the outset of his theological testament, because any novelties regarding such issues are denied by Luther. In fact, already in the Preface to SA Luther had revealed his sensitivity to being misrepresented when he complained about his opponents who "so shamelessly slandered us and wanted to keep the people on their side with their lies."[32]

In addition to Luther's assumption that the doctrine of the Trinity was an accurate summary of the biblical witness and rejecting the charge of innovation, there is yet a third reason for the apparent lack of overt biblical references in this article. There was in this instance no need for Luther to appeal to the higher authority of the Scriptures. He recognized basic agreement regarding the doctrine of the Trinity between the Roman Catholics and the Lutherans at this point. If both the Roman Catholics and the Lutherans agree, "it is not necessary to deal with [these articles] at greater length."[33]

---

29. Schlink, *Theology of the Lutheran Confessions*, xvii.

30. SA I, 4.

31. Thieme, *Luthers Testament*, 13 n. 1. It is interesting also with respect to the emphasis of this statement regarding the mode of Jesus' conception that Luther wrote this in 1538: "The Jews consider themselves very clever people because they can say that he [Jesus] was conceived by Joseph." The reformer then goes on to critique this position, in very strong terms (*The Three Symbols or Creeds of the Christian Faith*, 1538 [*WA* 50:262; *LW* 34:309]). Part of the explanation for Selnecker's insertion of *semper* into the Latin translation of SA I, 4 could be related to this concern.

32. SA, Preface, 7. Cf. also SA, Preface, 8 and 9.

33. SA I, 4.

The Catholic Faith

Luther's trinitarian convictions at the outset of SA reveal a number of significant features of his theology. First, Luther was clearly committed to the catholic, trinitarian faith as expressed in the ecumenical creeds of the early church. Luther shows himself to be self-consciously a Western catholic Christian.

Second, we recall that Luther wrote, "These articles are not matters of dispute or conflict."[34] Yet, what follows in SA was clearly a matter of both dispute and contention. Luther's expressed commitment to the Trinity provides the catholic starting point from which he moves to the controversial issues of SA. The Reformation debate, from Luther's perspective, is carried on always in the context of God's threefold revelation in the Scriptures.

Third, the careful reader of Luther's theology in SA I can detect here already the germ of the reformer's evangelicalism that is to be confessed in Part II. Part I, 4 is the longest of these opening articles and focuses explicitly on Christ's redeeming work. In the transition from SA I to SA II, Luther reveals that his evangelical doctrine is intimately connected with his understanding of the Trinity. For Luther, the Christian faith is both catholic and evangelical.

34. SA I, 4.

5

The Evangelical Pillar of Luther's Theology

The second part is about the articles that pertain to the office and work of Jesus Christ, or to our redemption.

[I.] Here is the first and chief article:

That Jesus Christ, our God and Lord, "was handed over to death for our trespasses and was raised for our justification" (Rom. 4[:25]); and he alone is "the Lamb of God, who takes away the sin of the world" (John 1[:29]); and "the Lord has laid upon him the iniquity of us all" (Isa. 53[:6]); furthermore, "All have sinned," and "they are now justified without merit by his grace, through the redemption which is in Christ Jesus . . . by his blood" (Rom. 3[:23-25]).

Now because this must be believed and may not be obtained or grasped otherwise with any work, law, or merit, it is clear and certain that faith alone justifies us. In Romans 3[:26-28], St. Paul says: "For we hold that a person is justified by faith apart from works prescribed by the law"; and also, "that God alone is righteous and justifies the one who has faith in Jesus."

We cannot yield or concede anything in this article, even if heaven and earth, or whatever, do not remain. As St. Peter says in Acts 4[:12]: "There is no other name given among mortals by which we must be saved." "And with his bruises we are healed" (Isa. 53[:5]).

On this article stands all that we teach and practice against the pope, the devil, and the world. Therefore we must be quite certain and not doubt. Otherwise everything is lost, and pope and devil and everything against us will gain victory and dominance.

We have been employing the image of a building to describe the two fundamental theological motifs of SA. It is now time to mix this metaphor because, for Luther, these pillars of the Christian faith are as vibrant as they are strong, as dynamic as they are immovable. In the five verses of SA II, 1, Luther shows the life-giving substance of his theology. The vital nature of this article can be found as well in the remaining three articles of Part II, the polemics of which are all expressly related to this "first and chief article."[1] The lifeblood of this vibrant passage is strongly felt throughout all of SA.

---

1. Repeatedly in SA, as Luther criticizes the Roman Catholic theology and practice of his day, he evaluates the church of Rome as "contrary to the first article" (SA II, 2, 21; 2, 25; II, 3, 2; II, 4, 3.)

Over forty years ago, a Swedish interpreter of Luther, Einar Billing, sought to characterize the theology of the reformer. Billing brought together a cluster of images, all of which were designed to describe the same reality—that which gives Luther's theology its vital energy:

> Whoever knows Luther even but partially, knows that his various thoughts do not lie alongside each other, like pearls on a string, held together only by common authority or perchance by a line of logical argument, but that they all, as tightly as the petals of a rosebud, adhere to a common center, and radiate out like the rays of the sun from one glowing core, namely the gospel of the forgiveness of sins. Anyone wishing to study Luther would indeed be in no peril of going astray were he to follow this rule: never believe that you have a correct understanding of a thought of Luther before you have succeeded in reducing it to a simple corollary of the thought of the forgiveness of sins.[2]

Billing's words ring true with respect to SA. The forgiveness of sins is on virtually every page of Luther's theological testament.

The Word of God

Luther never wrote a treatise on the authority of the Bible. He did not express himself in terms of what recent generations might call the "inerrancy/errancy" debate.[3] Luther's use of biblical sources reveals his attitude toward them. Luther wanted his theology to be energized and nourished by the Scriptures. The operative metaphor employed here would put it this way: the word of God is the heart that pumps the lifeblood of the forgiveness of sin throughout Luther's theology. In Luther's language, "God's word should establish articles of faith and no one else."[4]

---

2. Einar Billing, *Our Calling* (Rock Island, Ill.: Augustana Book Concern, 1947), 7. Cf. also George Forell, *Faith Active in Love* (Minneapolis: Augsburg Publishing House, 1959), 64.

3. Bernhard Lohse summarizes Luther's view of the Bible: "The total breadth of Luther's understanding of the authority of Scripture can be represented by three quotations:

"'Neither councils, fathers, nor we, in spite of the greatest and best success possible, will do as well as the Holy Scriptures, that is, as well as God himself has done.'

"'The cloths in which the infant Jesus was wrapped 'are nothing but Holy Scripture, in which Christian faith lies wrapped up.'

"'God and the Scripture of God are two things, no less than the Creator and the creature are two things.'

"It is thus clear that Luther can describe the relationship between God and the Scripture in three ways: 1) he identifies the Bible and the Word of God; 2) he also describes the Word of God as the real content of the Bible without identifying this content with the external form in which we encounter it; 3) he also describes a dialectic relationship in which he differentiates the Bible and the Word of God by describing the one as the Creator and the other as the creature" (*Martin Luther*, 156).

4. SA II, 2, 15.

One could question the seeming absence of a biblical basis in the first part of SA. However, one cannot help being impressed with the manifold use of biblical texts in Part II, 1. Luther wanted a theology that flowed out of the word.

Here it is important for Luther to indicate the authoritative biblical basis for his distinctive theological emphasis. The reasons for such biblical proof run in the opposite direction from that which in Part I made explicit scriptural evidence unnecessary. First, in Part II, Luther wants to demonstrate to his opponents (as well as remind his followers and heirs to this legacy of faith) that forgiveness is not earned but comes through faith apart from works of law—and that this radical understanding of the Scriptures is indeed accurate. In Part I, the biblical basis of the doctrine of the Trinity could simply be assumed by the competing groups.

Second, in Part II, Luther is once again concerned to show the point of contact with his understanding of the gospel and formulations of the early church. At this juncture, the reformer appeals to the ancient and highest authoritative documents of the church catholic: the Old and New Testaments. The Lutheran understanding of forgiveness emphasized different aspects of Christian theology from the church's teaching in the generations leading up to the sixteenth century. Luther wants to demonstrate that authentic evangelicalism stems from the word of God—and itself *is* the word of God. In SA, Luther sought to ground his statements in the biblical sources.

In fact, Luther thought that the accepted theologies of sixteenth-century Roman Catholicism, and not his theology, contained the innovative and corrupted doctrines. In SA III, 12, 1, Luther expresses this judgment openly: "We do not acknowledge to them that they are the true church, and they are not the church." Furthermore, while preparing SA for publication in 1538, he put this conviction in writing once again when he wrote *The Three Symbols or Creeds of the Christian Faith:*

> Therefore I have decided . . . to publish the three symbols . . . so that I may again bear witness that I hold to the real Christian Church, which up until now has preserved these symbols or creeds, and not to that false, arrogant church, which is indeed the worst enemy of the real church.[5]

The third factor that made an appeal to Scripture imperative in Part II, 1 is that, whereas a common understanding of the Trinity could be assumed, the

---

5. *WA* 50:262; *LW* 34:201. Luther wrote the following words, also published in 1538: "Behold, this is the true catholic, universal Christian Church; it will surely not excommunicate or persecute us but will gladly accept and confirm our doctrine and regard us as dear brothers" (*Sermons on the Gospel of John*, 1538 [*WA* 46:1122–25; *LW* 24:310]).

centrality of the forgiveness of sin as God's primary work in Christ was clearly a—even the—matter of dispute between Lutherans and Roman Catholics. Luther emphasizes the importance of the issue of forgiveness in SA II, 1, 5: "We cannot yield or concede anything in this article. . . . On this article stands all that we teach and practice against the pope, the devil, and the world." The disputed nature of Luther's understanding of the gospel led him to make such explicit reference to the authoritative Scriptures.

Law, Gospel, and the Forgiveness of Sin

For Luther, the language of "the forgiveness of sin" (and, for that matter, "justification by faith") points to the same phenomenon as "the distinction between law and gospel."[6] This similarity is evident in a telling linguistic correspondence between these phrases. Each juxtaposes something negative with something positive. The negativity of the law lies in its "foremost" function: it points out the sin that is in each person's life. Unlike the law, sin is negative in and of itself: it is humankind's attempt to live life apart from a saving relationship with God in Christ. For Luther, because the reality of life apart from a restored divine-human relationship is so bad (i.e., without meaning, guilt-ridden, futile), sin can only be negative.

"Forgiveness" and "gospel" are unambiguously positive words. They define the new life offered in Christ. This new life in relationship with God, Luther wants to say, is indeed very good. The law points out the sin that is within each person, the gospel (i.e., the "good news") is the forgiveness of the sin made painfully evident by the law. Luther's distinction between law and gospel, then, functions to guarantee the proper proclamation of the good news of the forgiveness of sin.

Law

Luther began to build his theological edifice with the trinitarian (that is, for Luther, the scriptural) basis of Part I. Here, in SA II, 1 he adds another foundational pillar to his evangelical confession of faith: the distinction between the "law" and the "gospel." The law, however, appears to be rather muted. Luther entitled Part II with these words: "The second part is about the articles that pertain to the office and work of Jesus Christ, or to our redemption." Where is the law, here? Theodore Tappert's title in *BC* for the first article is "Article I: Christ and Faith."[7] Although the word "law" (*Gesetz*) does appear twice in

---

6. Cf. Luther's *Lectures on Galatians*, 1535 (*WA* 40:41–51; *LW* 26:4–12).

7. *BC*, 292.

Article 1, it would seem that its presence is not at the center of things. How can it be that this article speaks of both law and gospel?

Luther presupposes the role of the law in the law-gospel scheme as described in SA II, 1. His twofold notion of law, as defined in SA and elsewhere, is such a rich and differentiated concept that one might miss its subtle but pervasive presence in Part II, Article 1.[8]

In SA III, 2, Luther clarifies his understanding of law in a way that demonstrates its influence throughout SA II, 1. The reformer begins his discussion of law: "We maintain here that the law has been given by God, in the first place, to curb sin by means of the threat and terror of punishment and also by means of the promise and offer of grace and favor."[9] God created this "first" or "civil" use of the law as a means to order the affairs of humankind.[10] This function of the law is built into the structure of creation itself—if one abides by this kind of law, life is well ordered and people can live together in harmony. For Luther, until their disobedience caused them to endure the threatened punishment from God, Adam and Eve lived naturally according to the dictates of this sort of law. Unfortunately, this gift, like all the good gifts of creation, has "become obscured and useless through Adam's fall."[11] Thus, the presence of sin in the world has led to the failure of the law to fulfill its first function. As Luther puts it in SA, "All of this failed because of the evil which sin worked in humankind."[12]

In fact, "some became worse because of it. They are, therefore, enemies of the law, which prohibits what they want to do and commands what they do not want to do."[13] Becoming "worse" happens in two ways, says Luther. First, the law's presence can incite hatred of the law in those who desire to do what is forbidden and are unwilling to do what is commanded. This attitude of

---

8. There has been an ongoing debate among Luther scholars as to whether there are "two uses" or "three uses" of the law in Luther's theology. In SA, the reformer explicates but two uses, the "civil" and the "theological." Cf. SA III, 2. See also Werner Elert, *The Christian Ethos* (Philadelphia: Muhlenberg Press, 1957), 294ff.; Wilfried Joest, *Gesetz und Freiheit* (Göttingen, 1951); and Albrecht Peters, *Glaube and Werke* (Berlin, 1926).

9. SA III, 2, 1. This law is summarized for Luther in the "two tables" of the Ten Commandments (cf. SC I). This sort of law is, for Luther, natural law, the God-given moral sense of humankind.

10. The civil function of the law sets up an "if . . . , then" relationship with those whom it addresses. A good example of the law functioning in this way is: "If you speed in the presence of a police officer, then you will get a ticket." Most often, when an officer is present, people obey the traffic laws. They become automatically safer drivers—they do not become necessarily better drivers or better people, just safer and easier to live with.

11. *Confession concerning Christ's Supper*, 1528 (*WA* 26:505; *LW* 37:366). These words were quoted earlier with respect to the overall trinitarian emphasis in Luther's theology.

12. SA III, 2, 1.

13. SA III, 2, 2.

rebelliousness is really an expression of despair over one's inability to keep the law. Luther writes, "These are the coarse, evil people who do evil whenever they have an opportunity."[14]

Second, people are made "worse" when their attempts to keep the law lead to self-righteous complacency. It is possible actually to think of oneself as being in compliance with the law when it comes to civil or "first use" matters. For Luther, however, when people attempt to use such outward keeping of the law as a means to gain favor with God, they show that they have "become blind and presumptuous, allowing themselves to think that they can and do keep the law by their own powers. . . . This attitude results in hypocrites and false saints."[15] In Luther's thought, self-justification can lead to complacency.

The first use of the law—to "curb sin"—is not yet what Luther calls "the foremost office or power of the law."[16] This second, theological function is to point out the depth of human need for God's grace or the forgiveness of sin. Because of the power of sin in human life, no person can fully keep the law. Law, by means of its mere existence as a standard of conduct unattainable to sinful creatures, reveals the hopeless predicament within which sinful people live. The elusiveness and pervasiveness of their sinful cooperation with evil would otherwise be unknowable to sinners.[17]

This dynamic function of the law in Luther's theology is described by Thomas McDonough by means of "three metaphors: the law as mirror, as hammer, and as mask."[18] The law as mirror makes people aware of their sinfulness. The law, like an accurate mirror, shows people their true selves. Luther puts it this way in SA: "The law . . . reveals original sin and its fruits."[19]

The law as hammer takes this awareness and drives home "the totality of . . . sinfulness" to believers, so that they despair of their own works as means of gaining God's favor.[20] The law, functioning in this way, writes Luther, "is the thunderclap of God, by means of which both the obvious sinner and the false saint are destroyed."[21] God allows no one self-justification. God "drives them altogether into terror and despair."[22]

---

14. SA III, 2, 2.

15. SA III, 2, 3.

16. SA III, 2, 4.

17. Ibid.; Thieme, *Luthers Testament,* 38.

18. McDonough, *Law and Gospel,* 144. McDonough attributes this language to J. S. Whale.

19. SA III, 2, 4.

20. McDonough, *Law and Gospel,* 144.

21. SA III, 3, 2.

22. Ibid.

Here the law as mask is encountered. It is God who is ultimately at work through this strange work of the law to prepare the sinner for the good news of the gospel. The law is God's mask because, although it is God who allows the law to function as a hammer, the despair of humankind is not God's final goal. The law as hammer masks God's true, saving intention for humankind. Luther writes, "The law kills through sin . . . [but] with God, there is truly rich redemption from the great prison of sin."[23]

Thus there is an intimate connection between the law and sin, which is clarified in the reformer's article on "Sin," directly preceding the article on "Law," in Part III.[24] Luther writes:

> First, here we must confess (as St. Paul says in Rom. 5[:12]) that sin is from Adam, the one person through whose disobedience all people became sinners and subject to death and the devil. This is called the original sin, or the chief sin.
> The fruits of this sin are the evil works, which are forbidden in the Ten Commandments.[25]

The theological point of contact between sin and "the foremost office or power of the law" is that the law shows people their sin—and by doing so, drives them to their knees.[26] At the same time, the presence of sin in the world makes human beings unable to keep the demands of the law. Returning to Luther's words: The law "reveals original sin and its fruits. It shows human beings how deeply they have fallen and how their nature is completely corrupt."[27]

This analysis of the theological use of the law makes explicit the implicit role played by the law in SA II, 1. The sinful condition of human beings provides the context for the saving act of God in Christ. Humanity is in need of being saved from that which the law makes plain: sin. Part II, 1 shows the matrix or web of sin into which Christ came in order to redeem humanity: "That Jesus Christ, our God and Lord,"[28] affirms Luther, "was handed over to death for our trespasses." Christ "takes away the sin of the world." "The Lord

---

23. SA III, 3, 8.

24. SA III, 1. Even in the order of the articles discussed in Part III, Luther displays the law/gospel scheme that is so integral to his theology: Sin (Article 1), which is revealed by the law (Article 2), is confessed (Article 3) and forgiven by the gospel (Article 4).

25. SA III, 1, 1–2.

26. SA III, 2, 4.

27. Ibid.

28. Jesus Christ as "God and Lord" was described in SA I, 4.

has laid upon him the iniquity of us all." "Furthermore," writes Luther as he prepares to quote the apostle Paul once again: "'All have sinned.'"

These passages take on meaning for Luther when the law has performed its "foremost office or power," when it "reveals original sin and its fruits." [29] Otherwise, without the law working in this way, the gospel message is basically irrelevant. Salvation in Christ makes sense only to those who recognize that they are in need of being saved.

According to Luther, God has done that which sin prevents humanity from doing. God's law is fulfilled by Christ. God has acted in Jesus of Nazareth to "justify" or "redeem" sinful humankind.[30] In SA II, 1, Luther borrows biblical language, but it is also legal language—the language of forensic justice.

The use of such legal language in SA creates this kind of analogy: Humanity's relationship to God, which in the beginning was intended to be that of a child thriving in the nurturing, sustaining love of a caring Father, has become that of a criminal standing guilty and condemned in a court of law. The ordinary human response of a guilty party is to try to fulfill the law through the performance of deeds (plea bargaining, doing community service projects, promising to "go straight," etc.) that seek to appease the court. The defendant might try to demonstrate a truly reformed life, while at the same time repay the plaintiff for any damages.

In other words, the guilty party tries to use the means available in the law in order to overcome the fact that a crime has been committed. Such an approach leaves the law intact and the accused submits to it. However, Luther's explanation of the chief function of the law does not allow for this. The law, in Luther's view, is not a means to make restitution. In this case, the law

> must say to [people] that they have no God. They honor or worship strange gods. This is something that they would not have believed before without the law. Thus they are terrified, humbled, despondent and despairing. They anxiously desire help but do not know where to find it. They become enemies of God, murmuring, etc. This is what is meant by Romans 3, "The law brings wrath," and Romans 5[:20]: "Sin becomes greater through the law." [31]

---

29. SA III, 2, 4.

30. Recall that Luther introduces SA II with this title: "The second part is about the articles that pertain to the office and work of Jesus Christ, or to our redemption." SA II, 1, 1 refers to "our justification" and SA II, 1, 3 refers to "'All have sinned,' and 'they are now justified without merit by his grace, through the redemption which is in Christ Jesus . . . by his blood.'"

31. SA III, 2, 4–5. In this excerpt, Luther mistakenly refers to Romans 3. He quotes actually from Rom. 4:15.

The second use of the law shows humankind's complete inability to justify itself. The law, in effect, is that which rightly accuses the guilty criminal. This same law, one might say, then also compels the lawgiver or the judge to condemn and punish the accused party—to the fullest extent of the law.

For the criminal, that is indeed a horrible prospect and so it is understandable that the defendant would want to cut a deal with the court, promise to do better, and seek to pay off the debt. Unfortunately this approach to the problem simply does not work. According to Luther, sin is too pervasive and attempts to use the law to justify oneself are futile.

Gospel

We turn now to a discussion of the gospel because the good news is that the debt has been paid. The wrong has been righted. Justice and mercy are both fulfilled. The judge declares that the guilty party no longer stands condemned.

For Luther, this does not happen simply or easily. It is costly business. The defendant was guilty of a capital offense. Instead, however, of inflicting this punishment on the guilty one, the judge takes off the judicial robe, so to speak, and descends from the bench, in order to submit to the punishment in the place of the defendant. Quoting the apostle Paul, Luther puts it this way: "Jesus Christ, our God and Lord, was handed over to death for our trespasses."[32] The law is fulfilled by the only one capable of fulfilling it. For it is that very divine judge, the dispenser of justice, who personally pays the penalty that sinful humankind cannot pay. The righteousness of God is imputed to those who are unrighteous.

Because it is the judge who was willing to pay the ultimate price—even death—in order to save those who rightly deserved punishment, the guilty one is declared justified. God has taken care of the debt. The offender and the offended have been reconciled. New life is given when death was rightly called for. Luther puts it this way: "We receive a different, new, clean heart through faith (as St. Peter says). God wants to regard and does regard us as completely righteous and holy, for the sake of Christ our mediator."[33]

In this process, the original or intended relationship between God and humankind is restored. God ceases to be the harsh, unbending condemner and executioner but turns out to be indeed the caring, nurturing heavenly Father who was hidden behind the austerity of judgment and law. It is as if a parent (who is also the one injured by the misdeed) were to substitute himself or

32. SA II, 1, 1.
33. SA III, 13, 1.

herself for the child who had committed the crime, thereby taking the punishment.

This is the central point of Luther's understanding of the gospel as expressed in SA II, 1: in Jesus Christ, the merciful and loving God embraces the sinner. This new divine-human relationship, established with humankind by God in Christ, brings the forgiveness of sin.[34]

The message that announces the undeserved pardon to the ones deserving condemnation is the gospel of the forgiveness of sin. This is indeed good news for those who are under the burden of the law. Those who were bound have been set free. The new emphasis in Luther's theology, which was counter to the prevailing theology of the time, is that there was nothing done by the guilty party that earns or even contributes to this forgiveness. This was God in Christ's gratuitous work, performed and offered to the world as a gift. It is entirely the grace of God that made this possible. Luther's evangelicalism in SA reflects the good news of this word of grace, the justification of the godless.

Indeed, Luther's understanding of Christ's work that brings the forgiveness of sin is so significant and differentiated that here in "the first and chief article" the reformer moves beyond a simple "satisfaction theory"[35] of the atonement and embraces also the *Christus Victor*[36] motif. For Luther, no single metaphor or image of Christ's saving work seems capable of capturing the profundity of what God has done. Therefore the reformer also sees the saving deed of God in Christ in the context of a cosmic battle:

> On this article stands all that we teach and practice against the pope, the devil, and the world. Therefore we must be quite certain and not doubt. Otherwise everything is lost, and pope and devil and everything against us will gain victory and dominance.[37]

For Luther, the atoning and forgiving activity of God in Christ is not simply a past action, but it also has tremendous contemporary relevance. God's particular, historical work in Jesus Christ is finished and complete. Yet this saving work takes on its intended meaning for everyday life only when it is appropriated by people through the grace-engendered gift of faith. Therefore

---

34. SC VI, 6.

35. Cf. Gustaf Aulen, *Christus Victor* (New York: Macmillan Co., 1969), 81–100.

36. Ibid., 101–22. Aulen's book argues for this theory of the atonement as the primary atonement motif in Luther's theology. In the Foreword to the 1969 edition, however, Jaroslav Pelikan points to "the heterogeneity of [Luther's] pictures of the redemptive work of Christ" (p. xvi). SA II, 1, and its juxtaposition of these two traditional understandings of the atonement, would seem to validate Pelikan's interpretation.

37. SA II, 1, 5.

God continues to make the evangelical offer of forgiveness based on this deed to the world, so that people might believe. It is this belief, this faith, that justifies. It is in this sense that Luther can talk of "justification by faith."[38]

The soteriological problem in the life of any given person is this: How can the accused and guilty party actually come to *believe* in the forgiveness of sin, the verdict of the judge? What good does it do a prisoner to receive a pardon if he or she does not accept it and instead chooses to live behind bars?[39]

The analogy of the courtroom and legal system can be pushed only so far. There is a rather easily identifiable role in this drama for each of the members of the Trinity except one: the Holy Spirit. God the Father, who had taken on the role of the judge, is revealed actually to be that loving and merciful parent once again. God the Son is the means by which the debt is repaid and forgiveness won. These roles carry with them titles that are the common experience of most people: a father and a son. God the Holy Spirit is described in the Bible with a number of images (wind, fire, dove), none of which carry with them the personal associations of parent and child.

Still, the role of the Holy Spirit is critical in Luther's understanding of the drama of creation, fall, and redemption. According to Luther, the Spirit is active in the world to make both the law and the gospel known. Indeed, God the Holy Spirit is the particular person of the Trinity who is hidden behind the law's mask. Luther points succinctly to the Spirit's activity when he paraphrases the Gospel of John: "The Holy Spirit 'will convince the world of sin.'"[40]

That, however, is not all that the Holy Spirit does. The Spirit, in Luther's theology, enables people to believe. Without this empowering work, the sinful human person would be left to try to apprehend forgiveness through his or her own effort. The Spirit, who uses theological function of the law, however, simply does not allow for this. No amount of human striving can lay claim to this forgiveness. It must be believed. And this belief itself is a gift given by God the Spirit.

The vital role of the Spirit is implied when the reformer writes, "Now because this [i.e., the gospel, the forgiveness of sin] must be believed and may not be obtained or grasped otherwise with any work, law, or merit, it is clear and certain that faith alone justifies us."[41] The Spirit, as Luther made clear already in 1528, makes the redemptive act of God in Christ real in the lives of people:

38. Thieme, *Luthers Testament*, 44.
39. Ibid., 31.
40. SA III, 3, 1.
41. SA II, 1, 4.

But because this grace would benefit no one if it remained so profoundly hidden and could not come to us, the Holy Spirit comes and gives himself to us also, wholly and completely. He teaches us to understand this deed of Christ which has been manifested to us, helps us receive and preserve it, use it to our advantage and impart it to others, increase and extend it.[42]

Luther had put this conclusion in rather personal terms in 1529, when he wrote SC and offered this explanation of the third article of the Apostles' Creed:

I believe that by my own reason or strength I cannot believe in Jesus Christ, my Lord, or come to him. But the Holy Spirit has called me through the Gospel, enlightened me with his gifts, and sanctified and preserved me in true faith.[43]

The Holy Spirit, says Luther, makes it possible for Christians to believe the forgiveness of sin offered in Christ.

This is the basic, evangelical view of salvation that Luther presents in his theological testament: redemption is solely God's work on behalf of sinful and undeserving humankind. Part II, 1 of SA summarizes the redeeming deed of God in Christ and points to the means by which the meaning of this act is apprehended: faith. Throughout this scheme, the active grace of God is at work to justify sinners who stand guilty and condemned under the accusations of the law. The gospel (i.e., the *euangelion* of the New Testament) is that this forgiveness of sin is offered through Christ and made real in the lives of believers by the Spirit.

Luther's Evangelical Polemic

The distinction between law and gospel reflects Luther's highest theological priorities. This distinction also serves as the basis for what might be called Luther's "evangelical polemic" against his adversaries, particularly the Roman church. At the conclusion of SA II, 1 he writes: "We cannot yield or concede anything in this article, even if heaven and earth, or whatever, do not remain." Luther makes a positive, constructive theological statement in SA I and in SA II, 1. Then, at the end of SA II, 1 he moves directly into a heated polemical discussion of papal abuses against "the first and chief article." This article is the basis for the reformer's attack on the Mass (SA II, 2), foundations and monasteries (SA II, 3), and the papacy (SA II, 4).

---

42. *Confession concerning Christ's Supper*, 1528 (*WA* 26:505; *LW* 37:366).
43. SC II, 6.

Rome's Lack of Faith

Luther engages in theological battle in SA. Throughout this document there are many disparaging comments about the sixteenth-century church of Rome. Two telling references summarize the reformer's critique.

First, in the discussion of SA, Part I, we noted that Luther's original monograph ended with the words: "These articles are not matters of dispute or contention, for both parties believe and confess them." Luther's decision to strike out "believe and" for his final version of SA takes on significance in the light of the reformer's view of the role of the law and gospel in the life of faith.

This deletion in SA I, 4 reveals Luther's conclusion that his Roman Catholic opponents did not actually trust or *believe* what they confessed in the trinitarian creeds. Otherwise the theologies that grew out of adherence to these creeds would reflect faith in the promises of God. It is evident in SA that Luther identifies justification by faith versus justification by works as the essence of the issue at stake between Rome and himself. Luther's unwillingness to attribute belief to his adversaries in SA I underscores his analysis of the central problem with sixteenth-century Roman Catholicism: it confused law and gospel.

Both the reformer and his opponents had what could be termed "christocentric" theologies.[44] However, this Christocentrism functioned differently in Luther's theology than it did in Roman Catholic theology. This difference can be seen when SA is compared with a writing of John Cochläus, a Roman Catholic adversary of Luther who wrote a rebuttal to SA already in 1538. Cochläus writes:

> We do not want to place the little word "alone" either next to faith or to works. Because, although Christ is the chief thing, through whose grace, merit, and good deed we are justified (that is, we are separated from our sins); the means and instruments which are meritorious for the forgiveness of sins are many and manifold.[45]

For Cochläus to say that Christ is the "chief thing" (*heuptursach*) means something fundamentally different from Luther's understanding of Christ in the "chief article" (*Häuptartikel*).[46] In Cochläus's view, Jesus Christ is basically the same as the other available "means and instruments" that merit forgive-

---

44. Schott, "Christus und die Rechtfertigung," 193. The analysis here follows the arguments of Schott.

45. *Ein nöting und christlich bedencken auff des Luthers artickeln, die man gemeynem concilio fürtragen sol*, in *CC*, 18:10. Cf. Schott, "Christus und die Rechtfertigung," 193.

46. In the early modern German of the sixteenth century, the suffixes used by Cochläus (*heupt-*) and Luther (*Haupt-*) are variant spellings of the modern German word *Haupt*.

ness. Christ may be the most important part of the system, but other things are needful as well. Human works (e.g., church traditions [pilgrimages, relics, alms, indulgences, etc.] and submission to the pope's authority) play a necessary role in the scheme of salvation. Therefore Christ's saving work does not have independent standing but is tied to the performance of certain works by those who would want to be saved.[47] That is why Cochläus and his party refused to use the word "alone" to describe the sufficiency of faith. What resulted in the sixteenth-century Roman church was a rather intricate system of observances and practices that were seen as additional "means and instruments" for the obtaining of God's grace and favor.[48]

Luther thought that one could not have it both ways: the simultaneous emphasis on both faith and works in Cochläus's understanding of the church only confused the gospel with the law. The sixteenth-century church of Rome had taken on the role of authoritative mediator between Christ and humankind, and Luther thought this role was antithetical to the gospel.[49] As Luther puts it in SA II, 1, 2: "Jesus . . . alone is 'the Lamb of God, who takes away the sin of the world.'"[50] Or, as Luther puts it a little later in this article, "it is clear and certain that faith alone justifies us."[51] Cochläus would omit "the little word 'alone,'" with respect to faith. For Luther, however, it is precisely this that distinguished the gospel from the law.

What Luther is after here is to keep the focus of his critique on central matters. The problems in society and in the church, according to Luther, grow out of a basic misunderstanding of the work and message of Christ. The reformer thought that the proposed council of the church would only allow itself to address relatively trivial concerns and not get to the heart of the matter. He writes:

> If participants in the council were to deal with the chief concerns in the
> spiritual and secular orders that are against God, then their hands would
> be so full that they would indeed forget the child's games and foolish play

---

47. Thieme, *Luthers Testament*, 19.

48. Ibid., 20f.

49. Schwartzwäller, "Rechtfertigung und Ekklesiologie in den Schmalkaldischen Artikeln," 89–92.

50. Emphasis added.

51. Emphasis added. Luther explained this exegetically in *On Translating, An Open Letter*, 1530 (*WA 30*[II]; *LW* 35:188): "Here, in Romans 3, I knew very well that the word *solum* is not in the Greek or Latin text; the papists did not have to teach me that. It is a fact that these four letters *s-o-l-a* are not there. And these blockheads stare at them like cows at a new gate. At the same time they do not see that it conveys the sense of the text; it belongs there if the translation is to be clear and vigorous."

of long gowns, large shaved heads, broad cinctures, bishop's and cardinal's hats, crosiers, and similar sleight-of-hand.[52]

A helpful writing by Luther for interpreting his conclusion that the church of Rome did not believe what it confessed in the creeds is *The Three Symbols or Creeds of the Christian Faith,* written in March of 1538 while he was preparing SA for publication.[53] Lewis Spitz indicates the importance of this work in relationship to SA: "In this exposition of the creeds, Luther wished to elaborate on the brief theses in the first part of his Smalcald Articles 'on the lofty articles of the divine majesty.'"[54]

Spitz points to no external evidence that supports this claim, but internally there is a very telling passage that acts as a commentary on the role of belief in Christian theology and life. It is as though Luther has in mind SA I and his reconsideration of allowing for belief in the "lofty articles of the divine majesty" by the church of Rome:

> Thus the devil has work to do and attacks Christ in three lines of battle. One will not let him be God, another will not let him be human, and the third will not let him do what he has done. Each of the three wants to reduce Christ to nothing. For what does it profit you to confess that he is God, if you do not also *believe* that he is human? . . . What does it profit you to confess that he is human, if you do not also *believe* that he is God? What does it profit you to confess that he is God and human, if you do not also *believe* that he has become everything and done everything for you? . . . All three articles must be truly *believed.* . . . If one article is lacking, then all are lacking, for the faith is supposed to be and must be whole and complete.[55]

Erdmann Schott introduces his explication of SA by noting the relationship of Luther's striking out the words "believe and" in SA I, 4 and the above-quoted passage from the 1538 discussion of the creeds. Schott interprets: "With the third 'line of battle,' Luther has in mind the works-righteousness of the Roman church. . . . Rome will not allow Christ to do what he has done! Thus we meet the basic thought of *The Schmalkald Articles*."[56]

What has Christ "done"? Jesus Christ "has become everything and done everything for you," writes Luther in 1538. Schott correctly identifies the pri-

---

52. SA, Preface, 13. When Luther refers to "secular orders" here, he indicates his awareness of the social consequences of the church's confusion of law and gospel (cf. also SA, Preface, 12).

53. WA 50:262–83; *LW* 34:201ff.

54. *LW* 34:199. Otto Clemen, editor of *Die drei Symbola oder Bekenntnis des Glaubens Christi* in WA 50, writes: "With [this document] . . . Luther wanted to explicate further the rather short and scant statements of the first part of the Schmalkald Articles" (p. 256).

55. WA 50:269; *LW* 34:210. Emphases added.

56. Schott, "Christus und die Rechtfertigung," 192.

mary issue at stake in SA: trust in the sufficiency of Christ's work versus trust in human work(s).

The distinction between law and gospel takes on personal importance when this word is no longer simply salvation for "humankind." When this becomes real existentially, then one truly encounters what Luther meant by justification by faith.[57] For Luther, it is not so much that Christ "has become everything and done everything" in a general, objective sort of way. Rather, it is the fact that Christ has done what he has done *"for you"* (in Luther's German: *fur dich*) that makes this a word of good news.[58]

The gospel of the forgiveness of sin was the core of Luther's polemics against Rome because justification by faith was, for Luther, the lifeblood of Christianity.[59] Luther was convinced that the sacramental hierarchy of Rome had wrongly inserted itself into the scheme of salvation.[60] Specifically, the hierarchy and the sacraments (and "quasi sacraments") of the church of Rome had themselves become objects of belief, diverting the attention of the faithful away from Christ to one's own religious works (such as attendance at Mass, indulgences, pilgrimages) or the religious works of others (such as saints and their relics, priestly acts, the prayers of monks or nuns). This is why Luther's polemics in SA proceed the way they do. Luther felt compelled to protest in the strongest possible terms the abuses he saw in the church of his day.[61] His critique is based on his conclusion that the gospel, not the law, saves humankind. The problem with "the papists" was that they allowed, and even encouraged, other requirements or laws to be added to the gospel. This made the gift of God in Christ something more to be earned than received freely. Thus, for Luther, although adherents to the church of Rome confessed the creeds, they did not really believe or trust them. They trusted in various, supposed "good" works, not Christ.

The Pope as Antichrist

The second significant example of Luther's polemical stance against the Roman church is his conclusion that the pope is "the true antichrist or contra-

---

57. Cf. "The Methodological Principle," in Forell, *Faith Active in Love*, 44ff.; and Lennart Pinoma, *Der existentielle Charakter der Theologie Luthers* (Helsinki: Finnische Akademie der Wissenschaften, 1940).

58. Throughout the above-quoted passage from *The Three Symbols or Creeds of the Christian Faith*, Luther uses the second person singular: *du bekennest, du gleubest* (WA 50:269).

59. SA II, 1, 5.

60. Schott, "Christus und die Rechtfertigung," 204.

61. Thieme, *Luthers Testament*, 14. See also Schwartzwäller, "Rechtfertigung und Ekklesiologie in den Schmalkaldischen Artikeln."

christ."[62] When Luther used these words to describe the pope, he was not simply calling Paul III (who happened to be the pope at the time) names. Luther's language here, when placed in its historical and theological contexts,[63] indicates that Luther chose these words based on priorities that were foundational to his reformation theology.[64]

The earliest recorded condemnation of a pope as the antichrist occurred in 991, when Bishop Arnulf of Orleans called into question the moral character and personal abilities of Pope John XV at the Gallican Synod of Reims. Arnulf's words reflect the general tone of the medieval usage of "antichrist" to vilify the pope:

> If, holy fathers, we are bound to weigh in the balance the lives, the morals, and the attainments of the humblest candidate for the priestly office, how much more ought we to look to the fitness of him who aspires to be the Lord and Master of all priests! Yet how would it fare with us, if it should happen that the man the most deficient in all these virtues, unworthy of the lowest place in the priesthood, should be chosen to fill the highest place of all? What would you say of such a one, when you see him sitting upon the throne glittering in purple and gold? Must he not be the "antichrist, sitting in the temple of God, and showing himself as God"?[65]

As the medieval period progressed and the role of the papacy in European culture increased,[66] it became rather commonplace for would-be reformers to

---

62. SA II, 4, 10.

63. In the sixteenth century, the traditional understandings of the antichrist included the scriptural passages that had become commonly associated with the antichrist: Daniel 8; 1 John 2:18 and 4:3; Revelation 13–19. See also Hans Hillerbrand, "The Antichrist in the Early German Reformation: Reflections on Theology and Propaganda," in *Germania Illustrata: Essays on Early Modern Germany Presented to Gerald Strauss*, ed. Andrew Fix and Susan Karant-Nunn (Kirksville, Mo.: Sixteenth Century Journal Publishers, 1992), 3. For Luther, the pope as the antichrist should be seen as part of the reformer's theological understanding of the devil's role in history. Heiko Oberman has explored this at length in *Luther: Man between God and the Devil*. Oberman's conclusion agrees with Harmannus Obendiek, *Der Teufel bei Martin Luther: Eine theologische Untersuchung* (Berlin: Furche-Verlag, 1931). Obendiek writes (p. 235): "Luther cannot conceive of God and the world, the reconciling and redeeming work of Christ, Revelation and the Word of God, humankind and humankind's way to God, apart from the concept of the devil."

64. J. Michael Miller, a Roman Catholic scholar, has done this in a general way, in *The Divine Right of the Papacy in Recent Ecumenical Theology* (Rome: Università Gregoriana Editrice, 1980).

65. *Acta Concilii Remenses ac Sanctum Basolum: Monumenta Germaniae Historica* (Berlin, 1826–), *Scriptores* 3:672, trans. Philip Schaff, *History of the Christian Church* (New York, 1899), 6:292. See also Bernard McGinn, "Angel Pope and Papal Antichrist," *Church History* 47 (1978): 156.

66. McGinn, "Angel Pope," 157. See also Robin Barnes, *Prophecy and Gnosis* (Stanford, Calif.: Stanford University Press, 1988), 26.

hurl the charge of antichrist at the bishop of Rome.[67] Indeed, "not only dissi-
dents and heretics but even saints . . . called the bishop of Rome the 'antichrist'
when they wished to castigate his abuse of power."[68] Even though some medieval thinkers, such as Peter John Olivi, placed the pope as antichrist in an
eschatological and even apocalyptic framework,[69] they continued to use the
term primarily to question the lack of personal integrity and/or capability of
the particular pope under scrutiny.[70] Throughout the medieval period, as Bernard McGinn puts it, "the ultimate religious value of the papacy"[71] was rarely
if ever challenged.[72] On the whole, this remained the case, even as late medieval
"premonitions" identified "specific dates" for the arrival of the antichrist.[73]

Luther was aware that his conclusion regarding the papacy put him in the
context of this tradition, even when he reinterpreted it in the light of his understanding of the Word of God as law and gospel. When Luther published
John Purvey's commentary on Revelation in 1528, he noted, "We are not the
first ones who interpret the papacy as the kingdom of the antichrist."[74] Luther,
however, thought that he was doing something different from earlier papal
critics, such as John Hus, when he did not base his critique of the papacy
on the moral lapses of any particular pope but rather on the theology that
undergirded the pope's authority.[75]

According to Luther, the basic error of the Roman Catholic Church of his
day was idolatrous faith in works as opposed to faith in Christ alone. Because

---

67. McGinn surveys this usage in "Angel Pope," 160f. Hans Preuss traces the application of "antichrist" to popes back to the eleventh century; see Preuss, *Die Vorstellungen vom Antichrist im
späteren Mittelalter, bei Luther und in der konfessionellen Polemik* (Leipzig, 1906), 47f.

68. Empie and Murphy, eds., *Papal Primacy and the Universal Church* (Minneapolis: Augsburg,
1974), 25.

69. McGinn, "Angel Pope," 165f.

70. Richard K. Emmerson, *Antichrist in the Middle Ages* (Seattle: University of Washington Press,
1981), 70.

71. McGinn, "Angel Pope," 173.

72. This tradition was modified somewhat in the later medieval era, when Wycliffe and Hus,
though still using "antichrist" primarily to point out the moral failures of the popes, began to
question the validity of the papacy itself (Emmerson, *Antichrist*, 70f.). Robin Barnes (*Prophecy,*
42f.) writes: "Earlier critics of the church, for example, John Hus and Savonarola, had identified
the pope himself as the antichrist. But these critics had based their charge mostly on moral consid-
erations."

73. Hillerbrand, "The Antichrist," 5.

74. WA 26:136–38.

75. Luther distinguished himself from the reform program of John Hus at this very point (*LW*
32:82, WA 7:433, 1–7: *Defense and Explanation of All the Articles,* 1521).

the pope seeks to rule the church and, in Luther's view, perpetuates such idolatry, he personifies "the true antichrist or contrachrist."

In the late 1510s, Luther began to argue that the pope and papal government of the church were anti-Christian. Prior to 1517, Luther's position toward the pope was apparently quite positive.[76] Luther himself indicates this as he reflects on his career as a reformer in the 1545 preface to his Latin works, when he describes himself with these words:

> I was once a monk and a most enthusiastic papist when I began the cause. I was so drunk, yes, submerged in the pope's dogmas, that I would have been ready to murder all, if I could have, or co-operate willingly with the murderers of all who would take but a syllable from obedience to the pope.[77]

When this attitude began to change, there were indications of Luther's growing conviction that the pope was the antichrist.[78] This tentative notion became a hardened conviction in the early 1520s.[79] Once Luther had arrived at this conclusion, he consistently held to his conviction that the pope was the "antichrist."[80]

Theologically, Luther based his conclusion that the papacy was anti-Christian on three primary factors, exegetical, dogmatic, and eschatological, all of which flowed out of the heart of his theology as expressed in SA.

First, Luther's judgment regarding the pope has an exegetical or scriptural component. Because Luther could find no clear biblical foundation for papal

---

76. Remigius Bäumer, *Martin Luther und der Papst* (Münster: Verlag Aschendorff, 1970), 7. Bäumer cites a half dozen modern scholars who also conclude that, early in his life, Luther was rather positive toward the papacy.

77. *The Preface to Luther's Complete Latin Works*, 1545 (*LW* 34:328; *WA* 54:179f.). See also Bäumer, *Luther und der Papst*, 8.

78. E.g., *WABr* 1:279, 11–14 (letter to Wenceslaus Link, December 18, 1518). Hendrix (*Luther and the Papacy*, 117f.) leaves open the question as to when Luther first identified the pope as the antichrist. The sources, however, would seem to indicate that this date is rather precisely identifiable.

79. Two late 1520 treatises document Luther's growing conviction about the bishop of Rome: *Adversus execrabilem antichristi bullam* (*WA* 6:597–612) and *Why the Books of the Pope and His Disciples Were Burned* (*WA* 7:161–82; *LW* 31:379–95). Both works contain references to the see of Rome as the kingdom of the antichrist and are representative of Luther's break with Rome (see also Hendrix, *Luther and the Papacy*, 117).

80. Evidence that Luther's conviction about the pope as antichrist persisted throughout the rest of his life is one of his most vitriolic writings: *Against the Roman Papacy, an Institution of the Devil*, written in 1545 (*LW* 41:257; *WA* 54:206). See also Wenzel Lohff, "Would the Pope Still Have Been the Antichrist for Luther Today?" *Concilium* 4 (1971): 68f.

supremacy,[81] he rejected the claims of papal apologists who justified the primacy of the bishop of Rome by an appeal to divine institution (*de jure divino*).[82] Roman Catholic interpreters of Scripture and canon law argued that papal authority was bestowed by God and submission to the Roman see was therefore necessary for salvation.[83] Luther, however, pointed to 2 Thessalonians 2 and was unpersuaded.[84] For the reformer, "divine right" depended on explicit scriptural references that would make adherence to the doctrine in question necessary for salvation.[85] Because he found no obvious biblical basis for papal primacy, Luther wrote: "The pope is not the head of all Christendom 'by divine right' or on the basis of God's word (because that belongs only to the one who is called Jesus Christ)."[86]

With this, Luther pointed to the second major element in his judgment that the papacy was anti-Christian: the dogmatic component. Not only was papal dominance founded on faulty scriptural grounds, the sixteenth-century papacy was, according to Luther, heretical:[87] the papacy usurped Christ's lordship by its insistence on human cooperation with grace (that is, for Luther, "works-righteousness"). In SA II, 1 (Luther's "first and chief article"), the reformer sought to demonstrate once again the centrality of the distinction between law and gospel in the Scriptures. The pope's continued rejection of this

81. In SA (e.g., SA III, 7, 1) and elsewhere Luther contends that the traditional texts for papal primacy are really about the power of the keys given to the whole church, represented in any particular case by a local congregation (cf. Ulrich Pflugk: "Luther und der Papst," *Luther* 31 [1960]: 133, 137).

82. In 1521, Cardinal Cajetan, who exemplifies the response of papal defenders, wrote a treatise against Luther at the request of Leo X: *De divina institutione pontificatus Romani Pontificis*. Cajetan concluded: "The authority of the pope is immediately from God and revealed in Sacred Scripture." See Miller, *The Papacy*, 31.

83. Popular scriptural texts used to buttress this conclusion were Matthew 16 and John 21, from which it was argued that the papal authority that was bestowed on the apostle Peter was handed down by him to his successors at Rome. This became the foundation for assertions of papal primacy in canon law.

84. In SA II, 4, 15, Luther refers to 2 Thess. 2:4 and in SA II, 4, 11 he refers to 2 Thess. 2:8. See also Friedrich Brunn, *Ist der Papst der Antichrist?* (Dresden: Justus Naumann's Buchhandlung, n.d.), 13f.

85. Papal authority *de jure divino*, defined by Luther as being "on the basis of God's word" (SA II, 4, 1) or "ordered" or "commanded by God" (SA II, 4, 10), would require an unambiguous biblical mandate and even dominical institution. See also *BSLK*, 427 n. 3. In *Disputatio I. Eccii et M. Lutheri Lipsiae habita*, 1519 (*WA* 2:279$_{23f.}$), Luther wrote about "the Holy Scriptures, which are properly the *jus divinum*." See also BC, 322: Tr., 12.

86. SA II, 4, 1. Luther makes this point in his *Table Talks*: *WATR* 2:17; *WATR* 3:119; *WATR* 3:132; *WATR* 3:562.

87. According to Hillerbrand ("The Antichrist," 4), Origen also "saw the antichrist as a synonym for heresy."

interpretation, therefore, meant for Luther that the papacy did not serve the truth of the gospel.[88] Luther writes:

> And when we distinguish the pope's teaching from that of the Holy Scriptures, or place it next to them, then we find that the pope's teaching, when it is at its best, is taken from the imperial, pagan law and teaches about secular dealings and judgments, as his pronouncements show. Furthermore, they teach about ceremonies involving churches, clothing, foods, persons; along with child's play, fantasies, and foolish activities without number. In all these things, there is absolutely nothing about Christ, faith, and God's commandments.[89]

According to Luther, the papacy as the head of the Roman hierarchy promotes doctrines and practices that are contrary to the central doctrine of the Christian faith and Scriptures: the gospel of the forgiveness of sin through Christ alone.[90] In particular, one such doctrine that prompted Luther's conclusion about the anti-Christian nature of the papacy was articulated by Pope Boniface VIII in the famous 1302 papal bull *Unam Sanctam:* "It is altogether necessary to salvation for every human creature to be subject to the Roman pontiff."[91] This sentiment, which was explicitly reaffirmed by the Fifth Lateran Council on the eve of the Reformation, in 1516,[92] helped to convince Luther that the pope proclaims a message counter to or "anti-" Christ.[93] Thus Luther summarizes the main lines of his entire critique of the Roman Catholic Church in SA:

> In the end, this is nothing other than the devil himself who promotes his lies about masses, purgatory, monastic life, one's own works, and worship (which are the essence of the papacy) in contradiction to God. He damns, slays, and plagues all Christians who do not exalt and honor his abominations above all things. Therefore we can no more adore the devil himself

---

88. Walter Mostert, "Die theologische Bedeutung von Luthers antirömischer Polemik," *Lutherjahrbuch* 57 (1990): 72–92, interprets three basic aspects of Luther's understanding of the gospel as related to his polemics: "Grace" (pp. 83f.), "Law and Gospel" (pp. 85f.), and "The Lord's Supper" (pp. 86f.).

89. SA II, 4, 14.

90. SA II, 1, 4f.; II, 4, 3; 4, 14. See also Pflugk, "Luther und der Papst," 137.

91. Tappert, *BC*, 299 n. 4.

92. Carter Lindberg, "The Late Middle Ages and the Reformations of the Sixteenth Century," in *Christianity: A Social and Cultural History*, ed. Howard Clark Kee (New York: Macmillan Co., 1991), 309.

93. SA II, 4, 4. Pflugk summarizes Luther's opinion: "But since [the pope] does not follow faith, as the Scripture intends, he is the antichrist and everything he does serves only to corrupt Christianity" ("Luther und der Papst," 137).

as our lord or god than we can allow his apostle, the pope or antichrist, to rule us as our head or lord. His papal government is characterized by lying and murder and the eternal ruin of body and soul.[94]

The summary character of this passage is evident when it is placed in the context of Luther's overall argument in SA, Part II. Luther moves directly from a positive, constructive theological statement of the distinction between law and gospel (Article 1) to a heated attack on the Mass (Article 2). Then follows a discussion of foundations and monasteries (Article 3). Ultimately, then, Luther turns his attention to the papacy (Article 4).

Luther's critique here also corresponds rather closely to what we know of his experience. First, the Mass and its associated practices, which the reformer describes and criticizes in Article 2, can be seen as various additional means offered by the Roman church after baptism to secure or ensure one's salvation. Both personally and pastorally Luther had a firsthand acquaintance with the items he specifically criticizes in Article 2: "purgatory," "purgatorial masses for the dead," "vigils," "pilgrimages," "alms," "fraternities," "relics," "indulgences," and "the invocation of saints."

Second, when Luther was a young man, he sought out what he considered to be the surest road to assure his salvation: the way of monasticism. Luther's experience as a young monk had acquainted him with the monastic life that he calls, in SA II, 2, "blasphemous worship, established through human beings . . . as something better than the general Christian vocation and the offices and orders established by God."[95]

Third, Luther takes aim at the papacy, the institution that confronted him throughout his adult life when he began to speak out against what he perceived as the theological and practical abuses of the Roman church of his day.

Luther's polemic in SA ascends from the most down-to-earth and pervasive ecclesiastical reality in sixteenth-century European Christianity, the Mass, to the monastic life, and then to the apex of the system, the papacy. Each of the three targets of Luther's critique is explicitly evaluated and rejected on the basis of "the first and chief article," the reformer's understanding of the gospel as the forgiveness of sin.

The third component of Luther's understanding of the pope as antichrist lies in the eschatological emphasis of the reformer's theology.[96] In fact, both Luther's reformation career in general and SA in particular are deeply influ-

94. SA II, 4, 14.

95. SA II, 3, 2.

96. The above survey of the usage of "antichrist" prior to the sixteenth century would indicate that Luther's eschatological understanding of the antichrist is inherited from medieval traditions.

enced by the hope of Christ's imminent return.[97] The preface to the articles reflects this when it makes the transition to the main body of the document with this prayer: "O dear Lord Jesus Christ, hold a council and redeem your people through your glorious return! The pope and his people are lost."[98]

Specifically, Luther's consistent use of the German word *Endechrist* and its cognates to describe the pope and papal practice in SA is an obvious clue to his eschatological understanding of the term.[99] This usage is a return to a linguistic form that he had publicly rejected in 1522 (he preferred thereafter *Widerchrist*).[100] Luther's use of *Endechrist* relates to Middle High German connotations of this word, which clearly imply the arrival of the end time.[101]

Luther's expectation that history was nearly over adds an urgency to the reformer's sense of mission.[102] Luther understood the pope as antichrist as part of what Heiko Oberman calls the "three basic elements in the tradition usually referred to as 'apocalyptic' eschatology: the struggle between God and the devil, the approaching end of time, and the appearance of the antichrist."[103]

This apocalypticism encouraged Luther to see his mission as an attempt to rescue the pure proclamation of the word from the minions of the devil.[104] As he puts it in 1542:

> The pope is to us the true antichrist, who has the high, subtile, beautiful, hypocritical Devil; who sits immovably in Christendom, allowing the Holy Scriptures, Baptism, the Sacrament, the Keys, the Catechism, and marriage to remain. . . . However, he rules so deftly that he raises his "shit

---

97. George Forell has shown the pervasive role of eschatological concerns in Luther's theology and ethics in *Faith Active in Love,* 156f. Forell gives particular attention to Luther's identification of the pope as antichrist. Ulrich Asendorf also demonstrates the eschatological character of Luther's theology in *Eschatologie bei Luther* (Göttingen: Vandenhoeck & Ruprecht, 1967). The most recent monograph to deal at length with Lutheran eschatology is Robin Barnes's *Prophecy.* Barnes writes summarily that "eschatological tension pervaded Luther's whole world-view" (p. 36).

98. SA, Preface, 15.

99. Luther uses *Endechrist* in SA II, 4, 10 and II, 4, 14. He refers to papal practice and doctrine with the adjectival forms *endechristischen* in SA II, 2, 25 and *endechristichen* in SA III, 11, 1. See also Preuss, *Die Vorstellungen vom Antichrist,* 132.

100. WA 10$^{1.2}$:47 (Advent sermon on Matthew 21:1-9). In spite of Luther's expressed preference for *Widerchrist* over *Endechrist,* he did on occasion revert to his former usage, as is evident from his 1528 comment about "das recht Endchristisschs regiment" (*Confession concerning Christ's Supper,* WA 26:507; LW 37:367).

101. BSLK, 430 n. 6. See also WA 10^{1}.2:47 n. 2

102. Oberman, *Luther: Man between God and the Devil,* 79.

103. Oberman, "*Teufelsdreck,*" 440. See also Barnes, *Prophecy,* 44.

104. Preuss, *Die Vorstellungen vom Antichrist,* 102f. See also Barnes, *Prophecy,* 43.

laws" [*Drecktal*], his Koran, and his human doctrine above God's word. Baptism, the Sacrament, the keys, prayer, the gospel, and Christ himself are not used by Christians anymore, rather Christians must trust their own works in order to become blessed. Upon this all foundations, monasteries, and all his kingdom are based. This devil cheats . . . the elect of God.[105]

The fundamental issue at stake here, and throughout his career, is, for Luther, faith in Christ versus faith in something or someone else.[106] The reformer assumes that faith is an essential part of human life and people naturally seek to believe in something. This belief may be completely sincere and well-meaning. Sincerity, however, is not the issue at stake for Luther. Sincere faith may be idolatrous faith. In the Large Catechism of 1529, Luther puts it this way:

> The trust and faith of the heart alone make both God and an idol. If your faith and trust are right, then your God is the true God. On the other hand, if your trust is false and wrong, then you have not the true God. For these two belong together, faith and God. That to which your heart clings and entrusts itself is, I say, really your God.[107]

This understanding of faith helps explain Luther's conclusion about the pope in SA. The pope by self-definition sat at the summit of an ecclesiastical system that, in Luther's estimation, put obstacles between people and God's grace. This papal position made the office itself contrary to the gospel. Luther evaluated the Roman church and concluded that its system encouraged believers to trust in something other[108] than the pure grace of God. The pope as head of the church, therefore, is a tempter who invites people to idolatry. Faith in various supposed good works is substituted for faith in Christ. This is why Luther writes in SA that

> the papacy is also pure enthusiasm. The pope boasts that "all laws are in the shrine of his heart" and that what he decides and judges in his churches is supposed to be spirit and law—as if it is equal to or above the

---

105. *WA* 53:395f. *Verlegung des Alcoran Bruder Richardi Prediger Ordens. Berdeutscht und herausgegeben durch D. M. Luther,* 1542. The translation of *Drecktals* as "shit laws" is used by Oberman in "*Teufelsdreck*," 444.

106. SA II, 1, 5, at the conclusion of "the first and chief article," which summarizes Luther's view of Christ and faith, the reformer writes: "On this article stands all that we teach and practice against the pope, the devil, and the world. Therefore we must be quite certain and not doubt. Otherwise everything is lost, and pope and devil and everything against us will gain victory and dominance."

107. LC I, 2–3.

108. E.g., various observances, a *de jure divino* hierarchy, an *ex opera operato* understanding of the sacraments.

Scriptures or the spoken word. All of this is the old devil and old snake which also made Adam and Eve into enthusiasts. The devil led them from the external word of God to "spirituality" and their own presumption—and even this was still accomplished by means of other, external words.[109]

Luther thought that both the papists and the enthusiasts expressed the same basic sin: they trusted in something other than the clear Word of God (the enthusiasts: ecstatic experiences; the Roman Catholics: works commanded by the see of Rome).[110] Since Luther believed that God's saving grace revealed in Christ was given through the Holy Spirit precisely to undeserving, sinful people (or as Luther puts it in SA: "'All have sinned,' and 'they are now justified without merit by his grace, through the redemption which is in Christ Jesus...by his blood'"),[111] all who want to substitute their own works for belief in Christ are essentially trying to play God.[112] Because the pope as presiding bishop of the church fostered this sort of theology, he personified for Luther the "antichrist."

Luther did not use the epithet "antichrist" because of the immorality or ineptitude of any single pope. The reformer had concluded that the institution of the papacy itself was the problem because it was contrary to the clear Word of God.[113] Any specific moral lapses on the part of Leo X, Hadrian VI, Clement VII, or Paul III were not the real issues.[114] The question of the reformation of the church was, for Luther, a question about the theological substance of Christianity itself. To be on one side of the issue meant to be "Christian." To be on the other side of the issue meant to be "anti-Christian."[115]

Luther's designation of the pope as antichrist in SA functions in at least

---

109. SA III, 8, 4–5.

110. Mostert, "Die theologische Bedeutung von Luthers antirömischer Polemik," 81f. See also Hans-Martin Barth, *Der Teufel und Jesus Christus in der Theologie Martin Luthers* (Göttingen: Vandenhoeck & Ruprecht, 1967), 86f., 108 n. 342, 111f.

111. SA II, 1, 3.

112. SA II, 4, 13 reads: "[The pope] has had to set himself up as equal to and even greater than Christ, as the head and lord of the church and ultimately the entire world. He allows himself to be called an earthly god and even tries to command the angels in heaven."

113. This emphasis is actually evident throughout Luther's reformatory career. One sees it as early as the "Open Letter to Pope Leo X," which prefaced *The Freedom of a Christian* in 1520 (*WA* 7:44; *LW* 31:336). It is evident in SA in 1536, where Luther in no way bases his use of the term on the personal character of Paul III. It is also evident in his infamous 1545 tract, *Against the Roman Papacy, an Institution of the Devil* (*LW* 31:261–376; *WA* 54:206–99), where the point of Luther's argument is based on papal obfuscation of the gospel. See also Barth, *Der Teufel und Jesus Christus*, 107.

114. Mostert, "Die theologische Bedeutung von Luthers antirömischer Polemik," 73f.

115. Ibid., 72.

two ways. On one hand, the pope symbolizes and epitomizes for Luther the entire Roman Catholic Church.[116] The reigning pontiff is the obvious head of the church's hierarchy, and thus, when Luther calls the pope the antichrist, he summarily declares his dissatisfaction with the entire church of Rome, the whole Roman communion.[117]

On the other hand, Luther's identification of the papacy with the Roman church is not consistent. Luther does not always view the pope as the personi-fication of the entire Roman Catholic Church. The papacy, dominated as it is by the antichrist, is over and against those elements of the true church that still exist under the papacy. The antichrist is a diabolical fiend, sent from the devil to ruin the church.[118] Therefore Luther writes in SA,

> The holy Christian church can survive quite well without such a head. It would have been much better if such a head had not been raised up by the devil. The papacy is not necessary in the church, because it exercises no Christian office, and the church must continue and exist without the pope.[119]

Here Luther recognizes that the Roman church is still a part of the church of Christ and thus the proper object for the subtle attacks of the antichrist. The fact that Luther sees the papacy overtaken by Satan in order to serve dia-bolical ends, points (albeit negatively) to Luther's continuing conviction that within the sixteenth-century Roman Catholic Church there were still true ex-pressions of Christ's church.[120]

In the end, the distinction between law and gospel serves as the theological basis for Luther's critical comments about the church and the bishop of Rome. Luther called the pope the antichrist because he saw the papacy as a diabolical purveyor of justification by works as opposed to justification by faith alone.

---

116. Luther seems to accept that the pope fulfills what modern scholars call a "petrine function" within the church (i.e., the papacy can serve as a focus or symbol of Christian unity). Cf. George Tavard, "What Is the Petrine Function?" in Empie and Murphy, *Papal Primacy*, 208–12.

117. When Luther left the Bundestag at Schmalkalden because he was too ill to participate, John Bugenhagen took what both he and Luther presumed to be the reformer's will during the night of February 26–27, 1537. These words open this document: "I know, praise be to God, that I did right to storm the papacy with the word of God, for it is an abomination to God, Christ, and the gospel" (quoted from Haile, *Luther*, 219).

118. Schott, "Christus und die Rechtfertigung," 206.

119. SA II, 4, 5–6.

120. Luther had made a similar point in 1528, in his work *On Anabaptism* (*WA* 26:147): "If the pope is the antichrist, as I most certainly believe, he must not sit and rule in the place of the devil but in the temple of God . . . since if he is to be the antichrist, he must be found among the Christians" (quoted from Forell, *Faith Active in Love*, 168 n. 25).

For Luther, papal insistence on meritorious works instead of, or in addition to, faith is what makes the pope "the true antichrist or contrachrist," because "the true catholic, universal Christian church will not excommunicate or persecute us, rather, it will heartily and gladly receive and ratify our doctrine and count us as dear brothers." [121]

The Schmalkald Articles have been characterized as one of Martin Luther's more pugnacious works, written somewhat late in his career and perhaps reflecting the aging reformer's increasing bitterness over the stalled progress of the German Reformation.[122] However true such a characterization might or might not be, it risks missing what Luther (and those closest to him) thought to be the main issue at stake in their efforts to reform the church. For Luther, the gospel of the forgiveness of sin by grace alone, apart from works of the law, is the distinctive feature of the Christian proclamation. Any theology (be it Roman Catholic, Anabaptist, Reformed, or Evangelical) that violated this *sine qua non* of the church's message was open to the charge of being labeled by Luther as "anti-Christian."

---

121. *Sermons on John 14–16* (WA 46:11$_{22-25}$; *LW* 24:310). See also SA III, 12, 2.

122. Increased scholarly attention to the "older Luther" has shed new light on the last fifteen years of the reformer's life and revised the oversimplified characterization of Luther in his last years as bitter, disappointed, and perhaps even demented. E.g., Edwards, *Luther's last Battles;* Kittelson, *Luther the Reformer;* Oberman, "*Teufelsdreck*"; von Loewenich, *Martin Luther: The Man and His Work;* Eike Wohlgast, *Die Wittenberger Theologie und die Politik der evangelischen Stände: Studien zu Luthers Gutachten in politischen Fragen* (Gütersloh, 1977).

6

Luther's Catholic Evangelicalism and the Christian Life

On the Gospel:
We now want to return to the gospel, which gives more than one kind of counsel
and help against sin, because God is overwhelmingly rich in his grace: first,
through the spoken word, in which the forgiveness of sins is preached to the
whole world (which is the particular office of the gospel); second, through Bap-
tism; third, through the Holy Sacrament of the Altar; fourth, through the power
of the keys and also the mutual conversation and consolation of the brothers
and sisters. Matthew 18[:20]: "Where two or three are gathered," etc.[1]

Article 4 is central to Luther's concerns in SA III. Both the material that precedes it and what follows it refer explicitly to what is presented here. For example, as he nears the conclusion of Article 3, Luther indicates what is to come:

> The gospel does not give consolation and forgiveness in only one way—but rather through the word, sacraments, and the like (as we shall hear). With God, there is truly rich redemption . . . (as Psalm 129[130:7-8] says).[2]

Article 4 itself also indicates what is to come in SA, Part III. Luther's list of the various ways in which the gospel becomes meaningful and relevant in human life forms the order of succeeding topics to be addressed in SA III, as Articles 5–8 clarify and explicate SA III, 4.

On the Gospel

Beginning with Article 4, Caspar Cruciger began receiving Luther's dictation.[3] Perhaps this is why Article 4 appears to be misnamed.[4] The gospel is described

---

1. SA III, 4.

2. SA III, 3, 8. SA III, 3 is the longest of the articles in the document. This article includes an extended discussion separately subtitled by Luther "On the False Penance of the Papists" (*"Von der falschen Busse der Papisten,"* SA III, 10–45). This excursus in large measure gives Part III, Article 3 its extraordinary length, compared to the other articles of SA.

3. This was made necessary after Luther was stricken with a heart attack on December 18, 1536. There were two secretaries: Cruciger recorded SA III, 4 through SA III, 9; the second recorded SA III, 10 to SA III, 12; the rest of SA was recorded by Cruciger (R. Wetzel, "Caspar Cruciger als ein schreiber der Schmalkaldischen Artikel," in *Lutherjahrbuch* 54, 1987, 92; cf. also *UuA*, 60).

4. There are fifteen articles in SA III. They all received titles from Luther himself: "On Sin" (*"Von der Sunde,"* 44 lines), "On Law" (*"Vom Gesetze,"* 24 lines), "On Repentance" (*"Von der Busse,"* 278

as that "which gives more than just one kind of counsel and help against sin." But what is this "help"? The content of the gospel message itself is mentioned almost in passing as "the forgiveness of sin" in connection with the first way God's "overwhelmingly rich . . . grace" relates to human life—the spoken word. The rest of the article catalogs the other ways in which the gospel is communicated. One might have expected from an article entitled "On the Gospel," written by Martin Luther, something a little different from what is actually given here. A more accurate title for this section would perhaps be something like "The Means of Grace" or "Word and Sacrament" or "How the Gospel Comes to People."

However, this title describes something important about Luther's view of the relationship between the gospel and the Christian life. Luther is saying that the gospel word is not separable from the communication of it. In Part II, Luther had already summarized the specific content of the gospel and discussed its major abuses under the Roman Catholic system. Now, in Part III, he first describes the correlative elements of sin (Article 1) and law (Article 2). Penance (Article 3) is the transition from the law to the gospel. What is needed in Article 4 is not a reiteration of the content of the gospel message (that would be redundant, given Part II, 1) but a description of how this gospel becomes meaningful in human life. That is why this particular article, "On the Gospel," has the place and form it does in SA III. The unique word of grace that is the content of Christian preaching is proclaimed always in the context of human need. Through the speaking and hearing—and sacramental reception—of God's word, the gospel gives its multifaceted "counsel and help against sin."

By calling this article "On the Gospel," Luther expresses his conviction that the gospel is, for him, something active and dynamic.[5] It is not the mere transmission of ideas from one intellect to another. Nor is the gospel simply a sentimental, romantic story about the selfless sacrifice of Jesus of Nazareth. The gospel is something that "is done" or "happens" in the life of the believer as the forgiveness of sin is experienced daily in the Christian life.

---

lines), "On the Gospel" ("*Vom Evangelio*," 8 lines), "On Baptism" ("*Von der Taufe*," 11 lines), "On the Sacrament of the Altar ("*Vom Sakrament des Altars*," 20 lines), "On the Keys" ("*Von den Schlusseln*," 11 lines), "On Confession" ("*Von der Beicht*," 92 lines), "On Excommunication" ("*Vom Bann*," 8 lines), "On Ordination and Vocation" ("*Von der Weihe und Vokation*," 20 lines), "On the Marriage of Priests," ("*Von der Priesterehe*," 16 lines), "On the Church" ("*Von der Kirche*," 10 lines), "On Being Justified before God and on Good Works" ("*Wie man fur Gott gerecht wird und von guten Werken*," 19 lines), "On Monastic Vows" ("*Von Klostergelubden*," 7 lines), and finally, "On Human Regulations" ("*Von Menschensatzungen*," 22 lines).

5. Gritsch and Jenson (*Lutheranism*, 43) write of the "meta-linguistic character" of justification by faith as more than a "content-item of the gospel." They seek thus to underscore the pervasive and dynamic character of the gospel in Lutheran theology.

The Spoken Word

The first means by which the forgiveness of sin comes to humankind is through oral proclamation. The reformer actually broaches this topic in the preceding article, "On Repentance."[6] At the beginning of SA III, 3, Luther asserts that "the New Testament maintains this office of the law and teaches it."[7] This makes sense for Luther, because when the law has accomplished its theological function (showing people their sin and need for God's grace), the believer will then eagerly hear the "consoling promise of grace through the gospel."[8]

This promise, announced openly, is what Luther means when he writes in SA III, 4 about "the spoken word, in which the forgiveness of sins is preached to the whole world (which is the particular office of the gospel)." The purpose of preaching is to bear witness to the saving, forgiving deed of God in Christ. This announcement of forgiveness gives the gospel its character as "good" news. The "particular" word of grace, the proclamation of the message of forgiveness, is what is offered to the repentant sinner described in Article 3.

Once again Luther emphasizes that the forgiveness offered in Christ is always the forgiveness of one's *sin*. The work of God in Christ makes sense existentially (i.e., in the context of a particular life) in the light of the extremity of the situation confronting human beings.

This word of God is based on, and is derived from, the authoritative documents of the Scriptures.[9] Thus, for Luther, the word of God is not only the proclamation of the gospel, the word is (broadly speaking) also the Bible itself. The use of scriptural quotations to describe "the first and chief article" of redemption through Christ illustrates this clearly.

Finally, not only does Luther conceive of God's word as the proclamation of the gospel and the Scriptures themselves, he maintains that the word of God is also Christ himself. The life, death, and resurrection of Jesus is the source of Christian proclamation and the primary subject of the biblical witness. Luther firmly believed that Christ is that to which the opening of the Gospel of John refers: "And the word was made flesh and dwelt among us, . . . full of grace and truth."[10]

---

6. This structure of SA III, 3 is noteworthy. The opening nine verses present Luther's understanding of repentance and the gospel spoken in this context. Then follows a separately titled subsection, "On the False Penance of the Papists," which encompasses verses 10–45.

7. SA III, 3, 1.

8. SA III, 3, 4.

9. At this point, Luther compiles a number of Scripture passages to bolster his argument. Cf. SA III, 3, 4–8.

10. John 1:14.

Thus, Luther's notion of God's word is threefold: the proclamation of law and gospel is the word of God; the Scriptures are God's word; Christ himself is the incarnate word of God.

Baptism

For Luther, the gospel comes to humankind not only through oral proclamation but also through the sacrament of Baptism.[11] This represents the second "overwhelmingly rich" way that God offers help against sin.

At the outset of his article on baptism in SA, the reformer seeks once again to base his theology on the Scriptures: "Baptism is . . . commanded by God's institution, or, as Paul says, 'washing in the word.'"[12] The authoritative gospel word here is the command of Christ in Matthew 28 that "all nations" be baptized "in the name of the Father and of the Son and of the Holy Spirit."[13] This word carries with it the gracious promise of forgiveness because it is based on the institution and command of Christ in the Scriptures.[14] God's gracious promise, given in the Old Testament and fulfilled in the New Testament, is implied in the trinitarian formula. Thus God's grace is given to the person being baptized.[15] In Luther's understanding, the word of grace is spoken as the element is administered and thus the forgiveness of sin is actually given in the sacrament.

In SA III, 4, Luther rejects two different Roman Catholic explanations of this sacrament. Luther wants to safeguard baptism against both a "materialist" misunderstanding (that the water is somehow altered and in itself conveys the word of God) and a "spiritualist" misunderstanding (that the water is insignificant or unnecessary). The first he attributes to "Thomas and the Dominicans who forget the word (God's institution) and say that God has placed a spiritual power in the water which, through the water, washes away sin."[16] It appears to Luther that this scholastic position gives the water in and of itself some kind of efficacious power, apart from the sacramental act. The word in baptism, as Luther understands it, is not spoken to the water, so that the element is somehow transformed. Rather, the word of grace is addressed to the one who receives the sacrament. It is the one baptized who is transformed.

Still, in SA Luther speaks of "the word of God *in* water,"[17] because the

---

11. CF. "On Baptism," SA III, 5.

12. SA III, 5, 1; the quotation attributed to Paul is Ephesians 5:26.

13. SC IV, 4; LC IV, 4.

14. Matthew 28:19; Mark 16:16.

15. LC IV, 10.

16. SA III, 5, 2.

17. Luther writes: "Gottes Wort im Wasser" (SA III, 5, 1).

sacramental act requires the presence of the element. God in Christ has promised to use such earthly means to communicate the forgiveness of sin. This leads to a discussion of the second scholastic explanation of baptism that Luther rejects, an understanding he attributes to "Scotus and the Franciscans."[18] According to Luther, this position holds "that baptism washes away sin through the assistance of the divine will, that this washing takes place only through God's will, and this is not at all through the word and the water."[19] The reformer could not accept a position that, in effect, denies the integral role of the earthly, material element (water) in the sacrament. Indeed, Luther understood baptism as necessarily involving both the word and the water.[20]

This is why Luther, as he begins his article on baptism in SA, refers to three significant authorities (Christ, Paul, and Augustine) who emphasized the importance of the water together with the word:

> Baptism is . . . commanded by God's institution, or, as Paul says, "washing in the word." Moreover, Augustine says, "when the word has been added to the element it makes a sacrament."[21]

The sacrament of Baptism is an expression of the gospel that uses something earthly like water together with and in accordance with the word of God. Therefore Luther writes:

> It is not the water that produces these effects, but the word of God connected with the water, and our faith which relies on the word of God connected with the water. For without the word of God the water is merely water and no Baptism. But when connected with the word of God it is a Baptism, that is, a gratuitous water of life and a washing of regeneration in the Holy Spirit.[22]

Thus baptism bestows "victory over death and the devil, forgiveness of sin, God's grace, the entire Christ, and the Holy Spirit with his gifts."[23] All of this is offered as a free gift to the one baptized, regardless of the recipient's unworthiness or ignorance. Thus, according to Luther, God's grace even extends to "children because they also belong to the promised redemption which was accomplished through Christ."[24]

---

18. SA III, 5, 3.
19. Ibid.
20. Ibid.; LC V, 10.
21. SA III, 5, 1, 2. This quotation of Augustine is used by Luther also in LC V, 10.
22. SC IV, 10.
23. LC IV, 41.
24. SA III, 5, 4.

But what good does it do to baptize infants who have no understanding of what is happening? How can a baby have what Luther describes in SC as "faith which relies on the word of God connected with the water"?[25] First, small children can be baptized because it is God who acts, in Luther's view, not the person being baptized.[26] The person being baptized receives something (the gospel, the forgiveness of sin, new life), and Luther contends that children can receive these gifts as well as adults. The declaration of grace and mercy in the gospel is relevant to all people, regardless of their understanding or maturity (or lack of same).

Second, Luther did not view baptism as a simple, past event. The Christian is constantly reminded of God's mercy that was expressed definitively at baptism—even if one was not fully cognizant at the moment of this expression. This is important because babies obviously have no real understanding of what is happening to them at the baptismal font. Moreover, baptism has some very concrete consequences for the everyday Christian life:

> What does such baptizing with water signify?
> Answer: It signifies that the old person in us, together with all sins and evil lusts, should be drowned by *daily* sorrow and repentance and be put to death, and that the new person should come forth *daily* and rise up, cleansed and righteous, to live forever in God's presence.[27]

In a sense, Luther saw the whole of the Christian life related to what happened in baptism. Being baptized as an infant allows a Christian to live virtually his or her entire life nurtured by the certainty of God's grace which is unconditionally poured out in baptism. In fact, Luther could even say, "In Baptism, . . . Christians have enough to study and practice all their lives."[28] Put another way, "Thus a Christian life is nothing else than a daily Baptism."[29]

It is hard to miss the fact that this view of baptism corresponds rather dramatically with Luther's explanation of repentance (*Busse*) in SA III, 3. Repentance, in Luther's estimation, is both remorse (sometimes called "contrition") and faith. These responses to sin correspond to the word of God as law and gospel.[30] Contrition is "true suffering of the heart"[31] and arises from the

---

25. SC IV, 10.

26. LC IV, 10.

27. SC IV, 12, emphasis added. Cf. also LC IV, 77–88.

28. LC IV, 41.

29. LC IV, 65.

30. SA III, 3, 2, 4. Cf. also Schlink, *Theology of the Lutheran Confessions*, 141.

31. SA III, 3, 2.

theological function of the law in the life of the believer.[32] Somewhat later in Article 3, Luther writes, "Holy people . . . still have and feel original sin and also *daily* repent of it and struggle against it."[33]

Christian penance, however, does not stop there. When a believer admits to the sin that is within, and then seeks God's grace and mercy, repentance happens. In the language of SA: "To this [theological] office of the law, however, the New Testament immediately adds the consoling promise of grace through the gospel. This we should believe."[34] Both contrition and faith in the promise are involved in Luther's understanding of true penance.

Moreover, this repentance, like baptism, has an ongoing character:

> This repentance endures among Christians until death because it confesses the sin that remains in the flesh throughout life. As St. Paul bears witness in Romans 7[:23], he wars with the law in his members, etc., and he does this not by using his own powers but with the gift of the Holy Spirit which follows the forgiveness of sins. This same gift *daily* cleanses and expels the sins that remain and works to make people truly pure and holy.[35]

In LC, Luther expresses the relationship between penance and baptism this way: "Repentance, therefore, is nothing else than a return and approach to Baptism, to resume and practice what had earlier been begun but abandoned."[36] Baptism, understood in this way, as an outward sign of God's grace and favor, provides strength and comfort to those who seek forgiveness.[37] In this context, we can understand why Luther, when confronted with temptations or afflictions (*Anfechtungen*), could say, "If, then, the holy sacrament of baptism is a matter so great, gracious, and full of comfort, we should diligently see to it that we ceaselessly, joyfully, and from the heart thank, praise, and honor God for it."[38]

Here we see why Luther deliberated for some time about whether or not to retain the churchly, liturgical practice of penance as a sacrament.[39] We can

32. SA III, 3, 2.

33. SA III, 3, 43, emphasis added.

34. SA III, 3, 4.

35. SA III, 3, 40, emphasis added.

36. LC IV, 79.

37. LC IV, 44.

38. *A Sermon on the Sacrament of Baptism*, 1519 (*WA* 2:736; *LW* 35:42).

39. In 1520, Luther wrote *The Babylonian Captivity of the Church*. Toward the beginning of this pivotal work, he wrote: "To begin with, I must deny that there are seven sacraments, and for the present maintain that there are but three: baptism, penance, and the bread" (*WA* 6:501, 34; *LW* 36:18).

also see why Luther eventually concluded that only Baptism and the Lord's Supper were rightly to be counted as sacraments,[40] even though "confession and absolution should by no means be allowed to fall into disuse in the church."[41] Penance has a scriptural warrant (Matthew 4:17) but lacks Christ's explicit institution of a physical sign (although the laying on of hands could be seen as this physical sign, it was not specifically commanded by Christ).[42] Luther came to see that the sacrament of Baptism (and, as will become evident, the Lord's Supper too) is intimately connected to the ongoing, even daily, forgiveness of sin and therefore incorporates already what is most significant about penance.[43]

The Christian life, which for Luther begins with the sacrament of Baptism, is thus "a Baptized life":

> Therefore let everybody regard their Baptism as the daily garment which they wear all the time. Every day they should be found in faith and amid its fruits, every day they should be suppressing the old person and growing up in the new. If we wish to be Christians, we must practice the work that makes us Christians. But if anybody falls away from their Baptism let them return to it. As Christ, the mercy-seat, does not recede from us or forbid us to return to him even though we sin, so all his treasures and gifts remain. As we have once obtained forgiveness of sins in Baptism, so forgiveness remains day by day as long as we live, that is, as long as we carry the old person about our necks.[44]

The Holy Sacrament of the Altar

Luther understands the basis and function of "the Lord's Supper"[45] in a manner quite similar to Baptism. First, both of the sacraments have the authority

---

40. By the end of *The Babylonian Captivity,* he had come to a new conclusion: "Nevertheless, it has seemed proper to restrict the name of sacrament to those promises which have signs attached to them. The remainder, not being bound to signs, are bare promises. Hence there are, strictly speaking, but two sacraments in the church of God—baptism and the bread. For only in these two do we find both the divinely instituted sign and the promise of forgiveness of sins" (*WA* 6:572, 10; *LW* 36:124).

41. SA III, 8, 1 and 2.

42. "The sacrament of penance, which I added to these two, lacks the divinely instituted visible sign" (*WA* 6:572; *LW* 35:124).

43. In *The Babylonian Captivity,* Luther wrote these words, which are germane to the discussion of SA III, 3: "Therefore, when we rise from our sins to repent, we are merely returning to the power and the faith of baptism from which we fell. . . . It will therefore be no small gain to a penitent to remember above all their baptism" (*WA* 6:528, 17ff.; *LW* 36:59). Later in this document these words are found: "The sacrament of penance . . . is, as I have said, nothing but a way and a return to baptism" (*WA* 6:572; *LW* 35:124).

44. LC IV, 84–86.

45. SA III, 6.

of Christ's institution. In other words, the Lord's Supper and Baptism are both based on God's word. In LC, Luther writes about the Sacrament of the Altar in this way: "As in the case of Baptism, we shall first learn what is of greatest importance, namely, God's word and ordinance or command, which is the chief thing to be considered."[46] The scriptural basis for celebrating the Sacrament of the Altar is, according to Luther, clear and unambiguous. In fact, in his explanation of this sacrament in SC, the reformer brings together four different texts from the New Testament in order to describe the biblical foundation of the Lord's Supper.[47]

Second, like Baptism, the Sacrament of the Altar communicates the forgiveness of sin to those who receive it. Because the follower of Christ is continually in need of this forgiveness, the practical implications of the Lord's Supper for the everyday life of the Christian become clear. Forgiveness, based on the word of promise, is indeed the primary "benefit" of the sacrament:

> What is the benefit of such eating and drinking?
> Answer: We are told in the words "for you" and "for the forgiveness of sins." By these words the forgiveness of sins, life, and salvation are given to us in the sacrament.[48]

Third, like Baptism, the Lord's Supper is connected to a physical element. Quite straightforwardly Luther asserts in SA that "the bread and the wine in the supper are the true body and blood of Christ."[49] By giving himself in such a way, Christ uses the sacrament to nourish the recipient with true faith and the assurance of the forgiveness of sin.[50]

At this point the reformer was being rather controversial. First, by asserting at the very outset of the article on the Lord's Supper in SA that "the bread and the wine in the supper are the true body and blood of Christ," Luther takes a step away from the language agreed upon a few months earlier in WC. This common statement, specifically regarding the nature of Christ's presence in

---

46. LC V, 4.

47. "The holy evangelists Matthew, Mark, and Luke, and also St. Paul, write thus: 'Our Lord Jesus Christ, on the night when he was betrayed, took bread, and when he had given thanks, he broke it, and gave it to the disciples and said, "Take, eat; this is my body which is given for you. Do this in remembrance of me." In the same way also he took the cup, after supper, and when he had given thanks he gave it to them, saying, "Drink of it, all of you. This cup is the new covenant in my blood, which is poured out for many for the forgiveness of sins. Do this, as often as you drink it, in remembrance of me"'"(SC VI, 4).

48. SC VI, 5f.

49. SA III, 6, 1.

50. SA II, 2, 18, 24, 29; SC VI, 8; LC V, 23f. Here is a good example of what dogmaticians have called *finitum capax infiniti* in Luther's thought.

the sacrament, had been signed by representatives from southern and northern Germany in May 1536. It reflects its origin as a negotiated settlement and it is rather ambiguous at the very point it was supposed to clarify. On the one hand, WC I reads: "*With* the bread and wine the body and blood of Christ are truly and substantially present, offered and received."[51] On the other hand, in WC II one finds these words: "Yet they concede that, by the sacramental union, the bread is the body of Christ; i.e., they hold that when the bread is held out the body of Christ is at the same time present and truly tendered."[52]

In SA, Luther opted for language closer to the second statement by not using the preposition "with." Luther's usage here also represents a return to the simple use of the copula, which corresponds more closely to the biblical accounts of the Last Supper.[53]

Melanchthon was apparently concerned about Luther's formulation at this point, if we can trust the report of Landgrave Philip of Hesse.[54] After the Landgrave had entertained Melanchthon in Schmalkalden on February 10, he penned a note to Jacob Sturm, the mayor of Strassburg, stating that Melanchthon had told him Luther "did not originally formulate [this article] in this way, but rather according to the [*Wittenberg*] *Concord,* that with the bread the body of the Lord was given."[55] According to the Landgrave, Melanchthon then went on to caution against discussion of SA at Schmalkalden because of the potentially divisive nature of this article. In the end, Melanchthon recom-

---

51. Emphasis added. "Cum pane et vino vere et substantialiter adesse, exhiberi et sumi corpus Christi et sanguinem" (*CR* 3:75; trans. Jacobs, *The Book of Concord*, 2:254).

52. "Tamen concedunt sacramentali unione panem esse corpus Christi, hoc est, sentiunt porrecto pane simul adesse et vere exhiberi corpus Christi" (*CR* 3:76; trans. Jacobs, *The Book of Concord*, 2:255).

53. Luther had insisted on the same literal sense of Scripture in his famous dialogue with Zwingli at Marburg in 1529. Cf. Luke 22:19-20; 1 Corinthians 11:24-25; Matthew 26:26-28; Mark 14:22-24. The Greek reads *esti,* Luther translated this with *ist,* the Vulgate used *est.*

54. Melanchthon's concern here is a little surprising, because he had not voiced this at the December 1536 meeting of theologians at Wittenberg. At that time, of course, his only recorded objection to SA was in regard to the papacy. In fact, an analysis of Melanchthon's attitude toward SA would be a fascinating study. In spite of his apparent reservations about this aspect of Luther's theological legacy (e.g., the article on the Lord's Supper and the view of the papacy), he could also write: "[*The Schmalkald Articles*] contain the same teaching as that which is in the *Augsburg Confession* and the *Apology,* except for an added section on the primacy of the papacy" (letter to Veit Dietrich, January 20, 1537 [*CR* 3:238]). Yet another problematic aspect of Melanchthon's relationship to SA is that, despite his qualified subscription, he then went on to write Tr, a document quite compatible with the assertions of Luther in SA.

55. *UuA,* 105; cf. also Theodor Kolde, *Historische Einleitung in die symbolischen Bücher der evangelisch-lutherischen Kirche, deutsch und lateinisch.* Besorgt von J. T. Müller, erste Auflage (Gütersloh: C. Bertelsmann Verlag, 1912), xlviii.

mended that the estates remain pledged to "the [*Augsburg*] *Confession* and the [*Wittenberg*] Concord." [56]

Philip of Hesse's report of Melanchthon's position is puzzling, however, because Luther's original manuscript of SA shows that he had originally written, "We hold that *under* the bread and wine are the true body and blood of Christ in the Supper." [57] It is an open question whether or not the preposition "under" was dropped from SA III, 6 prior to the Wittenberg meeting of theologians in 1536. [58] Regardless, it appears that Melanchthon was familiar with an early form of this article that corresponded more closely to WC than Luther's final draft. Still, if Hesse's report is accurate, Melanchthon was misinformed as to what sort of prepositional phrase the reformer had originally employed in SA III, 6. [59]

Luther makes another statement that relates to WC in SA III, 6 when he writes: "The true body and blood of Christ . . . are extended to and received not only by pious but also by evil Christians." [60] This issue had been the source of considerable discussion during the deliberations regarding WC at Wittenberg in 1536. Luther wanted to make completely certain that the South Germans did not harbor any sacramentarian notions about the presence of Christ in the sacrament depending on the worthiness of the recipient. When this point was resolved the previous May, Luther said, "Then we are one. We recognize and accept you as our dear brothers in the Lord if this article is valid." [61]

Luther was convinced that the real presence of Christ is indeed given to all people who participate in the Lord's Supper. To those who receive the sacrament in faith (the only way to receive the sacrament rightly), the Lord's Supper

---

56. *UuA*, 106. The Latin version of AC 10 is curiously similar to Luther's formulation of SA III, 6: "De coena Domini docent, quod corpus et sanguis Christi vere adsint et distribuantur vescentibus in coena, Domini; et improbant secus docentes."

57. Emphasis added. "Halten wir, das vnter brod vnd wein sei der warhafftige leib vnd blut Christi im Abendmahl" (Zangemeister, *Die Schmalkaldischen Artikel*, 66).

58. *UuA*, 61, 105 n. 9.

59. Actually, Luther's original use of "under" in SA III, 6 and Melanchthon's misrepresentation of it as "with" point to an interesting ambiguity in Lutheran sacramental theology. In LC V, 8, Luther used both "in" and "under." AC 10 reads, "in coena Domini" and "unter der Gestalt des Brots und Weins." Ap 10, 1 reads, "in coena Domini vere et substantialiter adsint corpus et sanguis Christi." This kind of confusion helps to explain the eventual multiplication of prepositions ("in," "with," and "under") employed by the various Lutheran confessional documents. FCSD 7, 38 brings them all together: "in pane, sub pane, cum pane . . . im Brot, unter dem Brot, mit dem Brot." It is difficult to ascertain what is exactly at stake theologically in choosing one preposition over another.

60. SA III, 6, 1.

61. Köstlin and Kawerau, *Martin Luther*, 2:341.

is "the forgiveness of sins, life, and salvation."[62] Those who receive the Lord's Supper without believing the promise of Christ's real presence for them do so to their condemnation.[63]

Luther's conviction at this point stems from his view of and trust in the word. "This is my body, given for you" was the promise of Christ as he instituted this meal. Luther interpreted the sacrament as a means of grace and the wickedness or unworthiness of the recipient cannot invalidate the sure word of Christ.[64] As Luther put it: the Lord's Supper "is not founded on the holiness of human beings but on the word of God."[65]

Luther does not stop there. The reformer can even say that, because the Sacrament of the Altar brings with it the forgiveness of sin, it is specifically *for* wicked people.[66] At this point SA is quite clear: the word of God makes the sacramental promise valid, not the worthiness of either the presider or the recipient.[67]

These first two points of SA III, 6 (the real presence of Christ and the reception of this presence by "evil" Christians) relate to Luther's concerns about the "enthusiasts" or "sacramentarians" who, Luther thought, spiritualized the sacrament and conceived of it as a symbolic representation of Christ and not his real presence as a means of grace. The bulk of SA III, 6, however, is directed against two Roman Catholic positions. The first anti-Roman Catholic position taken by Luther is indicated by his assertion that "one should not give only one form of the sacrament."[68] Here the reformer refers to the practice of distributing only the bread to the laity during the Mass, while the priest also partakes of the cup. First, Luther points to "the sophists and the Council of Constance . . . that as much is given with one as with both."[69] By rejecting the scholastic notion of "sacramental concomitance,"[70] and the decree of a church

---

62. SC VI, 6; cf. also SC VI, 10; LC V, 33–35. WC reads: "the body and blood of the Lord are truly extended also to the unworthy (*indignis*)" (WC III; trans. in Jacobs, *The Book of Concord,* 2:255).

63. 1 Corinthians 11:29.

64. SC VI, 4, 6; LC V, 16.

65. LC V, 16; this same emphasis on the word of God is evident in this statement: "The word must make the element a sacrament; otherwise it remains a mere element" (LC V, 10).

66. LC V, 60–65.

67. SA II, 2, 4, 5; SA III, 6, 1; cf. also LC V, 16.

68. SA III, 6, 2.

69. Ibid.

70. This doctrine, based on the teaching of Alexander of Hales (d. 1245), was promulgated at the Council of Constance in 1415, which rejected Hussite demands for Communion in "both kinds." It was taught that "the *whole* Christ is truly present in *one* element or 'species.'" This led to the withholding of the cup from the laity (Gritsch and Jenson, *Lutheranism,* 71). BC, 311 n. 5.

council, the reformer returns to a major theme of the Lutheran Reformation: the authority of the Word of God is necessary to establish articles of faith.[71] Thus, once again, Luther seeks to base the critique of his opponents' position on the Scriptures: "One kind is still not the complete order and institution as founded and commanded by Christ."[72]

Therefore, because concomitance and its resulting implementation is not founded on the Scriptures and yet is made an official church dogma that determines sacramental practice, Luther feels justified in rejecting it in the strongest terms:

> Especially do we condemn and curse, in God's name, those who not only allow distribution in both forms to be omitted but also haughtily prohibit, condemn, and slander both forms as heresy. Thus they set themselves against and above Christ, our Lord and God, etc.[73]

The second aspect of Roman Catholic sacramental theology that Luther criticizes is the doctrine of transubstantiation. According to this dogma, priestly consecration of the elements is said actually to turn the substance of the bread and wine into the substance of the body and blood of Christ.[74] Luther rejects this understanding of the Sacrament of the Altar on a number of grounds. First, attributing to the priests (even if they are "rotten rascals")[75] the power to make Christ present is to allow them to be "against and above Christ, our Lord and God, etc."[76] It appeared to Luther that if a priest's consecration could cause the bread and wine to become the body and blood of Christ, then that priest and his liturgical action would control God's grace.

For Luther, faith is always directed to God revealed in Jesus Christ, and

---

71. SA II, 2, 15; Galatians 1:8. Here we encounter the *sola scriptura* principle.

72. SA III, 6, 3.

73. SA III, 6, 4.

74. This doctrine was promulgated at the Fourth Lateran Council of 1215, under Innocent III. Transubstantiation can be summarized: When a priest consecrated the bread and wine, their "substance" (a category derived from Aristotle that describes the essential being of something) is transformed into the substance of the true body and blood of Christ. This happens while the "accidents" (a complementary category of Aristotle that describes nonessential properties of something) remain the same. The appearance and taste of the bread and wine are nonessential "accidents," so they remain. Nevertheless, the substance is really changed into Christ's body and blood, when performed by a properly ordained priest. The benefits of the sacrament were then distributed *ex opere operato*. Cf. Gritsch and Jenson, *Lutheranism,* 71.

75. SA II, 2, 1.

76. SA III, 6, 4. The issue here is not that a priest might be, in fact, a "rascal." Donatism is expressly rejected by Luther in SA III, 6. The problem is that transubstantiation appears to Luther to grant priests the power to make Christ present in the Mass. Thus they could be seen as superior to Christ.

placing one's trust in anything else than Christ and the word of the gospel was simply idolatrous.[77] Because the liturgy of the Mass itself seemed to Luther to become the object of faith, and not Christ, transubstantiation was unacceptable to the reformer. Thus Luther wrote: "I, with God's help, would sooner allow myself to be burned to ashes before I would allow a 'Massling' [*Messeknecht*] (whether good or evil) and his work to be equal to or greater than my Lord and Savior, Jesus Christ."[78]

Moreover, transubstantiation is also rejected by Luther because he saw no convincing scriptural warrant for it. Luther's notion of the real presence is an attempt to express the clear meaning of the biblical text, not explain it. The reformer was rather nonspeculative at this point. The Scriptures offer no such "subtle sophistry," so Luther could say, simply, "that bread is and remains there, as St. Paul himself indicates."[79] Luther's view of the real presence of Christ in the sacrament was tied always to the sacramental act of both word and element given to the communicant. The believer trusts the word that declares, "Take, eat; this is my body which is given for you."[80] Luther understood that, as the promise of the forgiving presence of Christ's body and blood is spoken and the bread and wine are received, Christ is really present. To insist on a speculative explanation of Christ's presence in the sacrament was, for Luther, a doctrinal legalism that is against the word of God. In the end, transubstantiation is "directly contrary to the chief article, which says that it is not an evil or devout 'Massling' with his work, but rather it is the Lamb of God and Son of God who takes away our sin."[81]

The two sacraments of Baptism and the Lord's Supper are intimately related to each other in the daily life of the Christian because they are both means of grace (i.e., they communicate the forgiveness of sin and, thus, new life). Luther writes: "A Christian life is nothing else than a *daily* Baptism."[82] Similarly, the reformer writes about "the Lord's Supper . . . as a daily food and sustenance so that our faith may refresh and strengthen itself and not weaken in the struggle."[83] Thus the Christian life is indeed, for Luther, a sacramental life, a life of daily repentance as one receives the good news of the gospel through the word and the sacraments.

77. SA II, 1; LC I, 1–3.

78. SA II, 2, 10.

79. SA III, 6, 5.

80. SC VI, 4.

81. SA II, 2, 7.

82. LC IV, 65.

83. LC V, 24. Cf. also LC V, 39.

Edmund Schlink recommends a picture of spatial movement in order to summarize Luther's sacramental theology: "The total life is a daily 'return' to Baptism and a daily approach to the Lord's Supper."[84] We have seen that Luther does indeed use the language of "return," with respect to baptism.[85] However, this kind of movement is not the only image of the sacraments that the reformer uses. This metaphor could give one the impression that the Christian life could somehow be separated from the means of grace (as if there might be some "place" in the Christian life where one is without baptism and must return to it, or must "approach" the Lord's Supper). The point to be underscored here is that, for Luther, it is impossible to conceive of the life of a Christian apart from the word and the sacraments.

Therefore a different metaphor—also derived from Luther as well as from the New Testament—recommends itself. This metaphor is that in Baptism one is given a new birth and through the Lord's Supper this new life is nourished and sustained.[86] In 1519, Luther wrote: "We have, therefore, two principal sacraments in the church, Baptism and the bread. Baptism leads us into a new life on earth; the bread guides us through death into eternal life."[87] In 1529, Luther put it this way: "While it is true that through Baptism we are first born anew, . . . the Lord's Supper is given as a daily food and sustenance so that our faith may refresh and strengthen itself."[88]

Such an organic picture has the advantage of underscoring the constant dependence on God's grace with which Christians live. At baptism, Christians are "born again," or "reborn."[89] Luther consistently emphasizes the new life

84. Schlink, *Theology of the Lutheran Confessions*, 143; cf. also 141.

85. SC IV, 12; LC IV, 74f.

86. Schlink calls Luther's and the Lutheran confessional writings' doctrine of baptism "a doxology of grace" (Schlink, *Theology of the Lutheran Confessions*, 154). The organic metaphor recommended here seems to capture doxologically the pervasive character of the sacramental life (as one might praise and celebrate the birth of a healthy baby). The notion of "nourishment" is an overt reference to the eating and drinking that takes place in the Lord's Supper. Eric Gritsch also can speak of the sacrament as food, but he situates his metaphor in a rather different context than what we recommend: "The Lord's Supper is the combat ration of the church struggling to do God's will in the world" (*Lutheranism*, 75). Neither does he connect this image with baptism in the totality of the sacramental life as the new life image here attempts to do.

87. *The Blessed Sacrament of the Holy and True Body of Christ, and the Brotherhoods*, 1519 (*WA* 2:754, 1; *LW* 35:67).

88. LC V, 23, 24.

89. John 3:3. In *The Order of Baptism* (1523), Luther refers to baptism as a "new birth by which we are being freed from all the devil's tryanny, loosed from sin, death, and hell, become children of life, heirs of all the gifts of God, and God's very children and Christ's siblings" (*WA* 12:52; *LW* 35:103). It is important to differentiate clearly between the notion of rebirth discussed here and modern, fundamentalistic conceptions of being "born again." Luther understands the rebirth of

given in and through baptism[90] and the influence of that baptism throughout the Christian's existence. Once the sacrament has been administered, a person can no more deny that baptism occurred than one can deny the fact that he has been given life itself. This is an objective reality in one's life as a Christian: God's forgiving grace in Christ has been given.

Still, Christians, like rebellious children, seek to establish independence from God. They defiantly reject their birthright of grace and attempt to live on their own. The fault is not God's, nor does such a denial change the reality of baptism. The good and merciful divine intention is unconditionally declared in the sacrament.

There is, then, the need for continual, daily reconciliation between Christians and God. This revitalization of the intended divine-human relationship is available to those who recall that, in spite of everything, they have been born through the waters of baptism as children of God. Moreover, Christians are given the sustaining real presence of Christ in the "Holy Sacrament of the Altar." The offer of God's mercy, first made at baptism, is never withdrawn. In fact, God's grace and the forgiveness of sin are offered over and over again. This offer is made throughout one's life as a Christian by means of the Lord's Supper, the food that nourishes and sustains the Christian. This sacrament is a way in which God's very self is given to believers.

This picture of the total sacramental life incorporates two realities. First, the definitive, nonrepeatable, although continually influential, character of baptism is underscored. Second, the ongoing, nourishing, and sustaining character of the Lord's Supper is also maintained.

The Keys and Mutual Conversation

The doctrine of the keys takes its name from the Gospel of Matthew's account of Jesus' words at the occasion of Peter's famous confession of faith, "You are the Christ, the Son of the living God" (Matthew 16:16). In the context of his response, Jesus promises: "I will give to you the keys to the kingdom of heaven; and whatever you bind on earth shall be bound in heaven; and whatever you loose on earth shall be loosed in heaven."[91]

In medieval Roman Catholicism, this passage and its parallels became proof texts for the authority of the clergy to grant the forgiveness of sins and pronounce excommunication. "Binding" (or, as John put it, "retaining")

baptism as God's act, whereas modern American fundamentalism tends to connect being "born again" with adult conversion and the believer's personal commitment to live a Christian life.

90. SC IV, 12; LC IV, 41, 65, 76, 83–86.

91. Matthew 16:19 (Matthew 18:18; John 20:23).

meant excommunication. "Loosing" ("remitting," in John) meant forgiveness. Canon law concluded that the power symbolized by "the keys to the kingdom of heaven" was given specifically to Peter, who, because he was understood to be the preeminent apostle and first bishop of Rome, was permitted to pass this power on to his successor. The pope as the head of the ecclesiastical hierarchy in turn conveyed this power to priests through episcopal ordination and the laying on of hands.[92] In the late medieval Roman Catholic Church, the keys were seen as the ability of the clergy to retain or forgive sins. Thus the power of the keys was the clerical power to save or condemn.

Luther disagreed with the clericalism of this concept of the keys when he wrote in SA III, 7, 1: "The keys are an office and authority given to the church by Christ to bind and loose sins." The reformer does not conceive of the keys as a special power or authority given only to duly ordained priests, but to the church. In SA, excommunication and forgiveness are intrafamilial activities. This is why Luther can equate the power of the keys with "the mutual conversation and consolation of the brothers and sisters."[93] Luther understood the church in these matters primarily as the local congregation dealing with its own repentant and unrepentant sinners:

> But in this case, where souls are at stake, the congregation shall have a place as judge and helper. Paul was an apostle, yet he was not willing to excommunicate a person who was living in adultery with his stepmother [I Cor. 5:1]. But he called on the congregation to act. And when the congregation did not take any action, he did not either, because he was satisfied with whatever punishment the congregation meted out to him.[94]

The church consists of "holy believers and 'little sheep who hear the voice of their shepherd'"[95] along with "the word of God and true faith."[96] The word upon which the church is founded is, as we have seen, both law and gospel.

Thus a correspondence between the keys and law and gospel is indicated in SA:

> However, the "small" (that is, the truly Christian) excommunication is that we should not allow public, obstinate sinners to come to the sacra-

---

92. "The Catholic Church has always taught that this priesthood was instituted by the . . . Lord . . . , and that the power . . . of remitting and of retaining sins, was given to the apostles and to their successors in the priesthood" (chap. 1 of the twenty-third session of the Council of Trent [July 15, 1563], quoted in *The Church Teaches*, ed. John Clarkson et al. [St. Louis: Herder Book Co., 1955], 329).

93. Schlink, *Theology of the Lutheran Confessions*, 242.

94. *The Keys*, 1530 (WA 30[II]:502f.; LW 40:372).

95. SA III, 12, 2.

96. SA III, 12, 3.

ment and other assemblies of the church until they correct themselves and avoid sin. The preachers should not mix civil punishments together with this spiritual penalty or excommunication.[97]

The discipline of the keys should last only until the sinners repent and "correct themselves and avoid sin."[98] The keys for Luther do not only represent the discipline of law. In SA III, 8 the reformer straightforwardly ties the power of the keys to the forgiveness of sin in the confessional:

> Because absolution or the power of the keys is a comfort and help against sin and a bad conscience, and was instituted by Christ in the Gospel, confession and absolution should by no means be allowed to fall into disuse in the church.[99]

It is ultimately Christ, the Good Shepherd (*Hirt, Pastor*),[100] who forgives, and the church announces that forgiveness of sin to its members.[101] This is the gospel. The keys are included by Luther as one of the ways "the gospel . . . offers counsel and help against sin," because this God-given power can be a source of true consolation for the repentant sinner. On the authority of the Scriptures, the one seeking forgiveness may trust the word of absolution because Christ himself has authorized the church to announce it. This consolation is sure because it is founded on the clear basis of God's word and deed, not on the (for Luther) dubious basis of a proper contrition, confession, satisfaction, and absolution.[102]

In short, Luther's understanding of the power of the keys in SA corresponds to the distinction between law and gospel. For Luther, "to bind sins" is to pronounce excommunication, which is the judgment of the theological function of the law.[103] "To loose sins" is to declare forgiveness, which is the good news of the gospel.[104]

---

97. SA III, 9.

98. James Spalding points out that already in 1520, "Luther insisted the ban should only be used for the excommunicated person's improvement," in "Discipline as a Mark of the True Church in Its Sixteenth Century Lutheran Context," in *Piety, Politics, and Ethics: Reformation Studies in Honor of George Wolfgang Forell*, ed. Carter Lindberg (Kirksville, Mo.: Sixteenth Century Journal Publishers, 1984), 132.

99. SA III, 8, 1.

100. SA III, 12, 2.

101. SC V, 16, 27.

102. See "On the False Penance of the Papists," SA III, 3, 10–43.

103. SA III, 7, 1.

104. Ibid. In *On the Councils and the Church*, which Luther wrote while preparing SA for publication (*LW* 41:6), he made some very similar comments about the function of the keys in congregational life:

"God's people or holy Christians are recognized by the office of the keys exercised publicly. That is, as Christ decrees in Matthew 18[:15-20], if Christians sin, they should be reproved; and if they

Catholic Evangelicalism and the Christian Life

Karl Thieme rightly calls Article 4 "the pinnacle of the third part" of SA.[105] In this article, as well as in the entirety of Part III, Luther brings together the catholicity of SA I with the evangelicalism of SA II. Here Luther gives particular attention to the relationship between his central theological concerns and the concrete realities of the Christian life.

Part III shows us that the catholic-evangelical tension in Luther's theological program has some very concrete implications for the life of faith. Part III, 4 (and thus all of Part III) is a description of the life of the church, for it describes the various ways in which God acts to make known the reality of grace. Luther provides posterity with a brief catalog of what he considered to be the most important aspects of the Christian life: word, sacraments, church. These are the various ways by which the catholic evangelicalism of the Christian church becomes real in anyone's life of faith.

---

do not mend their ways, they should be bound in their sin and cast out. If they do mend their ways, they should be absolved. . . . Now where you see sins forgiven or reproved in some persons, be it publicly or privately, you may know that God's people are there." Luther then goes on to discuss the pastoral use of the keys in dealing with "tender and despairing" consciences (*WA* 50:631f.; *LW* 41:153).

105. Thieme, *Luthers Testament,* 49.

Conclusion

The Catholic Evangelicalism of the Schmalkald Articles

THIS BOOK IS A PROPOSAL FOR A NEW READING OF LUTHER—AND, BY EXTEN-sion, the Lutheran confessional writings—through the lens of the Schmalkald Articles. It is possible, and in many ways even preferable, to interpret Luther's basic theological program from its end point, represented by the Schmalkald Articles. Here is where we can see precisely what Luther thought the Reformation was really all about. Whatever enduring worth there might be to the work of Martin Luther (historically, ecumenically, pastorally, theologically), we find it expressed with particular pointedness and profundity in the Schmalkald Articles.

We have seen that Luther wrote SA under the compelling pressure of his perceived imminent death. This pressure gives SA its testamentary character and to a significant degree determines the form and content of the document. The form of SA as a short but comprehensive compendium of Luther's theology can be traced to the reformer's desire to describe the main features of his theological program before he died.

The Schmalkald Articles bring order to the theological commitments of Martin Luther in a particularly clear and pointed way.[1] The catholic pillar of SA is the trinitarian, creedal faith of the church. Luther then constructs an evangelicalism that emphasizes the distinction between law and gospel as the other foundational pillar of the Christian understanding of faith. Both of these pillars of Luther's theology are intended by the reformer to be grounded in the Word of God.

As the reformer's theological testament, SA contains what Luther himself saw as his highest, most important theological priorities. The resultant "catholic evangelicalism," with its trinitarian starting point and distinctive emphasis on the gospel of the forgiveness of sin, embodies the constructive features of the Lutheran theological Reformation as well as the primary Lutheran critique of the late medieval church.

---

1. Other writings in Luther's works that could be placed in the same genre as SA are Part III of *Confession concerning Christ's Supper* of 1528, SC of 1529, and *The Three Symbols or Creeds of the*

"Catholic evangelicalism" is, perhaps, an unfortunate choice of words. It is a bit cumbersome. It is not popular parlance. Still, if the foregoing is accurate, this phrase seems to capture in a nutshell what Luther was up to when he wrote SA. Furthermore, catholic evangelicalism is not merely a dry, impractical theological formula. In SA, Part III, Luther explores the significance of his understanding of catholic evangelicalism for the Christian life. The concrete worship life of the church, centered around word and sacrament, expresses the loving, gracious intention of the triune God revealed in Christ.

Luther mentioned in the summer of 1537 that he would not particularly mind if all his writings were to disappear, save *The Bondage of the Will* and the Small Catechism.[2] The reformer made his positive evaluation of these two works about a year before SA was published. Based on the research presented here, it is conceivable that, if SA had been an option, Luther might have added his theological testament to that short list of enduringly worthwhile works.[3]

The struggles with severe illness that Luther suffered during the middle 1530s make it possible that no other writing from Luther's pen was personally more significant to the reformer himself than SA. When we read SA, we read what the reformer wanted to bequeath theologically to the church and the world. When we read SA, we read Luther's theological testament.

Christian Faith of 1538. Cf. Franz Lau, "Luthers Schmalkaldische Artikel als eine Einführung in seine Theologie," *ZTK* 18 (December 1937): 293.

2. *WABr* 8:99–100; *LW* 50:172f. (letter to Wolfgang Capito, July 9, 1537).

3. One could argue that SA did indeed exist as an option for Luther to include on this list of works. However, SA was not published by Luther until June of 1538 and he made some further alterations in the text (not the least of these changes was the addition of the very important Preface, in which he calls SA "mein Zeugnis und Bekenntnis" [SA, Preface, 3]). Therefore the first edition of SA, the edition adopted in *The Book of Concord,* was not really complete in the summer of 1537.

Appendix A
The Schmalkald Articles
Martin Luther
Translated and Edited by William R. Russell

ARTICLES OF CHRISTIAN DOCTRINE, WHICH SHOULD HAVE BEEN PRESENTED by our side at the council in Mantua, or wherever else it might happen, and which were to indicate what we could or could not accept or give up, etc. Written by Doctor Martin Luther in the year 1537.[1]

The Preface of Doctor Martin Luther

[1]Pope Paul III called a council to meet at Mantua last year during Pentecost.[2] Afterward he moved it from Mantua, so that we still do not know where he intends to hold it, or whether he can hold it.[3] We on our side had to prepare for the possibility that, whether summoned to the council or not, we would be condemned. I was therefore instructed[4] to compose and collect articles of our teaching in case there was discussion about what and how far we would and could compromise with the papists, and in which things we thought we definitely had to persist and remain firm.

[2]So I collected these articles and presented them to our side.[5] They were

1. As a prefatory comment to his own manuscript of SA, Luther wrote this sentence in Latin on the cover: "In these things, there is sufficient doctrine for the life of the church. For the rest, in political and economic matters, there is sufficient law to bind us, so that beyond these burdens there is no need to fashion others. 'Today's trouble is enough for today' [Matt. 6:34]." It was not copied by Spalatin or included in any subsequent versions of SA. The translation here is based on "Die Schmalkaldischen Artikel," ed. Helmar Junghans, in *Martin Luther: Studienausgabe,* ed. Hans-Ulrich Delius (Berlin: Evangelische Verlagsanstalt, 1992), 5:350.

2. Paul III (d. 1549) published the council bull *Ad dominici gregis curam* on June 2, 1536. Pentecost in 1537 fell on May 23.

3. In 1538, when Luther wrote the Preface and published SA, the council had already been postponed twice and did not meet until December 1545 at Trent (Hubert Jedin, *A History of the Council of Trent* [London: Thomas Nelson & Sons, 1957], 1:313–54).

4. John Fredrick gave Luther this assignment on December 11, 1536. (See John Fredrick's letter to the theologians at Wittenberg, *WABr* 7:613f.) The bulk of SA was written during the next two weeks.

5. FCEp 4. It is not clear whether Luther here refers to a December 1536 gathering or select theologians at Wittenberg or to the Bundestag at Schmalkalden in February 1537.

accepted and unanimously confessed by us, and it was resolved that we should publicly present the articles as our confession of faith—if the pope and his adherents should ever become so bold as seriously, genuinely, and without deception or treachery to convene a truly free council,[6] as would be his duty.

[3]But the Roman court is so dreadfully afraid of a free council and so shamefully flees from the light that it has deprived even those who are on the pope's side of their hope that he will ever tolerate a free council, much less actually convene one. They are understandably greatly offended and are troubled when they observe that the pope would as soon see all of Christendom lost and every soul damned as allow himself or his followers to be reformed even a little and permit limits on his tyranny.

Therefore I wanted to make these articles available through the public press at this time, in case I should die before a council could take place (as I fully expect and hope). I wanted to do this, both because the scoundrels, who flee from the light and avoid the day, go to such great pains to postpone and hinder the council, and so that those who live and remain after me will have my testament and confession, in addition to the confession that I have already published.[7] I have held fast to this confession until now and, by God's grace, I will continue to hold to it. [4]What should I say? Why should I complain? I am still alive—every day I write, preach, and teach. Yet there are such poisonous people, not only among the adversaries, but false believers who want to be on our side and who dare to use my writings and doctrine directly against me. They let me look on and listen, even though they know that I teach otherwise. They want to conceal their poison with my work and mislead the poor people by my name. What will happen in the future after my death?[8]

[5]Should I indeed respond to everything while I am still living? Certainly. But then again, how can I alone stop all the mouths of the devil, especially those (they are, however, all poisoned) who do not want to hear or pay attention to what we write? Instead, they devote all their energy to one thing: how they, without any shame at all, might twist and corrupt our words and every letter. I will let the devil (or ultimately God's wrath) answer them as they merit it. [6]I often think of the good Gerson, who doubted whether one should make good writings public. If one does not, then many souls that could have been saved are neglected. But if one does, then the devil is there with innumerable vile, evil mouths that poison and distort everything so that it bears no fruit. [7]Still, what they gain one sees in the daylight. For although they so shame-

6. AC, Preface, 21, and *Against the Roman Papacy, an Institution of the Devil*, 1545 (*LW* 41:265–70).

7. *Confession concerning Christ's Supper*, Part III, 1528 (*LW* 37:360).

8. SA, Preface, 3; SA III, 15, 3. *Confession concerning Christ's Supper*, 1528 (*LW* 41:162, 360).

lessly slandered us and wanted to keep the people on their side with their lies, God has continually furthered his work. God has made their number less and less, while our number grows larger and larger. God allows them to be ruined with their lies and continues to do so.

[8]I must tell a story: A doctor, sent here to Wittenberg from France, told us openly that his king was persuaded beyond the shadow of a doubt that there was no church, no government, no marriage among us, but rather everything went on in public as with cattle,[9] and all did what they want. [9]Now imagine, how will we be viewed on that day before the judgment seat of Christ, by those who have represented as pure truth such great lies to the king and to foreign lands through their writings? Christ the Lord and Judge of us all knows quite well that they lie and have lied. They will have to hear the judgment; that I know for sure. May God bring to repentance those who can be converted. For the rest, there will be eternal suffering and woe.

[10]I return to the subject: I would indeed very much like to see a true council, so that many matters and people might be helped. Not that we need it, for through God's grace our churches are now enlightened and supplied with the pure word and right use of the sacrament, an understanding of the various created orders, and true works. Therefore we do not ask for a council for our sakes. In such matters, we know there is nothing good to hope for or expect from the council. Rather, we see in bishoprics everywhere so many parishes empty and deserted[10] that our hearts are ready to break because of it. And yet, neither bishops nor cathedral canons ask how the poor people live or die—people for whom Christ died. And should not these people hear this same Christ speak to them as the true shepherd with his sheep?[11] [11]It horrifies and frightens me that Christ might cause a council of angels to descend upon Germany and totally destroy us all like Sodom and Gomorrah, because we mock him so blasphemously with the council.[12]

[12]In addition to such necessary concerns of the church, there are also innumerable, important things in the secular estate that need improvement: There is disunity among the princes and the estates. Greed and charging interest have burst in like a great flood and have attained a semblance of legality. Recklessness; lewdness; extravagant dress; gluttony; gambling; pompousness;

9. This could be a reference to the supposed lewdness of the Wittenbergers.

10. In 1538 it was reported in Wittenberg that there were some six hundred vacant parishes in the bishopric of Würzburg (*WATR* 4:4002). *On the Councils and the Church*, 1539 (*LW* 41:12, 135).

11. John 10:3. SA III, 12, 2.

12. The Latin translation: "pretext of a council." For the story of Sodom and Gomorrah, see Genesis 19.

all kinds of vice and wickedness; disobedience of subjects, servants, workers, all the artisans; extortion by the peasants[13] (who can count them all?) have so taken over that one could not set things right again with ten councils and twenty imperial diets. [13]If participants in the council were to deal with the chief concerns in the spiritual and secular orders that are against God, then their hands would be so full that they would indeed forget the child's games and foolish play of long gowns, large shaved heads,[14] broad cinctures, bishop's and cardinal's hats, crosiers, and similar sleight-of-hand. If we already had fulfilled God's command and precept in the spiritual and secular orders, then we would have found enough time to reform food, clothes, shaved heads, and chasubles. But if we swallow such camels and strain out gnats, let logs stand, and dispute about specks,[15] then we might also be satisfied with such a council.

[14]I, therefore, have provided only a few articles, because we already have received from God so many mandates to carry out in the church, in the government, and in the home that we can never fulfill them. What help is it to make many decretals and regulations in the council, especially if we neither honor nor observe these chief things commanded by God? It is as if we expect God to honor our magic tricks while we trample his real commands underfoot. But our sins burden us and do not permit God to be gracious to us, because we also do not repent and want to defend every abomination.

[15]O dear Lord Jesus Christ, hold a council and redeem your people through your glorious return! The pope and his people are lost. They do not want you. Help us who are poor and miserable, who sigh[16] to you and earnestly seek you, according to the grace you have given us through your Holy Spirit, who with you and the Father lives and reigns, forever praised. Amen.

[PART ONE]

The first part of the articles is about the lofty articles of the divine majesty, namely:

1. That Father, Son, and Holy Spirit, three distinct persons in one divine essence and nature, is one God, who created heaven and earth, etc.

2. That the Father was begotten by no one, the Son was begotten by the Father, the Holy Spirit proceeds from the Father and the Son.

---

13 LC I, 226, 235; *Appeal for Prayer against the Turks,* 1541 (*LW* 43:220); Heerpredigt wider den Türken, 1529 (*WA* 30[II]:181[20ff.]); *To the Saxon Princes,* 1545 (*LW* 43:279).

14. The distinctive haircut, "the tonsure," worn by medieval monks.

15. Matt. 23:24; 7:3-5.

16. Rom. 8:26.

3. That neither the Father nor the Holy Spirit, but the Son became a human being.

4. That the Son became a human being in this way: he was conceived by the Holy Spirit without male participation and was born of the pure, holy Virgin Mary.[17] After that, he suffered, died, was buried, descended to hell, rose from the dead, ascended to heaven, is seated at the right hand of God, in the future will come to judge the living and the dead, etc., as the Apostles' and the Athanasian symbols,[18] and the common children's catechism, teach.[19]

These articles are not matters of dispute or conflict, for both sides confess them.[20] Therefore it is not necessary to deal with them at greater length.

[PART TWO]

The second part is about the articles that pertain to the office and work of Jesus Christ, or to our redemption.

Here is the first and chief article:[21,22]

[1]That Jesus Christ, our God and Lord, "was handed over to death for our trespasses and was raised for our justification" (Rom. 4[:25]); [2]and he alone is "the Lamb of God, who takes away the sin of the world" (John 1[:29]); and "the Lord has laid upon him the iniquity of us all" (Isa. 53[:6]); furthermore, [3]"All have sinned," and "they are now justified without merit[23] by his grace, through the redemption which is in Christ Jesus . . . by his blood" (Rom. 3[:23-25]).[24]

---

17. The Latin translation: "always virgin" (*semper virgine*). AC 3, 1 and FCSD 8, 24.

18. Luther uses the Latin word *symbolon*. The creeds were known as "symbols." Cf. TCS I and II. Cf. also *The Three Symbols or Creeds of the Christian Faith*, 1538 (*WA* 50:262–83; *LW* 34:197–229). Regarding Luther's attitude toward the creeds, see F. Kattenbusch, *Luthers Stellung zu den öcumenischen Symbolen* (Giessen, 1883).

19. SC II, 3, 4; LC II, 25–33.

20. In Luther's rough draft of his original manuscript, he had first written, "both parties believe and confess them." Luther's Sermon on Epiphany, January 13, 1538 (*WA* 46:138₁₇f.); *The Three Symbols or Creeds of the Christian Faith*, 1538 (*LW* 34:210f.); *Brief Confession concerning the Holy Sacrament*, 1544 (*LW* 38:310); and Karl Thieme, *Luthers Testament wider Rom in seinen Schmalkaldischen Artikeln* (Leipzig: A. Deichert, 1900), 14–17.

21. AC 2; AC 4: AC 6; AC 20; ACAp 4; SA III, 13; FCEp 3; FCEp 5; FCSD 3; FCSD 5.

22. "Chief article" (German: *Häuptartikel*) is a technical term that Luther uses regularly in SA. His various usages of this word (particularly the use of the prefix *Häupt* or *Haupt* in compounds) indicates a particular item of significance for Luther. *Häupt* is translated here consistently as "chief." Cf. ACAp 4, 2.

23. Luther's translation differs from the Greek, which reads, "as a gift."

24. *WA* 30ᴵᴵ:632f., 636f., 640–43. Here is a so-called satisfaction theory of the atonement (Gustaf Aulen, *Christus Victor* [New York: Macmillan Co., 1969], 81–100).

[4] Now because this must be believed and may not be obtained or grasped otherwise with any work, law, or merit, it is clear and certain that faith alone justifies us.[25] In Romans 3[:26-28], St. Paul says: "For we hold that a person is justified by faith apart from works prescribed by the law"; and also, "that God alone is righteous and justifies[26] the one who has faith in Jesus."

[5] We cannot yield or concede anything in this article,[27] even if heaven and earth, or whatever, do not remain. As St. Peter says in Acts 4[:12]: "There is no other name given among mortals by which we must be saved." "And with his bruises we are healed" (Isa. 53[:5]).

On this article stands all that we teach and practice against the pope, the devil, and the world.[28] Therefore we must be quite certain and not doubt. Otherwise everything is lost, and pope and devil and everything against us will gain victory and dominance.[29]

Article 2

[1] The mass under the papacy has to be the greatest and most terrible horror, as it directly and violently opposes this chief article. Nevertheless it has been the highest and finest of all the various papal idolatries. The papacy contends that this sacrifice or work of the mass (even when done by a rotten rascal) helps people out of sin, both here in this life and beyond in purgatory, even though only the Lamb of God ought and has to do this, as mentioned above, etc. Nothing is to be yielded or given up from this article also, because the first article does not allow it.

[2] And where there were reasonable papists, we would want to speak with them in a friendly way like this: "Why do you hold so firmly to the mass?"

1. Indeed, it is no more than a mere little human invention, not commanded by God. And we are allowed to drop all human inventions, as Christ says in Matthew 15[:9]: "In vain do they worship me with human precepts."

[3] 2. It is an unnecessary thing that you can easily omit without sin and danger.

[4] 3. You can receive the sacrament in a much better and more blessed way (indeed, it is the only blessed way), when you receive it according to Christ's

---

25. SA III, 13, 1. *On Translating, An Open Letter,* 1530 (*LW* 35:181ff., 187f., 193–99).

26. Luther uses the same word, *gerecht,* to mean both "righteous" and "justifies."

27. The Latin translation: "nor can any believer concede or permit anything contrary to it."

28. *Die Promotionsdisputation von Palladius und Tilemann,* 1537 (*WA* 39¹:205f.); Explication of Psalm 127:1, 2 (*WA* 40ᴵᴵᴵ:232).

29. The German word *Recht* is translated here as "dominance."

institution. Why do you want to force the world into misery and destitution for specious reasons, which you have made up (especially when you can have it otherwise in a better and more blessed way)?

[5] Let it be publicly preached to the people that the mass, as a human trifle, may be omitted without sin. No one would be damned who does not observe it but rather would be blessed quite well in a better way without the mass. Indeed, what does it matter if the mass falls of its own accord, not only among the ignorant folk but also among all pious, Christian, reasonable, and God-fearing hearts? How much more would this be the case if they were to hear that the mass is a dangerous thing, fabricated and invented without God's word and will?

[6]4. Because such innumerable, unspeakable abuses have arisen throughout the whole world with the buying and selling of masses, one should rightly give it up (if only to curb such abuses), even if it did have something useful and good in it. Moreover, one should give it up in order to guard forever against such abuses, because it is completely unnecessary, useless, and dangerous—and one can have all things that are more necessary, useful, and certain without the mass.

[7]5. The mass is and can be nothing but a work of a human being (even a rotten rascal), as the canon of the mass and all the books[30] say. One wants to be able to reconcile oneself and others to God, acquire the forgiveness of sins, and merit grace with it (When it is observed in this way, it is observed best. Should it be otherwise?). Thus we should and must condemn and repudiate the mass, because it is directly contrary to the chief article, which says that it is not an evil or devout "Massling" with his work, but rather it is the Lamb of God and Son of God who takes away our sin.[31]

[8]If one would want to "make a good impression,"[32] then one cannot seriously celebrate the sacrament or commune by oneself for the sake of one's personal devotion.[33] If a person seriously desires to commune, then that person administers the sacrament for certain and in the best way according to Christ's institution. However, to commune oneself is a human notion, uncer-

30. Liturgical works of the medieval period make reference to "Handing over that which Pope Gelasius, the 50th Primate of Saint Peter, first ordained in the Canon" (Guillaume Durandus, *Rationale divinorum officiorum* [1478], IV:35, 12).

31. John 1:29.

32. The "good impression" here may refer to the communicant's justification before God. Cf. *WA* 50:203 n. 1, and *BSLK* 418 n. 4.

33. Cochläus wrote that private masses are "nowhere forbidden in the Scriptures or by the churches, but rather are much more commanded as can be shown in the Decretals and numerous canons" (*CC*, 16f.).

tain, unnecessary, and even forbidden. Such a person does not know what he or she is doing, because, without God's word, the person is following a false human notion and innovation. [9]Thus it is not correct (even if everything else would otherwise be in order) that one should use the common sacrament of the church for one's own devotional life and play with it to favor oneself without God's word and outside the church community.

[10]This article on the mass will be the sum and substance of the council because, if it were possible for them to concede to us every other article, they could not concede this one. As Campegio said at Augsburg, he would sooner allow himself to be torn to pieces before he would let go of the mass.[34] In the same way I, with God's help, would sooner allow myself to be burned to ashes before I would allow a "Massling" (whether good or evil) and his work to be equal or greater than my Lord and Savior Jesus Christ. Thus we are and remain forever separated and against one another. They rightly recognize this: if the mass falls, the papacy falls. Before they would allow that to happen, they would kill us all, if they could do it.

[11]Moreover, this dragon's tail,[35] the mass, has produced many noxious pests and the excrement of numerous idolatries:

[12]First, purgatory. Because they are occupied with purgatorial masses for the dead and vigils after seven days, thirty days, and a year, and, finally, with the Common Week, All Saints' Day, and Soul Baths, the mass seems only to be used on behalf of the dead, although Christ founded the sacrament only for the living. Purgatory, therefore, with all its splendor, requiems, and transactions, is to be regarded as a manifestation of the devil because it is also against the chief article, that Christ alone (and not human works) ought to help souls. Beyond this, nothing about the dead is commanded or encouraged.[36] For these reasons, one may well want to abandon it, even if it were neither error nor idolatry.

[13]The papists, at this point, use Augustine[37] and some of the fathers, who have supposedly written about purgatory, and think that we do not see why

---

34. Luther mentions this event a number of times: *Dr. Martin Luther's Warning to His Dear German People,* 1531 (*WA* 30^{III}:311$_{25}$; *LW* 47:45); *Glosse auf das vermeinte kaiserliche Edikt,* 1531 (*WA* 30^{III}: 352$_{25-28}$, 362$_{29-31}$); *WATR* 3:3502 (recorded December 12, 1536—precisely while Luther was writing SA) and 3732. Melanchthon had reported on Campegio's strong conviction concerning this point at Augsburg, in 1530 (*CR* 2:168ff., 246ff., 254f.).

35. Rev. 12:3; 20:2. *The Keys,* 1530 (*LW* 40:376).

36. *Confession concerning Christ's Supper,* 1528 (*LW* 37:369).

37. *City of God,* Book 21, chapter 24.

and how they use such passages.[38] Saint Augustine does not write that there is a purgatory and cites no writing that persuades him to it. Instead, he leaves the matter undecided and says simply that his mother asked to be remembered at the altar or at the sacrament.[39] Now all of this is certainly nothing but the human thoughts of a few persons, who can establish no article of faith, which God alone can do. [14]But our papists use such human words in order to make us believe that their shameful, blasphemous, accursed fairs of soul masses make an offering in purgatory, etc. They will never prove such a thing from Augustine. When they have given up their purgatorial "mass fairs" (something Augustine never dreamed of), then we might discuss with them whether Saint Augustine's word, apart from Scripture, ought to be tolerated and whether the dead are to be remembered at the sacrament. [15]It is not valid for them to formulate articles of faith on the basis of the holy fathers' works or words. Otherwise, their food, clothes, houses, etc., would also have to be articles of faith—as they have done with relics. The fact is that[40] God's word should establish articles of faith and no one else, not even an angel.[41]

[16]Second, the result has been that evil spirits have caused much rascality. They have appeared as human souls.[42] They have demanded masses, vigils, pilgrimages, and other offerings with unspeakable lies and cunning, [17]which we all held as articles of faith, according to which we had to live. The pope confirms this, as does the mass along with all the other horrors. Here there is also nothing to yield or surrender.

[18]Third, pilgrimages. Here they also sought masses, the forgiveness of sins, and God's grace. The mass determined everything. Now, it is positively certain that such pilgrimages, without God's word, are not commanded, nor are they necessary. We could have it all in a much better way, without any sin

---

38. Cochläus writes: "We can prove that such a belief and use has been in the Christian church continually from the apostles to the present. Among the Greeks and in the eastern church, St. Dionysius (a disciple of Paul), Origen, Athanasius, Chrysostom, Cyril, Damascus, etc., have borne witness to it. Among the Romans in the western church, the four eminent teachers: Ambrose, Jerome, Augustine, and Gregory bear witness to it along with all other Latin theologians and canons lawyers" (CC, 18–19).

39. Confessions, Books 11 and 13.

40. The Latin translation: "We have another rule, namely, that . . ."

41. SA II, 2, 13–15 was not a part of Luther's original manuscript or the copy made by Spalatin and subscribed at Schmalkalden in 1537. Luther inserted this paragraph into the text prior to SA's publication in 1538 (WA 50:205–6; UuA, 41–42).

42. Luther apparently refers here to the reports of apparitions by Gregory the Great (d. 604), Dialog. IV, chapter 40 (MSL 67, 396f.), and Peter Damian (d. 1072), Opusculum 34, chapter 5 (MSL 145, 578f.).

or danger. We could dispense with it. Why would one allow the neglect of one's own parish, God's word, wives and children, etc., which are necessary and commanded, but run after unnecessary, uncertain, shameful, devilish imps? [19]Only because the devil has taken over the pope, causing him to praise and confirm such practices so that the people are indeed routinely separated from Christ by their own works and become idolaters. Is this not the most evil thing in pilgrimages? Aside from the fact that it is an unnecessary, uncommanded, unwise, and uncertain, and even harmful thing. [20]Here, therefore, there is also nothing to yield or concede, etc. And let it be preached that it is unnecessary as well as dangerous. Then see where pilgrimages stand.[43]

[21]Fourth, fraternities. The monasteries, foundations, and vicars have assigned and conveyed to themselves (by lawful and open sale) all masses, good works, etc., for both the living and the dead. They are not only purely human trifles, without God's word, completely unnecessary and not commanded; but they are also contrary to the first article of redemption, and therefore they can in no way be tolerated.

[22]Fifth, relics.[44] Here a good many open lies and follies are based on the bones of dogs and horses.[45] The devil laughs at such rascality. They should have long ago been condemned, even if there were something good in them. In addition, they are also without God's word, neither commanded nor advised. It is a completely unnecessary and useless thing. [23]The worst is that relics were also to have produced an indulgence and the forgiveness of sin as a good work and act of worship, like the mass, etc.

[24]Sixth, precious indulgences belong here. They are given to both the living and the dead (but for money). The pitiful Judas or pope sells the merits of Christ together with the superabundant merits of all the saints and the entire church, etc. All of this is not to be tolerated, not only because it is without God's word, not necessary, and not commanded; but because it is contrary to the first article. Christ's merit is not acquired through our work or our pennies, but through faith by grace, without any money and merit; not by the authority of the pope, but rather through the sermon or by the preaching of God's word.

On Prayer to Saints

[25]Prayer to the saints is also one of the anti-Christian abuses that is in conflict with the first, chief article and destroys the recognition of Christ. It is

---

43. The Latin translation: "Thus they will spontaneously perish."

44. Cochläus writes that the church fathers, "Jerome . . . , Ambrose, Augustine, Basil, Chrysostom, etc.," approved of relics (*CC*, 25).

45. Luther referred to these supposed bones of the saints in *Predigten des Jahres 1546*, Nr. 4, January 26 (*WA* 51:138$_{5-8}$). Cf. also *On the Councils and the Church*, 1539 (*WA* 50:642$_{23ff}$; *LW* 41:165).

neither commanded nor recommended, has no example from the Scripture, and we have everything a thousand times better in Christ—even if it were a precious possession, which it is not.[46]

[26]Although the angels in heaven pray for us (as Christ himself also does), and in the same way also the saints on earth or perhaps in heaven pray for us, it does not follow from this that we ought to appeal to them; pray; conduct fasts for them; hold festivals; celebrate masses; make sacrifices; establish churches, altars, worship services; and serve them in other ways; and consider them as helpers in need and assign all kinds of aid to them and attribute a specific function to particular saints, as the papists teach and do. That is idolatry. Such honor belongs to God alone. [27]You as a Christian and saint on earth can pray for me, not only in the case of a particular need but in all necessities. But on account of that, I ought not idolize you, appeal to you, hold a celebration, conduct a fast, sacrifice, have a mass in your honor, and base my saving faith on you. I can honor, love, and thank you otherwise quite well in Christ. [28]Now if such idolatrous honor is taken away from the angels and dead saints, then the honor that remains will not hurt anyone, indeed, it will soon be forgotten. When usefulness and help, both physical and spiritual, are no longer expected, then the saints will be left in peace, both in the grave and in heaven. Whether for nothing or out of love, no one will think much about them, esteem them, or honor them.

[29]In summary, we cannot tolerate and must condemn what the mass is, what has resulted because of it, and what depends on it, so that we might hold, use, and receive the holy sacrament by faith, unspoiled and with certainty according to the institution of Christ.

Article 3

[1]In former times, foundations and monasteries were established, with good intentions, for the education of learned people and decent women. They should be returned to such use so that we might have pastors, preachers, and other servants of the church, as well as other necessary persons for earthly government, for the cities and lands, and also well brought up young women to be mothers and housekeepers, etc. [2]Where they are not willing to serve in this way, it is better if one allows them to become deserted or torn down than that they, with their blasphemous worship, established through human beings, should be held as something better than the general Christian vocation and

---

46. Cochläus writes: "We know that praying to saints has been done consistently in the church from the time of the Apostles and it is not forbidden in the Scriptures" (*CC*, 28).

the offices and orders established by God. All this is also contrary to the first and chief article of redemption of Jesus Christ. Furthermore, they (like all other human inventions) are also not commanded, not necessary, not useful— and they make for a dangerous and a vain, futile effort. The prophets call such worship *aven*, which means "empty effort."[47]

Article 4

[1]The pope is not the head of all Christendom "by divine right" or on the basis of God's word[48] (because that belongs only to the one who is called Jesus Christ).[49] The pope is only bishop or pastor of the church at Rome and of those who willingly or through human invention have joined themselves to him (this is his secular authority).[50] They are not under him as a lord, rather beside him as a brother and companion, to be Christians as also the ancient councils[51] and the era of St. Cyprian[52] demonstrate. [2]But now, however, no bishop dares to call the pope "brother," as at that time, but rather must call him his "most gracious lord," as if he were a king or emperor. We will not, ought not, and cannot impose this upon our consciences. But whoever wants to do it, such a person does it without us.

[3]It follows from this that everything which the pope has undertaken and done on the basis of such false, offensive, blasphemous, arrogant power has been and still is a purely diabolical affair and business, which corrupts the

---

47. The Hebrew word *aven* literally means "wickedness," "emptiness," "vanity," "futility." Luther translated it here with *Mühe*, which properly means "effort," "trouble," "labor," "pain." Luther connects *Mühe* with the prophet's denunciation of worship that was "done without feeling and with an evil conscience" (Isa. 1:13, WADB 11¹:28) and "false teaching and works" (Isa. 29:20, WADB 11¹:94). *Mühe* is for Luther a technical term (the same word he used in the previous sentence) to point to what he considered to be the vanity (i.e., the *aven*) of monastic life (with its, from Luther's perspective, empty ritual and/or liturgical formality). *Der Prophet Habakuk ausgelegt*, 1526 (WA 19:357f.); Isa. 29:20 and 41:29 (WADB 11¹:94, 127); *Vorlesung über Jesaias*, 1527–30 (WA 31ᴵᴵ:11, 181, 307).

48. Tr 12.

49. Eph. 1:22; 4:15; 5:23; Col. 1:18.

50. This refers to the secular power of the pope, the "patrimony of Peter." 1 Peter 2:13.

51. E.g., the councils of Nicea (A.D. 325), Constantinople (A.D. 381), Ephesus (A.D. 431), and Chalcedon (A.D. 451). Canon IV of the Council of Nicea stipulates that bishops should be elected by their own churches in the presence of one or more neighboring bishops.

52. Cf. Tr. 14. Cyprian (d. 258), as bishop of Carthage, addressed Pope Cornelius as his "very dear brother" (MSL 3:700, 703, 708, 731, 796, 830). Ambrose (d. 397), bishop of Milan, and Augustine (d. 430), bishop of Hippo, addressed the bishops of Rome in their day with similar appellations (MSL 16:1124; MSL 33:758, 764; *Corpus scriptorum ecclesiasticorum latinorum* 44:652, 669).

entire holy Christian church[53] (insofar as it depends on him) and negates the first, chief article on the redemption of Jesus Christ (outside of what belongs to the physical government, through which God allows much good to happen for a people through a tyrant and rascal).

[4]All his bulls and books, in which he roars like a lion (the angel of Revelation 12 indicates this),[54] state that no Christians can be saved unless they are obedient and submit to him in all things—what he wills, what he says, what he does.[55] All of this (which says quite a bit) is nothing other than: "If you believe in Christ and have everything that is necessary for salvation in him, then it is nevertheless nothing and all is vain if you do not hold to me as your god, submit to me and obey." Still, it is obvious that the holy church was without the pope, at the very least, for over five hundred years,[56] and even today the Greek church and many churches that use other languages have never been under the pope and still are not. [5]Thus it is, as it has often been said, a human fiction. It is not commanded. There is no need for it. And it is useless. The holy Christian church can survive quite well without such a head. It would have been much better if such a head had not been raised up by the devil. [6]The papacy is not necessary in the church, because it exercises no Christian office, and the church must continue and exist without the pope.

[7]And I assert that the pope should want to renounce his claim so that he would not be supreme in the church "by divine right" or by God's command. However, in order that the unity of Christendom might be preserved against the sects and heretics, we might accept a head in which all others are held together. Such a head could now be elected by the people and it would remain in their power and by their choice whether to change or depose this head. This is virtually the way the council at Constance handled the popes, deposing the three[57] and electing the fourth. Now I assert (says I) that it is impossible for

53. Cf. SA II, 4, 5. "The holy Christian church" is a quotation from the German translations of the Nicene and Apostles' Creeds, which had been used in Germany since the 1400s. Cf. TCS I; TCS II.

54. Luther actually quotes Rev. 10:3. The reformer made the same mistake in *On the Councils and the Church*, 1539 (*WA* 50:578; *LW* 41:90).

55. The most exteme medieval papal claim for such authority is expressed in Boniface VIII's 1302 bull *Unam Sanctam:* "We declare, say, define, and pronounce that it is altogether necessary to salvation for every human creature to be subject to the Roman pontiff" (quoted from *The Book of Concord*, ed. Theodore Tappert [Philadelphia: Fortress Press, 1959], 299 n. 4).

56. Luther thought that Gregory I (d. 604) was the last bishop of Rome prior to the rise of the papacy per se. Tr 19.

57. John XXIII was deposed at Constance on May 29, 1415. Gregory XII abdicated on July 4, 1415. Benedict XIII was deposed on July 26, 1415. Martin V was elected pope on November 11, 1417.

the pope and the chair of Rome to renounce such things and to want to accept this view, because he would have to allow his entire government and order to be overthrown and destroyed with all his laws and books. In summary, he cannot do it.

And even if he were to do it, Christianity would not be helped in any way. There would be many more sects than before, [8]because they would not have to submit to such a head on the basis of God's command but rather from human goodwill. The head of this church would rather easily and quickly be despised, until it would finally have not even one member. It would no longer have to be at Rome or at some other set place,[58] but wherever and in whatever church God would provide a suitable man for it. Oh, that would be a complicated and disorganized setup!

[9]Therefore the church cannot be better ruled and preserved than if we all live under one head, Christ, and all the bishops are equal according to the office—although they may be unequal in their gifts[59]—holding diligently together one unanimous doctrine, creed, sacraments, prayers, and performing works of love, etc. St. Jerome writes that the priests at Alexandria ruled the church together in common, as the apostles also did and afterward all bishops in all of Christendom,[60] until the pope elevated himself over all.

[10]This[61] shows authoritatively that he is the true antichrist or contrachrist, who has raised himself over and set himself against Christ because the pope will not let Christians be saved without his authority, which amounts to nothing. It is not ordered or commanded by God. [11]This is called precisely, "setting oneself over God and against God," as St. Paul says.[62] Neither the Turks nor the Tartars, as great enemies of Christians as they are, do such a thing. They allow whoever desires it to have faith in Christ, and they receive physical tribute and obedience from the Christians.

[12]The pope, however, will not allow faith, but rather says that if one is obedient to him, then one will be saved. We do not intend to do this, even if we have to die in God's name on account of it. [13]All of this stems from his

58. The papal residence had been at Avignon, France, from 1309 to 1377.

59. 1 Cor. 12:4, 8-10; Rom. 12:6-8.

60. Luther refers to two passages from Jerome, which he employs in other contexts as well (e.g., WA 2:228f., 259; WABr 1:392). The citations of Jerome are from Commentary on the Epistle to Titus, 1:5, 6 (MSL 26:562); and Epistle to Euangelus the Presbyter, no. 146 (MSL 22:1194).

61. The Latin translation of SA: "this doctrine."

62. 2 Thess. 2:4. Luther regularly applied this text to the papacy. Cf. Hans Preuss, Die Vorstellungen vom Antichrist im späteren Mittelalter, bei Luther und in der konfessionellen Polemik (Leipzig, 1906), 156.

claim to be head of the Christian church[63] "by divine right." Therefore he has had to set himself up as equal to and even greater than Christ, as the head and lord of the church and, ultimately, the entire world. He allows himself to be called an earthly god and even tries to command the angels in heaven.[64]

[14]And when we distinguish the pope's teaching from that of the Holy Scriptures, or place it next to them, then we find that the pope's teaching, when it is at its best, is taken from the imperial, pagan law[65] and teaches about secular dealings and judgments, as his pronouncements show. Furthermore, they teach about ceremonies involving churches, clothing, foods, persons; along with child's play, fantasies, and foolish activities without number. In all these things, there is absolutely nothing about Christ, faith, and God's commandments.[66]

In the end, this is nothing other than the devil himself who promotes his lies about masses, purgatory, monastic life, one's own works, and worship (which are the essence of the papacy) in contradiction to God. He damns, slays, and plagues all Christians who do not exalt and honor his abominations above all things. Therefore we can no more adore the devil himself as our lord or god than we can allow his apostle, the pope or antichrist, to rule as our head or lord. His papal government is characterized by lying and murder and the eternal ruin of body and soul,[67] as I have demonstrated in many books.[68]

[15]These four articles will furnish them with enough to condemn at the council. They neither can nor will allow us the smallest little portion of these articles. Of this we may be certain. We can depend upon the hope that Christ our Lord has attacked his enemies and will carry the day, both by his Spirit and at his return.[69] Amen.

[16]At the council, we will not stand before the emperor or the secular

63. Gratian, *Decretum,* Part I, dist. 21, chap. 3, and dist. 22, chaps. 1–2.

64. On June 27, 1346, Pope Clement VI published the bull *Ad memoriam reducendo,* in which he is said to have commanded the angels "to lead to heaven the souls of the pilgrims who might die on their way to Rome" during the jubilee year of 1350.

65. Luther refers here to Roman law. *WATR* 2:3470.

66. *WATR* 4:4515 and *WATR* 6:6863.

67. FCSD, 10, 20.

68. *Explanations of the 95 Theses,* 1518 (*WA* 1:571; *LW* 31:152); *Proceedings at Augsburg,* 1518 (*WA* 2:20; *LW* 41:281); *The Leipzig Debate,* 1519 (*WA* 2:161; *LW* 31:318); *Disputatio I. Eccii et M. Lutheri Lipsiae habita,* 1519 (*WA* 2:341–43); Letter from Luther to Hieronymus Dungersheim, December 1519 (*WABr* 1:567); Letter from Luther to Hieronymus Dungersheim, December 1519 (*WABr* 1:601–3); Letter from Justus Jonas to Luther, June 1530 (*WABr* 5:432).

69. 2 Thess. 2:8.

authority, as at Augsburg,[70] where they issued a most gracious summons[71] and in goodness allowed the matters to be heard. We will stand before the pope and the devil himself, who does not intend to listen, but only to damn, murder, and drive us to idolatry. Therefore we must not kiss his feet or say, "You are my gracious lord." Rather, we ought to speak as the angel spoke to the devil in Zechariah [3:2], "The Lord rebuke you, O Satan!"

[PART THREE]

We could discuss the following things or articles with learned, reasonable people or among ourselves. The pope and his kingdom do not value these things, because conscience[72] is nothing to them. Money, honor, and power are everything.

[Article 1:] On Sin

[1] First, here we must confess (as St. Paul says in Rom. 5[:12]) that sin is from Adam, the one person through whose disobedience all people became sinners and subject to death and the devil. This is called the original sin, or the chief sin.

[2] The fruits of this sin are the evil works, which are forbidden in the Ten Commandments: unbelief, false belief, idolatry, being without the fear of God, presumption, despair, blindness, and, most of all, not knowing or honoring God. After that, there is swearing with God's name, not praying, not praying for others, not honoring God's word, being disobedient to parents, murdering, promiscuity, stealing, deceit, etc.

[3] This original sin has caused such a deep, evil corruption of nature that reason does not comprehend it; rather, it must be believed on the basis of revelation from the Scriptures[73] (Psalm 50[74] and Rom. 5[:12], Exod. 33[:20], Gen. 3[:6ff.]). The scholastic theologians, therefore, have taught pure error and blindness against this article:

---

70. Luther refers here to the imperial diet that was held at Augsburg in the summer of 1530. It was at that occasion that the Augsburg Confession was presented to Emperor Charles V.

71. On January 21, 1530, Charles V's proclamation for the Diet of Augsburg included these words: "to listen to, understand, and consider each belief, opinion, and viewpoint between us in love and kindness, so that we might come to Christian truth." *Dr. Martin Luther's Warning to His Dear German People,* 1531 (*WA* 30[III]:287, 292; *LW* 47:24f., 30).

72. Luther uses a Latin word, *conscientia.*

73. FCEp 1, 9.

74. The Vulgate (Latin Bible) numbered the Psalms differently from modern English versions. Here Luther refers to Ps. 51:6-7.

[4]First, that after the fall of Adam, the natural powers of human beings were still whole and uncorrupted. As the philosophers[75] taught, a person had, by nature, sound reason and goodwill.

[5]Second, that the human being has a free will, either to do good and reject evil or to reject good and do evil.[76]

[6]Third, that the human being could, by using natural powers, keep and carry out every command of God.

[7]Fourth, that human beings could, from natural powers, love God above all things[77] and their neighbors as themselves.

[8]Fifth, that if a person does as much as possible, then God will certainly give grace to that person.[78]

[9]Sixth, that if someone wants to go to the sacrament, it is not necessary to have a proper intention to do good, but it is enough for that person not to have an evil intention to commit sin,[79] because nature is so completely good and the sacrament is so powerful.

[10]Seventh, that there is no basis in Scripture that the Holy Spirit with his grace is necessary for a good deed.[80]

[11]These and many similar things have come from a lack of understanding and ignorance about both sin and Christ our Savior. We cannot allow these purely pagan teachings, because, if these teachings were right, then Christ died in vain.[81] There would be no guilt or sin in humankind for which he had to die—or he would have died only for the body and not for the soul, because the soul would be healthy and only the body would be mortal.

[Article 2:] On Law

[1]We maintain here that the law has been given by God, in the first place, to curb sin by means of the threat and terror of punishment and also by means of the promise and offer of grace and favor. All of this failed because of the evil which sin worked in humankind. [2]Some became worse because of it. They are, therefore, enemies of the law, which prohibits what they want to do

---

75. E.g., Plato (d. 347 B.C.) and Aristotle (d. 322 B.C.).

76. FCSD 2, 33.

77. E.g., John Duns Scotus (d. 1308), *Commentary on the Sentences*, III, Distinction 27, Question 1.

78. E.g., Gabriel Biel, sent. II, d 27 q i, art. 3, dub. 3 0. Cf. also Heiko Oberman, *The Harvest of Medieval Theology* (Durham, N.C.: Labyrinth Press, 1983), 468.

79. Cf. SA III, 3, 17, and the note in that place.

80. FCSD 2, 33.

81. Gal. 2:21.

and commands what they do not want to do. On account of this, where they are not restrained by punishment, they do more against the law than before. These are the coarse, evil people who do evil whenever they have an opportunity.

[3]Others become blind and presumptuous, allowing themselves to think that they can and do keep the law by their own powers (as has just been said above about the scholastic theologians).[82] This attitude results in hypocrites and false saints.

[4]The foremost office or power of the law is that it reveals original sin and its fruits.[83] It shows human beings how deeply they have fallen and how their nature is completely corrupt. The law must say to them that they have no God. They honor or worship strange gods. This is something that they would not have believed before without the law. Thus they are terrified, humbled, despondent, and despairing. They anxiously desire help but do not know where to find it. They become enemies of God, murmuring,[84] etc. [5]This is what is meant by Romans [4:15]: "The law brings wrath,"[85] and Romans 5[:20] "Sin becomes greater through the law."

[Article 3:] On Repentance

[1]The New Testament maintains this office of the law and teaches it, as Paul does and says, in Romans 1[:18]: "The wrath of God is revealed from heaven against all."[86] Also Romans 3[:19-20]: "So that the whole world is guilty before God" and "no human being will be justified in his sight"; and Christ says in John 16[:8]: The Holy Spirit "will convince the world of sin."

[2]Now this is the thunderclap of God, by means of which both the obvious sinner and the false saint[87] are destroyed.[88] God allows no one righteousness and drives them altogether into terror and despair. This is the hammer (as Jer. [23:29] says): "My word is a hammer which breaks the rocks to pieces."

---

82. SA III, 1, 6.

83. Rom. 3:20; 7:7; SA III, 1, 3.

84. Rom. 5:10; Exod. 16:8; Luke 15:2; 19:7.

85. Luther mistakenly refers to Romans 3.

86. Cf. FCSD 5, 14.

87. Cf. SA III, 2, 2–3.

88. This metaphor is an echo of Luther's famous 1508 encounter with the lightning bolt on the outskirts of Stotternheim. This event prompted him to enter the monastery. Cf. Roland H. Bainton, *Here I Stand: A Life of Martin Luther* (New York: New American Library, 1950), 15. SA III, 3, 30.

This is not "active contrition,"[89] a contrived remorse, but "passive contrition,"[90] the true suffering of the heart, the suffering and pain of death.

[3]This is what is known as the beginning of true repentance. Here a person must listen to a judgment such as this: "There is nothing in any of you—whether you appear publicly to be sinners or saints.[91] You must all become something other than what you are now, and act in another way, no matter who you are now and what you do. You may be as great, wise, powerful, and holy as you could wish, but here no one is godly," etc.[92]

[4]To this office of the law, however, the New Testament immediately adds the consoling promise of grace through the gospel.[93] This we should believe. As Christ says in Mark 1[:15]: "Repent and believe in the good news."[94] This is the same as, "Become and act otherwise, and believe my promise." [5]And before Jesus, John the Baptizer was called a preacher of repentance—though for the forgiveness of sins. That is, he convicted them all and made them into sinners, so that they would know what they were before God and would recognize themselves as lost people. In this way they were prepared for the Lord. They received the forgiveness of sins expectantly and receptively. [6]Jesus himself says in Luke [24:47]: "You must preach repentance and forgiveness of sins in my name to all nations."

[7]But where the law exercises such an office alone, without the assistance of the gospel, there is[95] death and hell. Humankind has to despair, like Saul and Judas, as St. Paul says: "The law kills through sin."[96] [8]On the other hand, the gospel does not give consolation and forgiveness in only one way—but rather through the word, sacraments, and the like (as we shall hear). With God, there is truly rich redemption from the great prison of sin (as Psalm 129 [130:7-8] says).

[9]Now we must compare the false penance of the sophists with true repentance, in order that they both might be better understood.[97]

---

89. Luther uses a Latin phrase, *activa contritio.*

90. Luther uses a Latin phrase, *passiva contritio.*

91. The Latin translation: "in your own opinion."

92. Rom. 3:10-12. See also SA III, 3, 33.

93. FCSD 5, 14. *WA* 7:24.

94. See also Matt. 3:2; Luke 3:15.

95. The Latin translation: "nothing else but."

96. Rom. 7:10; for Saul, see 1 Sam. 28:20 and 31:4; for Judas, see Matt. 27:3-5.

97. Cochläus writes, "[Luther] leaves out the beginning, middle, and end of the true gospel that, above all, teaches us to do Penance" (*CC*, 42).

On the False Penance of the Papists[98]

[10]It is impossible that they should teach correctly about penance, because they do not recognize true sin. As mentioned above,[99] they hold nothing right about original sin, but rather they say that the natural powers of humankind have remained whole and uncorrupted. They say that reason can teach correctly and the will can rightly act according to it. They say that God surely gives his grace if a person does as much as is within that person, according to human free will.

[11]From this it must follow that they only do penance for actual sins, such as evil thoughts to which they consent (because evil impulses, lust, and inclinations were not sin), evil words, and evil works (which they could have well avoided by means of their free will).

[12]They divide such penance into three parts.[100] There is remorse, confession, and satisfaction, with the following comfort and pledge: if a person experiences true remorse, confesses, and makes satisfaction, then that person, by these actions, merits forgiveness and pays for sins before God. In this way, they have instructed the people who come to penance to have confidence in their own works. [13]From this came the phrase that was spoken from the pulpit when they said the general confession on behalf of the people: "Spare my life, Lord God, until I might repent of my sins and improve my life."[101]

[14]Here there was no Christ. Nothing was mentioned about faith, but they hoped to overcome and wipe out sin before God with their own works. We also become priests and monks with this intention: we wanted to set ourselves against sin.

[15]Remorse was handled in this way: because no one could recall all of one's sins (particularly those of an entire year),[102] the person found another way out.[103] If an unknown sin was remembered later, then one was also to be remorseful for it and confess it, etc. Meanwhile, one was commended to God's grace.

[16]Moreover, since no one knew how great the remorse should be, so

---

98. ACAp 12, 98–178.

99. SA III, 1, 4–11.

100. Luther discusses these three respective parts of repentance in what follows: SA III, 3, 12–21.

101. This phrase, or its equivalent, dates back to at least the tenth century and was spoken by the pastor, in behalf of the congregation, at the conclusion of the sermon. *BSLK* 439 n. 3.

102. At the Fourth Lateran Council (1215), it was stipulated that all who had reached the age of discretion (seven years) must confess their sins to a priest at least once a year.

103. Luther uses an idiom, which, translated literally, is, "they mended the coat" or "patched the hide" (*flickten sie den Pelz*).

that one might certainly have enough before God, one was given this comfort: whoever could not have contrition,[104] that is, have remorse, then that person should have attrition.[105] I like to call this a halfway or beginning remorse because they themselves have not as yet understood either word and they still know even less about what they mean than I do. Such attrition was counted as contrition when they went to confession.

[17]And when it happened that some said they could not repent or be sorrowful for their sins, as might happen in fornication or revenge, etc., they were asked whether they at least wished or willingly desired to have remorse. When they would say "yes" (because who would say "no," except the devil himself?), it was considered to be remorse and their sins would be forgiven on the basis of such a good work. Here they pointed to St. Bernard as an example, etc.[106]

[18]Here we see how blind reason stumbles into the things of God and seeks comfort in its own works, according to its own presumption. It cannot think about Christ or faith. If we look at this now in the light, then such remorse is a contrived and imaginary idea. It comes from one's own powers, without faith, without knowledge of Christ. Given this, a poor sinner who had thoughts of lust or revenge would have rather laughed than cried, except if the person had truly confronted the law or been plagued by the devil with a sorrowful spirit. Otherwise, it is certain that such remorse would be pure hypocrisy and would not kill the desire for sin. The person had to have remorse, but would rather sin more—if it would have been without consequences.

[19]Confession was like this: everyone had to enumerate all of one's sins (which is an impossible thing). This was a great torment. Whatever the person had forgotten could be forgiven only when it was remembered—and then it still had to be confessed. With that, one could never know whether one had confessed perfectly enough or whether confession could ever end. At the same time, people were pointed to their works and told that the more perfectly they confessed and the more ashamed they were and the more they humbled themselves before the priest, the sooner and better they would do enough to deal with their sin. Such humility would certainly earn the grace of God.[107]

[20]Here also there was neither faith nor Christ, and the power of the

104. Luther uses a Latin word: *contritionem.*

105. Luther uses the Latin word: "attrition." Regarding the scholastic theory of *contritio* and *attritio,* see O. Scheel, *Martin Luther* (1930), 288f.

106. *Treatise on Grace and Free Will,* IV, 10 (MSL 182, 1007).

107. Cf. Peter Abelard (d. 1142), *Ethica seu scito te ipsum,* chap. 24 (MSL 178, 668), and *Epitome theologiae christianae,* chap. 36 (MSL 178, 1756).

absolution was not told to them. Rather, their comfort was based on the enumeration of sins and humiliation. It is not possible to count what torments, rascality, and idolatry such confession produced.[108]

[21]Satisfaction is truly the most intricate[109] of the three because no one could know how much should be done for each individual sin, much less for all sins. Here they came up with only one bit of advice: impose a few satisfactions, which one could easily uphold, such as saying the Lord's Prayer five times, fasting for a day, etc. They then directed those with leftover penance to purgatory.

[22]Here, as well, there was only pure misery and destitution. Some imagined that they would never get out of purgatory because, according to the ancient canons, each mortal sin carried with it seven years of penance.[110]

[23]Still, confidence was placed on our work of satisfaction and, if the satisfaction would have been perfect, then confidence would have been placed totally upon it and neither faith nor Christ would be of any use. But this confidence was impossible. If they would have done penance for a hundred years in this way, they would still not have known whether they were penitent enough. This means always doing penance but never arriving at repentance.

[24]At this point, the holy chair of Rome[111] established indulgences in order to help the poor church.[112] With these, the pope forgave and remitted the satisfaction, first for seven years in a particular case, and then for a hundred years, etc. The indulgences were then divided among the cardinals and bishops, so that one could grant a hundred years and another could grant a hundred days. However, the pope reserved for himself the right to remit the entire satisfaction.[113]

[25]Only after this practice began to bring in money and the market in bulls became lucrative did the pope come up with the jubilee year and attach it to Rome—which offered the forgiveness of all penalties and guilt.[114] The people came running, because everyone wanted to be set free from the

---

108. The Latin translation inserts a reference to Chrysostom's "Sermon on Penance" (MSG 48, 754).

109. The Latin translation: "perplexing."

110. *47 canones poenitentiales,* by Astesanus (d. 1330).

111. The pope, as head of the church, was seen as the occupant of the chair or throne (Latin: *cathedra*) of St. Peter.

112. "The poor church" appears to be a reference to the sad state to which churchly penance had deteriorated as well as an ironic reference to the financial situation in Rome.

113. Plenary indulgences were instituted in 1095 by Pope Urban II in connection with the first crusade.

114. Luther refers here in German to the Latin expression *remissio poenae et culpae,* which dates back liturgically to the mid-thirteenth century.

heavy, unbearable burden. This is called "finding and digging up the trea-sures of the earth."[115] Immediately, the popes pressed further and established many jubilee years to follow one another. The more money he swallowed, the wider the pope's gullet became. Therefore he sent his legates across the lands, until all the churches and every home were influenced by the jubilee year. [26]Finally, he squeezed into purgatory with the dead—first with masses and the establishment of vigils; after that, with indulgences and the jubilee year. In the end, souls became so cheap that one could be sprung for a nickel.[116]

[27]That still did not help anything. Although the pope taught the people to rely on and trust in such indulgences, he himself once again made the pro-cess uncertain when he asserted in his bulls, "Whoever desires to partake of the indulgence or the jubilee year should be remorseful, go to confession, and give money."[117] We have heard above that such remorse and confession were uncertain and hypocritical.[118] Similarly, no one knew which soul might be in purgatory and no one knew which few had felt real remorse and confessed. In this way, the pope took the money and comforted them with his authority and indulgence and still directed them to their uncertain works.

[28]Now, there were a few who did not consider themselves guilty of any real sins (that is, of thoughts, words, and deeds), myself and others like me, who wanted to be monks and priests in monasteries and foundations. We fasted, kept vigils, prayed, held masses, used rough clothing and furniture, etc., in order to resist evil thoughts. With earnestness and intensity we wanted to be holy. Still, the hereditary, inborn evil did something while we slept, which is its manner (as St. Augustine[119] and St. Jerome,[120] along with others, confess). Each one still held that some of the others were so holy, as we taught, that they were without sin and full of good works. On this basis, we transferred and sold our good works to others, since we did not need them all to get to heaven. This is certainly true, and there are seals, letters, and examples available.

[29]Such people do not need repentance, because, if they do not consent

---

115. Dan. 11:43. Christians in the medieval and late medieval period used this passage to express their conviction that the devil would show the antichrist where the concealed riches of the earth were hidden, so that the people could bring them to the antichrist (Preuss, *Die Vorstellungen vom Antichrist im späterem Mittelalter*, 20).

116. Luther apparently refers to the infamous verse of the indulgence preachers: "When the coin in the coffer rings, the soul from purgatory springs!"

117. Penance and confession, beginning in the middle of the thirteenth century, were regularly connected with indulgences.

118. SA III, 3, 16–23.

119. *Confessions,* Book II, Chapter 2, and Book X, Chapter 30.

120. *Epistle to Eustochius* 22:7.

to evil thoughts, then for what would they be remorseful? What would they confess, when they avoid evil words? For what would they want to make satisfaction, when their deeds were guiltless? They could sell their over-and-above righteousness to other, poor sinners. The Pharisees and scribes in the time of Christ were such saints.[121]

[30]At this point, the fiery angel St. John, the preacher of true repentance, comes to destroy everyone together with a single thunderclap, saying, "Repent!"[122] Some people think this way: "We have already done penance." [31]Others think: "We do not need repentance." [32]John says, "All of you together repent! On the one hand, you are false penitents; on the other hand, they are false saints. You all need the forgiveness of sins because you all still do not know what true sin is, let alone that you ought to repent of it or avoid it. You are no good. You are full of unbelief, stupidity, and ignorance regarding God and his will. Because God is present here, we all must receive grace upon grace from his fullness,[123] and no human being can be justified before God without it. Therefore, if you want to repent, then repent in the right way. Your penance does not do it. You are hypocrites who think you do not need repentance.[124] You are a brood of vipers.[125] Who assured you that you will escape the wrath to come?" etc.[126]

[33]St. Paul also preaches this way in Romans 3[:10-12] and says, "No one has understanding." "No one is righteous." "No one seeks God." "No one does good, not even one. They have become worthless and forsaken." [34]Also, Acts 17[:30]: "But now God commands all people everywhere to repent." He says, "all people"—no single human being is excluded. [35]This repentance teaches us to recognize sin; that is, we are all lost. Neither hide nor hair of us is good and we must become absolutely new people.

[36]This repentance is neither incomplete and partial, like that which does penance for actual sins, nor is it uncertain. It does not deliberate over what is a sin or what is not a sin. Instead, it simply lumps everything together[127] and

---

121. The Latin translation: "and hypocrites."

122. Matt. 3:2. Regarding the fiery angel, see Mal. 3:1 and M. Henschel, "'Der feurige Engel S. Johannes': Zu einer Stelle in Luthers Schmalkaldischen Artikeln," *Lutherjahrbuch* 31 (1964): 76. See also Matt. 11:10 and SA III, 3, 2.

123. John 1:16.

124. In the last two sentences, Luther makes a wordplay with *Busse*, using it to mean both "penance" and "repentance."

125. Matt. 3:7.

126. Matt. 3:7; Luke 3:7.

127. Luther uses an idiom, "*stosst alles in Haufen.*"

says, "Everything is pure sin with us." What is it that we would want to spend so much time searching, dissecting, or distinguishing? Therefore, here as well, remorse is not uncertain, because there remains nothing that we would like to consider as a possession that could pay for sin. Rather, there is plain, certain despair about all that we are, think, say, or do, etc.

[37]Similarly, such confession also cannot be false, uncertain, or partial. Whoever confesses that "everything is pure sin with them"[128] bring together all sins and allow no exceptions. None are forgotten. [38]Thus satisfaction is also not uncertain. It is not our uncertain, sinful work but rather the suffering and blood of the innocent "Lamb of God, who takes away the sin of the world."[129]

[39]John preached about this repentance and, after him, Christ in the Gospels, and we also. With this repentance, we knock to the ground the pope and everything that is built upon our good works, because it is all built upon a rotten, flimsy basis: good works or law. There are no good works, only purely evil works. No one keeps the law (as Christ says in John 7[:19]), but all transgress it. Therefore the structure is merely false lies and hypocrisy, even when it is most holy and at its best.

[40]This repentance endures among Christians until death because it confesses the sin that remains in the flesh throughout life.[130] As St. Paul bears witness in Romans 7[:23], he wars with the law in his members, etc., and he does this not by using his own powers but with the gift of the Holy Spirit which follows the forgiveness of sins.[131] This same gift daily cleanses and expels the sins that remain and works to make people truly pure and holy.[132]

[41]The pope, theologians, lawyers, and all human beings know nothing about this. Rather, it is a doctrine from heaven, revealed through the gospel, and the godless saints are forced to call it heresy.

[42]Some fanatical spirits might come again. (Perhaps some already are at hand, just as I saw for myself at the time of the disturbance.)[133] They maintained that, if any who once receive the Spirit or the forgiveness of sin or become a believer, might sin after that, then such sin would not hurt those who

---

128. SA III, 3, 36.

129. John 1:29. See also SA II, 1, 2.

130. FCSD 2, 34–35.

131. Rom. 8:2.

132. Cf. SC IV, 12; FCSD 2, 33–34.

133. Luther's view of the "spirits" and "enthusiasts" was colored by the disturbances at Wittenberg in the early 1520s, led by Andreas von Karlstadt and "the Zwickau prophets," Thomas Münzer and the Peasants' War [1525], and "The Kingdom of God" at Münster [1534–35].

continue to remain in faith. They shout, "Do what you will! If you believe, then nothing matters. Faith eradicates all sin," etc. They say, in addition, that if someone sins after receiving faith and the Spirit, then that person never really had the Spirit and faith. I have seen many such people and I am concerned that such a devil is still in some.

[43]Therefore it is necessary to know and teach that when holy people somehow fall into a public sin (such as David, who fell into adultery, murder, and blasphemy against God), then faith and the Spirit have left (this sets aside the fact that they still have and feel original sin and also daily repent of it and struggle against it). The Holy Spirit does not allow sin to rule and dominate so that a person acts on it, but the Spirit controls and resists, so that sin is not able to do what it wants. However, if sin does what it wants, then the Holy Spirit and faith are not there. As John says (1 John 3:9; 5:18): "Those who have been born of God do not sin and cannot sin." And it is still the truth (as the same St. John writes [1:8]): "If we say we have no sin, we deceive ourselves, and the truth of God is not in us." [134]

[Article 4:] On the Gospel [135]

We now want to return to the gospel, which gives more than just one kind of counsel and help against sin, because God is overwhelmingly rich in his grace: first, through the spoken word, in which the forgiveness of sins is preached to the whole world (which is the particular office of the gospel); second, through Baptism; third, through the Holy Sacrament of the Altar; fourth, through the power of the keys and also the mutual conversation and consolation of the brothers and sisters. [136] Matthew 18[:20]: "Where two or three are gathered," etc. [137]

---

134. SA III, 3, 42–45 was added to the text by Luther as he prepared the document for publication in 1538. The emphasis here would seem to be directed against John Agricola and the "antinomians," who taught that the law did not apply to Christians. There was a heated controversy over this issue among the Wittenberg theologians in the middle and late 1530s. These paragraphs were not part of the document Agricola subscribed in December of 1536. Cf. *Die Schmalkaldischen Artikel*, 1537, 1538 (*WA* 50:239f.); Zangemeister, *Die Schmalkaldischen Artikel*, 65f.

135. From this point forward, because of an apparent heart attack, Luther was forced to dictate the rest of SA. Caspar Cruciger recorded SA III, 4–9 and 13–15. Another, unknown secretary recorded SA III, 10–12. R. Wetzel, "Casper Cruciger als ein Schreiber der 'Schmalkaldischen Artikel,'" *Lutherjahrbuch* 54 (1987), 92.

136. Luther uses a Latin phrase: *per mutuum colloquium et consolationem fratrum.* The origin of this formula is obscure.

137. Luther wrote: "Where two are gathered."

[Article 5:] On Baptism

[1]Baptism is nothing other than the word of God in water, commanded by God's institution, or, as Paul says, "washing in the word."[138] Moreover, Augustine says, "When the word has been added to the element it makes a sacrament."[139] [2]Therefore we do not agree with Thomas[140] and the Dominicans who forget the word (God's institution) and say that God has placed a spiritual power in the water which, through the water, washes away sin. [3]We also do not agree with Scotus[141] and the Franciscans who teach that baptism washes away sin through the assistance of the divine will, that this washing takes place only through God's will, and this is not at all through the word and the water.

On the Baptism of Children

[4]We maintain that we should baptize children because they also belong to the promised redemption which was accomplished through Christ.[142] The church ought to extend it to them.

[Article 6:] On the Sacrament of the Altar

[1]We maintain that the bread and the wine in the supper are the true body and blood of Christ[143] and they are extended to and received not only by pious but also by evil Christians.[144]

[2]And one should not give only one form of the sacrament. And we do not need the lofty science that was taught to us, that as much is given in one form as is given in both. This is how the sophists and the Council of Constance teach.[145] [3]Even if it were true that as much is given with one as with both,

---

138. Luther quotes a Latin version of Eph. 5:26: *lavacrum in verbo.*

139. *Tractate 80,* on John 3 (MSL 35, 1840). Augustine's actual words were, "When the word is added to the element it makes a sacrament." Luther referred to this statement in other contexts: LC IV, 18; LC V, 10. Cf. also *Luther, Aufzeichnung über Augustins Worte: "Accedat verbum ad elementum et fit sacramentum,"* no date (*WABr* 12:399–401).

140. Thomas Aquinas, *Summa theologiae,* III, Question 62, Article 4.

141. John Duns Scotus (d. 1308), *Commentary on the Sentences* IV, Distinction 1, Question 2.

142. Matt. 19:14.

143. In Luther's rough draft of his original manuscript, he had first written, "We maintain that under the bread and the wine in the supper there is the body and blood of Christ." WC reads, "with the bread and wine the body and blood of Christ are truly and substantially present, offered and received. . . . The bread is the body of Christ." AC 10, 1; *WA* 50, 242.

144. WC reads, "the unworthy also eat, so they hold that the body and blood of the Lord are truly extended also to the unworthy, and that the unworthy receive, where the words and institution of Christ are retained." *BSLK,* 451 n. 1.

145. *WA* 39¹:13–38.

one kind is still not the complete order and institution as founded and commanded by Christ. [4]Especially do we condemn and curse, in God's name,
those who not only allow distribution in both forms to be omitted but also
haughtily prohibit, condemn, and slander both forms as heresy. Thus they set
themselves against and above Christ, our Lord and God, etc.

[5]We have absolutely no regard for the subtle sophistry[146] concerning
transubstantiation. They teach that bread and wine leave or lose their natural
substances and only the form and color of the bread remain, but is no longer
real bread. It is closest to Scripture to say that bread is and remains there, as
St. Paul himself indicates: "The bread that we break" and "Eat of the bread." [147]

[Article 7:] On the Keys

[1]The keys are an office and authority given to the church by Christ[148] to bind
and loose sins. These are not only the rude and well-known sins but also the
subtle, secret ones that only God knows. As it is written, "But who can detect
one's own errors?" [149] And Paul himself complains in Romans 7[:23] that he
served, with his flesh, the "law of sin." [2]It is not within our power, but it
is God's alone, to judge which, how great, and how many sins there are. As it
is written: "Do not enter into judgment with your servant, for no one living is
righteous before you." [150] And Paul also says in 1 Corinthians 4[:4]: "I am not
aware of anything against myself, but I am not thereby acquitted."

[Article 8:] On Confession

[1]Because absolution or the power of the keys is a comfort and help against
sin and a bad conscience, and was instituted by Christ in the Gospel,[151] confession and absolution should by no means be allowed to fall into disuse in the
church—especially for the sake of weak consciences and young, immature
people who are being examined and instructed in Christian doctrine.

[2]The enumeration of sins, however, ought to be free for each individual
with respect to what each one wants or does not want to enumerate. As long
as we are in the flesh we will not lie if we say, "I am a poor person, full of
sin." [152] Romans 7[:23] puts it this way: "I feel in my members another law."

---

146. In 1520, Luther called transubstantiation an "illusion of St. Thomas and the pope" (*The
Babylonian Captivity of the Church*, WA 6:456$_{36}$; *LW* 44:199).

147. 1 Cor. 10:16; 11:28.

148. Matt. 16:19; 18:18.

149. Ps. 19:12.

150. Ps. 143:2.

151. Matt. 16:19.

152. 2 Esdras 7:68.

Because private absolution[153] is derived from the office of the keys, we should not neglect it but hold it in high esteem and worth, just as all the other offices of the Christian church.

[3]In these things, which concern the spoken, external word, it is certain to maintain this: God gives no one his Spirit or grace apart from the external word which goes before. We are thus protected from the enthusiasts, that is, the spirits, who boast that they have the Spirit apart from and before contact with the word. They judge the Scriptures or the word accordingly, interpreting and stretching them however it pleases them. Münzer did this, and there are still many who do this today. They want to be shrewd judges between the spirit and the letter, but they do not know what they say or teach.[154] [4]The papacy is also pure enthusiasm. The pope boasts that "all laws are in the shrine of his heart"[155] and that what he decides and judges in his churches is supposed to be spirit and law—as if it is equal to or above the Scriptures or the spoken word.[156] [5]All of this is the old devil and old snake which also made Adam and Eve into enthusiasts. The devil led them from the external word of God to "spirituality" and their own presumption—and even this was still accomplished by means of other, external words. [6]Similarly, our enthusiasts also condemn the external word, but they themselves still do not keep silent. They chatter and write so as to fill the world—as if the Spirit could not come through the Scriptures or the spoken word of the apostles. But the Spirit must come through their writings and words. Why do they not abstain from their preaching and writing until the Spirit himself comes into the people apart from and in advance of their writings? They boast that the Spirit has come into them without the preaching of the Scriptures. There is no time here to debate these matters more extensively. We have dealt with them sufficiently elsewhere.

[7]Also, both those who believe prior to baptism and those who receive faith in baptism have it through the external word which goes before. Adults who have reached the age of reason must have already heard, "Whoever believes and is baptized will be saved,"[157] even though they were at first without faith and after ten years received the Spirit and baptism. [8]In Acts 10[:1ff.], Cornelius had for a long time heard from the Jews about a future Messiah, through whom he would be justified before God. His prayers and alms were

---

153. Luther uses a Latin phrase: *absolutio privata.*

154. AC 5, 4.

155. *Corpus juris canonici,* Book VI, I, 2, c. 1.

156. Tr 6.

157. Mark 16:16.

acceptable in such faith (Luke calls him "righteous and God-fearing [10:2, 22]), and not without such a preceding word or hearing could there be faith or righteousness. But St. Peter had to reveal to him that the Messiah (on whose future coming he had, until then, believed) now had come. His faith in the future Messiah ought not hold him captive along with the hardened,[158] unbelieving Jews, but he ought to know that he now needs to be saved by the present Messiah and not, like the Jews, deny or persecute him.

[9]In summary: enthusiasm is implanted in Adam and his children, from the beginning to the end of the world. It is given to them and they are poisoned by the old dragon. It is the origin of the power and might of all the heresies, even that of the papacy and Mohammed. [10] Therefore we should and must insist that God does not want to deal with us human beings, except by means of his external word and sacrament. Everything that is attributed to the Spirit apart from such a word and sacrament is of the devil. [11]Also, God wanted to appear to Moses first in the burning bush and by means of the spoken word.[159] No prophet, neither Elijah nor Elisha, received the Spirit apart from or without the Ten Commandments. [12]John the Baptist was not conceived without Gabriel's preceding word,[160] and he did not leap in his mother's womb without Mary's voice.[161] [13]St. Peter says: the prophets did not prophesy "by human will" but "by the Holy Spirit" as "holy people of God."[162] Without the external word, they were not holy and much less would the Holy Spirit have moved them to speak while they were still unholy. Peter says they were holy when the Holy Spirit speaks through them.

[Article 9:] On Excommunication

We maintain that the "great" excommunication, as the pope calls it, is a purely secular penalty and does not touch us who are servants of the church. However, the "small" (that is, the truly Christian) excommunication is that we should not allow public, obstinate sinners to come to the sacrament or other assemblies of the church until they correct themselves and avoid sin. The preachers should not mix civil punishments together with this spiritual penalty or excommunication.[163]

158. Exod. 4:21; 7:13; 10:20; 11:10; 14:4.

159. Exod. 3:2ff.

160. Luke 1:13-20.

161. Luke 1:41-44.

162. 2 Peter 1:21.

163. The *excomunicatio major* excluded a person from both the church and political communities, while the *excommunicatio minor* restricted a person only from the sacrament. The biblical foundation for excommunication was found in Matt. 18:15ff.

[Article 10:] On Ordination and Vocation

[1]If the bishops want to be true bishops and embrace the church and the gospel, then, for the sake of love and unity (and not out of necessity), we might allow them to ordain and confirm us and our preachers—if all the pretense and fraud of unchristian ceremony and pomp are set aside. However, they are not and do not want to be true bishops. [2]Rather, they are political lords and princes who do not want to pay attention to preaching, teaching, baptizing, communing, or any proper work or office of the church. In addition, they drive out, persecute, and condemn those who are called to such an office. Still, the church must not remain without servants on their account.[164]

[3]Therefore, as the ancient examples of the church and the fathers teach us, we want to and should ourselves ordain suitable persons to such an office. They have not been able to forbid or prevent us, even in accordance with their own laws, because their laws say that those who are ordained by heretics should be regarded as ordained and remain ordained.[165] Similarly, St. Jerome wrote about the church at Alexandria that it had originally been ruled by the priests and preachers together, without bishops.[166]

[Article 11:] On the Marriage of Priests

[1]The bishops have forbidden marriage and burdened the godly estate of priests with perpetual celibacy—and they have had neither the authority nor the right. Rather, they have dealt with it like anti-Christian, tyrannical, wicked rascals. With this, they have given the occasion for all kinds of horrible, enormous, innumerable sins of unchastity. They are still stuck in these things. [2]Now, they have as much power to make a young woman out of a young man or to make a young man out of a young woman as they do to abolish sexual distinctions altogether. They have also had little power to separate or inhibit such creatures of God so that they should not honestly and conjugally live with one another. [3]Therefore we do not want to comply with their mis-

---

164. FCSD, 10, 19.

165. Gratian, *Decretum,* Part I, dist. 68, chap. 1; Part III, dist. 4, chap. 107. Cochläus writes: "Luther says too much when he says, 'those who are ordained by heretics should be regarded as ordained and remain ordained,' according to our papal laws. That only applies to those heretics who ordain according to the order and usage of the church, as the Arians, Donatists, Pelagians, etc., did. They used the churchly form of consecration. Their children, who were baptized by them need not be baptized again. Similarly, their priests and deacons, who were ordained by consecrated bishops, do not have to be reordained. However, Luther will never show, either from St. Jerome or from papal law, that we should consider the mockery of a bishop's ordination by Luther or Bugenhagen (performed without oil or charism, against the order of the Christian church and without properly ordained bishops in attendance) a real ordination" (*CC,* 48).

166. SA II, 4, 9.

erable singleness. We do not tolerate it. We maintain that marriage is free, as God ordered and founded it. We do not want to disrupt or inhibit God's work. St. Paul says it would be "a teaching of demons."[167]

[Article 12:] On the Church

[1]We do not acknowledge to them that they are the church, and they are not the church.[168] [2]We do not want to hear what they command or forbid in the name of the church, because, God be praised, a seven-year-old child[169] knows what the church is: holy believers and "little sheep who hear the voice of their shepherd."[170] [3]This is why children pray in this way, "I believe in one holy Christian church."[171] This holiness does not exist in surplices, shaved heads, long albs, and their other ceremonies they have devised over and above the Holy Scriptures. Its holiness exists in the word of God and true faith.

[Article 13:] On Being Justified before God and on Good Works[172]

[1]I have no idea how to change what I have consistently taught about this until now, namely, that we receive a different, new, clean heart through faith (as St. Peter says).[173] God wants to regard and does regard us as completely righteous and holy, for the sake of Christ our mediator. Although sin in the flesh is still not completely gone or dead, God will still not count it or consider it.

[2]After such faith, renewal, and forgiveness of sin, good works follow, and whatever in these works is still sinful or imperfect should not be even counted as sin or imperfection, for the sake of Christ. The human being should be called and should be completely righteous and holy, according to both the person and his or her works from the pure grace and mercy that have been poured and spread over us in Christ. [3]Therefore we cannot boast about the great merit of our works, where they are viewed without grace and mercy. Rather, as it is written, "Let the one who boasts, boast in the Lord."[174] [4]If

---

167. 1 Tim. 4:1.

168. Luther called the pope "a damned heretic and schismatic" in D. M. Luthers Appellation an ein christlich frei Concilium verneuert, 1520 (WA 7:89).

169. Seven was the earliest age of discernment (WA 51:524 n. 6).

170. John 10:3. FCSD 10, 19.

171. The Latin translation: "I believe in the holy Catholic or Christian church." Luther quotes from a German translation of the creed that had been in use in Germany since the fifteenth century. TCS I, 3; TCS II, 3; AC 6 and 7; SC II, 3; LC II, 3.

172. LC II, 47–50.

173. Acts 15:9.

174. 1 Cor. 1:31; 2 Cor. 10:17.

one has a gracious God, then everything is good. Furthermore, we say also that if good works do not follow, then the faith is false and not true.

[Article 14:] On Monastic Vows

[1]Because monastic vows are in direct conflict against the first and chief article, they should simply be done away with. Christ spoke in Matthew 24[:5] about those who say, "I am Christ," etc. [2]Those who vow to live a monastic life believe that they lead a better life than common Christians, and through their works intend to help not only themselves but others to get to heaven. [3]This is known as denying Christ, etc. They boast, on the basis of St. Thomas, that monastic vows are equal to baptism. This is blasphemy against God.[175]

[Article 15:] On Human Regulations

[1]The papists say that human regulations effect the forgiveness of sins or merit salvation. That is unchristian and damnable. As Christ says, "In vain do they worship me, teaching human precepts as doctrines."[176] Also, the letter to Titus [1:14]: "those who reject the truth." [2]Furthermore, it is not right when they say that it is a mortal sin to break such human regulations.[177]

[3]These are the articles on which I must stand and on which I intend to stand, God willing, until my death. I know of nothing in them that can be changed or conceded. If anyone does so, it is on that person's conscience.[178]

[4]Finally, the papal bag of tricks is still filled with foolish, childish things such as the consecration of churches, baptizing bells, baptizing altar stones, and inviting the donors who give money for these things to the rites. This baptizing is a mockery and an effrontery to Holy Baptism. We ought not tolerate it.

[5]Moreover, there is the consecration of candles, palms, spices, oats,

---

175. The last sentence of SA III, 14 was written into the text of the original manuscript by Luther himself, presumably when he reviewed his dictation of SA III, 4 to SA III, 15 (*UuA*, 68).

176. Matt. 15:9.

177. Cochläus writes, "Whoever breaks these traditions out of wickedness, with contempt for the priests and bishops, and leads the weak and simple into defiance and scandal (as Luther's followers do daily—eating meat and breaking fasts, etc.), without doubt commit a serious mortal sin" (*CC*, 57).

178. SA III, 15, 3 is out of place here. Perhaps Luther meant them to be part of an extended subscription, but these words were separated from his signature. Both the original 1538 publication of SA and the 1580 *Book of Concord* suggested a break in Luther's train of thought here when they began this paragraph with an ornamental initial.

cakes, etc.[179] Nevertheless, this cannot be called or be consecration. Rather, this is pure mockery and deception. For such innumerable magic tricks, we commend them to their God and to themselves until they become tired of them. We intend to be unmolested with these things.

Subscriptions to the Schmalkald Articles

Dr. Martin Luther subscribes

Dr. Justus Jonas, rector, subscribes with his own hand

Dr. John Bugenhagen, Pomeranian, subscribes

Dr. Caspar Cruciger subscribes

Nicholas Amsdorf of Magdeburg subscribes

George Spalatin of Altenburg subscribes

I, Philip Melanthon,[180] also regard the above articles as true and Christian. About the pope, however, I maintain that if he would allow the gospel, we might allow to him his superiority over the bishops which he has "by human right." We could make this concession for the sake of peace and general unity among those Christians who are now under him and might be in the future.

John Agricola of Eisleben subscribes[181]

Gabriel Didymus subscribes[182]

I, Dr. Urban Rhegius, superintendent of the churches in the Duchy of Lüneburg, subscribe for myself and in the name of my brothers and in the name of the church of Hanover

I, Stephen Agricola, as minister to the Elector, subscribe

And I, John Draconites, professor and minister of Marburg, subscribe

I, Conrad Figenbotz, subscribe to the glory of God that I have believed and I preach and I believe firmly as above

I, Andreas Osiander, minister of Nürnberg, subscribe

Master Veit Dietrich, minister of Nürnberg

---

179. On Holy Saturday, the "old fire" was extinguished in the church, the "new fire" was lit and sprinkled with holy water. At the Easter Vigil, the Easter candle was consecrated and lit from this "new fire." On Candlemass (February 2), candles were consecrated. On Palm Sunday, palms were consecrated. On the Assumption of Mary (August 15), herbs, flowers, ears of corn, honey, grape-vines, etc., were consecrated. On St. Stephen's Day (December 26), oats were consecrated. On Easter Sunday, unleavened Easter cakes were consecrated. *BSLK,* 462 n. 8.

180. Melanchthon began using "Melanthon" in 1531 (Heinz Scheible, "Luther and Melanchthon," *LQ* 4, 3 [Autumn 1990]: 330f.).

181. The first eight subscriptions to SA were obtained at a gathering of theologians at Wittenberg, in December 1536.

182. Didymus signed SA in January 1537.

I, Erhard Schnepf, preacher of Stuttgart, subscribe

Conrad Oettinger of Pforzheim, preacher of Duke Ulrich

Simon Schneeweiss, servant of the church in Crailsheim

I, John Schlagenhaufen, pastor of the church of Köthen, subscribe

Master George Helt of Forchheim

Master Adam of Fulda, preacher of Hesse

Master Anton Corvinus

I, John Bugenhagen, subscribe again, in the name of Master John Brenz, who, when leaving Schmalkalden, directed me to do both orally and in a letter, which was shown to these brothers who have subscribed [Luther's articles][183]

I, Dionysius Melander, subscribe to the Augsburg Confession, the Apology to the Augsburg Confession, and the Wittenberg Concord on the subject of the Eucharist

Paul Rhodius, superintendent of Stettin

Gerard Oemcken, superintendent of the church of Minden

I, Brixius Northanus, minister of the church of Christ which is at Soest, subscribe the articles of the Reverend Father Martin Luther and acknowledge that I have believed and taught likewise and, by the Spirit of Christ, will likewise believe and teach

Michael Caelius, preacher of Mansfeld, subscribes

Master Peter Geltner, preacher of Frankfurt, subscribes

Wendal Faber, pastor of Seeburg in Mansfeld

I, John Aepinus, subscribe[184]

---

183. Brenz's note to Bugenhagen reads: "I have read, and again and again, the Confession and Apology presented at Augsburg by the Most Illustrious Prince, the Elector of Saxony, and by the other princes and estates of the Roman Empire, to his Imperial Majesty. I have also read the Formula of Concord concerning the sacrament, made at Wittenberg with Dr. Bucer and others. I have also read the articles written at the Assembly at Schmalkalden in the German language by Dr. Martin Luther, our most revered preceptor, and the tract concerning the Papacy and the Power and Jurisdiction of Bishops. And, according to my mediocrity, I judge that all these agree with Holy Scripture, and with the belief of the true and lawful Catholic Church. But although in so great a number of most learned men who have now assembled at Schmalkalden I acknowledge that I am the least of all, yet as I am not permitted to await the end of the assembly, I ask you, most renowned man, Dr. John Bugenhagen, most revered Father in Christ, that your courtesy may add my name, if it be necessary, to all that I have above mentioned. For I testify in this my own handwriting that I thus hold, confess and constantly will teach, through Jesus Christ, our Lord. Done at Schmalkalden, Feb. 23, 1537" (*BSLK*, 466).

184. Aepinus (d. 1553) had originally subscribed SA thus: "John Apins of Hamburg subscribes. Concerning the superiority of the pontiff, we agree with all the representatives from Hamburg and assent to the sentences of Reverend Philip which were added at the end." He then reconsidered and signed without reservation (*UuA*, 126 [*WA* 50:254 n. 18]).

Likewise, I, John Amsterdam of Bremen

I, Fredrick Myconius, pastor of the church of Gotha in Thuringia, subscribe for myself and in the name of Justus Menius of Eisenach

I, John Lang, doctor and convener of the church of Erfurt, in my name
and on behalf of my coworkers in the gospel, namely,[185]

The Rev. Licentiate Ludwig Platz of Melsungen

The Rev. Master Sigismund Kirchner

The Rev. Wolfgang Kiswetter

The Rev. Melchior Weittmann

The Rev. John Thall

The Rev. John Kilian

The Rev. Nicholas Faber

I, The Rev. Andrew Menser, subscribe in my own hand

And I, Egidius Melcher, have subscribed with my own hand

185. The final ten subscriptions were obtained in March 1537, when Luther and his entourage
stopped in Erfurt on their way back to Wittenberg from Schmalkalden (*UuA*, 137 n. 1).

Appendix B

Names and Terms

Agricola, John (d. 1566). Teacher at the University of Wittenberg from 1519 (the same year he served as Luther's secretary at the Leipzig debate with John Eck). He began to speak publicly against the use of law in the church in the late 1520s. Agricola became a chief protagonist in the "antinomian controversy" at Wittenberg in the mid-1530s. He fell out of favor with both Melanchthon and Luther and went to Berlin as court preacher for the Elector of Bradenburg. He was the main Protestant architect of the Augsburg Interim.

All Saints' Day, November 1. Remembrance day for the dead, dating back to the tenth century. *WA* 30[II]:252, 260 n. 38; *Exhortation to All Clergy Assembled at Augsburg*, 1530 (*WA* 30[II]:351$_{20}$; *LW* 34:57).

Amsdorf, Nicolaus von (d. 1565). A student and, later, a professor at the University of Wittenberg. Von Amsdorf, a close friend of Luther, was with the reformer at Leipzig in 1519 and at Worms in 1521. Luther ordained him Bishop of Naumburg in 1543. After Luther's death, von Amsdorf saw himself as a defender of orthodox Lutheran teaching, most notably against George Major's assertion that "good works are necessary for salvation."

antichrist/anti-Christian (German: *Endechrist/lich*). In 1522 (Advent Postil, *WA* 10[I,2]:47), Luther had publicly expressed his dissatisfaction with *Endechrist* as the inherited, popular German translation of the Latin *Antichristus*. He preferred *Widerchrist*. In SA, however, Luther returned to *Endechrist* as all references to the antichrist, except in SA II, 4, 10. SA II, 2, 25; SA II, 4, 10, 14; SA III, 11, 1; *Brief Confession concerning the Holy Sacrament* (*LW* 38:310). Luther often pointed to the money matters of the Roman church as evidence of the anti-Christian nature of the papacy. E.g., *On the Papacy in Rome, Against the Most Celebrated Romanist in Leipzig*, 1520 (*WA* 6:289; *LW* 39:60); *To the Christian Nobility of the German Nation concerning the Reform of the Christian Estate*, 1520 (*WA* 6:416; *LW* 44:141); *Einer aus den hohen Artikeln des päpstlichen Glaubens*, 1537 (*WA* 50:80$_{17f.}$); *Luthers Vorrede über den Propheten Daniel*, 1541 (*WADB* 11[II]:100$_{10f.}$).

article(s). The traditional translation of *Artikel* into English, when used with respect to SA. This translation, although obvious and understandable, does not completely capture the force of what Luther is trying to communicate. The articles in the Lutheran confessional writings are not a series of encyclopedia or newspaper "articles" about the Christian faith. Other possible translations of *Artikel* are "basics," "things," "staples," "essentials," "properties," "goods," "inventory," etc. With this in mind, however, the traditional rendering of *Artikel* as "Article" is retained throughout the text.

Augustine of Hippo (d. 430). One of the most influential thinkers in Christian history. As bishop of the North African town of Hippo, Augustine synthesized Neoplatonic categories with the Scriptures and thus set the trajectory of Christian theology for at least the next thousand years. His most seminal works are *The City of God, The Confessions,* and *The Trinity.*

Bernard of Clairvaux (d. 1153). Abbot of the Cistercian monastery at Clairvaux, France, in the first half of the twelfth century. A noted preacher and hymn writer, Bernard played a decisive role in shaping the popular piety of his day.

Bugenhagen, John (d. 1558). A native of Wollin, Pomerania; sometimes referred to as Pomeranus or Pomer. He came to Wittenberg in 1521, and after a decade as pastor of the City Church, he began to lecture at the university, in the theological faculty. Bugenhagen collaborated with Luther in translating the Bible and contributed greatly to the organization of Protestant churches of northern Germany and Denmark.

bull, papal (German: *Bullen*). Papal decrees at the time were sealed with leaden fasteners (in Latin, *Bulla*) and were known popularly as "bulls." SA II, 4, 4.

Campegio, Lorenzo (d. 1539). Papal legate at the Diet of Augsburg in 1530.

canons, cathedral, and foundation (German: *Tumherrn*). Associations of secular priests and associations of women, connected to a cathedral or collegiate church. The women lived under a rule, but did not take perpetual vows as did nuns. The chapter schools were taught by the canons: men taught the boys and women taught the girls. See A. Werminghoff, *Verfassungsgeschichte der deutschen Kirche im Mittelalter* (2nd ed., 1913), 143–52, 190f. SA, Preface, 10.

chief- (German: *Häupt-/Haupt-*). A technical term that Luther uses regularly in SA. His various usages of this word (particularly the use of the prefix *Häupt,* in compounds) indicates a particular item of significance for Luther. *Häupt* is translated as "head" or "chief." ACAp IV, 2; SA, Preface, 13, 14; SA II, 2, 1, 7, 12, 25; SA II, 3, 2; SA II, 4, 3.

Cochläus, John (d. 1552). One of Luther's most ardent Roman Catholic controversialists. He wrote a point-by-point rebuttal to SA already in 1538. He referred to the numerous good reasons for the pope to postpone the council—not the least of which was the poor response by German prelates (*CC*, 61f.). See SA II, 4, 4.

Common Week, the. The seven-day period following St. Michael's Day (September 29) when numerous masses were said on behalf of the dead. *WA* 30^{II}:252, 260 n. 37; *Exhortation to All Clergy Assembled at Augsburg*, 1530 (*WA* 30^{II}:351$_{16}$; *LW* 34:56). See SA II, 2, 12.

Constance, Council of. A general council of the church, which met in the southern German city of Constance from 1414 to 1418. This council defined the sacramental doctrine of concomitance, burned John Hus at the stake, and ended the "great schism" of the Western church. SA III, 6, 2; *Vorrede zu Tres epistolae Ioannis Hussii*, 1536 (*WA* 50:16–19); *WATR* 3:3502, 3542; *Against the Roman Papacy, an Institution of the Devil*, 1545, (*WA* 54:208–10; *LW* 41:265–69).

correct(ly) (German: *gerecht/recht*). In SA, and more generally in both medieval and modern German, *Recht(en)*, as adjective, noun, and adverb, has a variety of meanings. Other possible translations are "right, righteousness, privilege, power, reason, dominance, justice, justify, law, claim, title, truth, legitimacy, authority, administration of justice," etc. See SA, Preface, 2, 10, 12; II, 1, 3; II, 4, 10, 14; III, 3, 2, 3, 9, 10, 12, 18, 27, 30, 32, 40, 42; III, 6, 5; III, 8, 4; III, 9; III, 10, 1, 3; III, 11, 1; III, 13, title, 1, 2, 4; III, 15, 2; Subscription #7.

Cruciger, Caspar (Creutziger) (d. 1548). Served as pastor of the Wittenberg castle church and professor of theology before becoming rector of the university in 1533. Cruciger assisted Luther in his translation of the Bible and participated in important theological debates and conferences. He took the ailing Luther's dictation of SA III, 4 to SA III, 11 and recorded many of Luther's famous "Table Talks." He was instrumental in reforming Leipzig in 1539, and he recorded Luther's dictation of SA III, 4.

Didymus, Gabriel (d. 1558). A former Augustinian monk who was pastor at the Electoral residence of Torgau; signed SA in January 1537. He was not present at Schmalkalden.

Dietrich, Veit (d. 1549). Was converted to Lutheranism in the early 1520s and became Luther's private secretary in 1527, accompanying the reformer to Marburg in 1529 and to the Coburg castle in 1530. Dietrich was a pastor in Nürnberg from 1535 until his death.

divine right, by (Latin: *jure divino*). A technical phrase in the medieval church used to underscore the divine institution and legitimacy of various church structures and practices. This phrase is used in distinction to "by human right" (*jure humano*). In *Disputatio I. Eccii et M. Lutheri Lipsiae habita*, 1519 (*WA* 2:279$_{23f.}$), Luther wrote about "the Holy Scriptures, which are

properly the *jus divinum.*" SA II, 4, 1, 7, 13 and Melanchthon's subscription
to SA.

dominance (German: *gerecht/recht*). In SA, and more generally in both medieval and modern German, *Recht(en)*, as adjective, noun, and adverb, has
a variety of meanings. Other possible translations are "right, correctness,
righteousness, privilege, power, reason, justice, justify, law, claim, title,
truth, legitimacy, authority, administration of justice," etc. SA, Preface, 2,
10, 12; II, 1, 3; II, 4, 10, 14; III, 3, 2, 3, 9.

Dominicans (German: *Predigermönchen*). Literally, the "preacher monks." The
Dominicans are known as the Order of the Preachers. SA III, 5, 2.

enthusiasts (German: *Enthusiasten*). Luther tended to lump the so-called radical Reformation or left-wing Reformation together under such labels.
Other favorite terms of derision Luther used to vilify these Protestant opponents were "fanatics" (German: *Schwärmer*) and "fanatical spirits" (German: *Rottengeister*). SA III, 3, 42; SA, II, 2, 11; III, 8, 3, 5, 9; Luther said
this in his 1539 tract *On the Councils and the Church:* "Münzer called us
Wittenberg theologians 'scholars of the book' (*Schriftgelehrten*) and himself a 'scholar of the spirit' (*Geistgelehrten*), and after him, many other follow his lead" (*WA* 50:646$_{33f.}$; *LW* 41:170); also, *Against the Heavenly Prophets in the Matter of Images and Sacraments*, 1525 (*WA* 18:136–39; *LW*
40:146–49); Luther's sermon on Pentecost, 1544 (*WA* 21:468f.); *Predigt am
2. Adventsonntag, nachmittags*, December 10, 1531 (*WA* 34^{II}:487$_{2f.}$); *Commentary on I Corinthians 15*, 1532 (*WA* 36:491, 499–506; *LW* 28:67, 75–82);
Freder, Dialogus dem Ehestand zu Ehren, 1545 (*WA* 54:173$_{5–7}$); Letter from
Luther to Spalatin, April 12, 1522 (*WABr* 2:493); Letter from Thomas
Münzer to Luther, July 9, 1523 (*WA* 3:104–6); Letter from Luther to
Spalatin, August 3, 1523 (*WABr* 3:120); Letter from Luther to John Briess-
mann, July 4, 1524 (*WABr* 3:315); *On War against the Turk*, 1529 (*WA*
30^{II}:107$_{18}$ [and n. 3]; *LW* 46:161). Heiko Oberman, *Luther: Man between
God and the Devil* (New Haven: Yale University Press, 1989), 292.

estates (German: *Ständ(en)*). *See* orders (of creation).

excrement (German: *Geschmeiss*). See Luther's Sermon on Matthew 21:14ff.,
February 13, 1538 (*WA* 47:404$_{12}$) and *Brief Confession concerning the Holy
Sacrament*, 1544 (*WA* 54:160$_{27}$; *LW* 38:310). SA II, 2, 11.

fanatical spirits (German: *Rottengeister*). Luther tended to lump the so-called
radical Reformation or left-wing Reformation together under such labels.
Other favorite terms of derision Luther used to vilify these Protestant opponents were "fanatics" (German: *Schwärmer*) and "enthusiasts" (German:
Enthusiasten). SA II, 2, 11; SA III, 3, 42; SA III, 8, 5, 6, 9. *See* enthusiasts.

foolishness/foolish activities (German: *Närrenswerk/Narrenswerk*). SA, Preface, 13; SA II, 4, 14; SA III, 15, 4.

Franciscans (German: *Barfussenmönchen*). Literally, the "barefoot monks." The Order of Friars Minor was known for its vow of poverty that could include a prohibition on owning shoes. SA III, 5, 3.

fraternities (German: *Bruderschaften*). In the eighth century, monasteries began to form "societies" within themselves that were obligated to pray for and perform works of piety on behalf of deceased brothers. In the late medieval period, societies arose that were based in parishes (either groups of clergy, lay and clergy together, or groups of lay people), which were designed to fulfill religious obligations. Concerning Luther's opinion of these societies, cf. *The Blessed Sacrament of the Holy and True Body of Christ, and the Brotherhoods,* 1519 (*WA* 2:754–58; *LW* 35:67–73). Cf. also A. Werminghoff, *Verfassungsgeschichte der deutschen Kirche im Mittelalter* (2nd. ed., 1913), 149 n. 4. SA II, 2, 21.

Gerson, Jean (d. 1429). One of the most influential theologians in the ecclesiastical conflicts of the late 1300s and early 1400s. He was a moderate conciliarist whose meditative emphasis influenced medieval mysticism greatly. Gerson was highly valued by Luther, particularly in the reformer's earlier years. Luther refers to Gerson's *De laude scriptorum,* XI (*J. Gersonis opera omnia,* ed. M. Louis Ellies du Pin [1706], 2:702). SA, Preface, 6.

head- (German: *Häupt-/Haupt-*). *See* chief-.

hocus-pocus (German: *Gaukelei/Gäukelei*). A term used by Luther to mock various pious practices of the sixteenth-century Roman Catholic Church, which he considered rather superstitious. Other possible translations include "magic," "tricks," and "sleight-of-hand." SA, Preface, 14; SA III, 12, 3; SA III, 15, 4, 5. *WATR* 5:634$_{11ff.}$; *WATR* 5:636$_{26ff.}$; *On the Councils and the Church,* 1539 (*LW* 41:17).

horror (German: *Greuel*). Rather often used by Luther to describe the papacy and papal practices. It also has the sense of "abomination," "abhorrence," "disgust." SA II, 2, 16; SA II, 2, 17. Philipp Deitz, *Wörterbuch zu Dr. Martin Luthers Deutschen Schriften* (Hildesheim: Georg Olms Verlagsbuchhandlung, 1961), 1:165.

invention, human (German: *Menschenfundl[in]*). A compound word used by Luther to describe the Roman Catholic practices that may or may not be permissible, but because they are invented by human beings and not commanded by God, they are not necessary. SA II, 2, 2; II, 3, 2; II 4, 1.

John "the Steadfast" (d. 1532). Elector Prince of Saxony from 1525 to 1532. He played a pivotal role in lodging the evangelical "protest" at the second

Diet of Speyer. He signed the Augsburg Confession of 1530 and helped to influence his son toward the Lutheran cause.

John Fredrick "the Magnanimous" (d. 1554). Elector Prince of Saxony from 1532 to 1554, nephew of Fredrick the Wise and son of John the Steadfast. A committed and theologically aware Lutheran, John Fredrick commissioned Luther to write what was to become SA, in December of 1536. See SA, Preface, 1.

Jonas, Justus (d. 1555). An intimate friend and close collaborator with Luther. He was with Luther at Worms (1521); attended the wedding of Luther and Katherine von Bora and bore witness to the subsequent consummation of the marriage (1525); he was at Marburg (1529) and at Luther's death (1546), and he preached Luther's first funeral sermon at Eisleben. Jonas had considerable humanistic training, which he used to translate important Reformation works (e.g., Luther's *Bondage of the Will* and Melanchthon's *Loci*) from Latin into German. Jonas was dean of the theological faculty at Wittenberg for a decade (1523–33), lecturing on both the Old and the New Testament. As a church visitor in Saxony, he wrote the new church ordinances enacted there as a result of the Reformation.

jubilee year (German: *Guldenjahr*). Literally, "golden year" or "money year." In 1300, Boniface VIII published the bull *Antiquorum habet fida*, thus instituting a jubilee year, which promised a plenary indulgence for all who made a pilgrimage to Rome. Pope Sixtus IV established a papal indulgence for the dead in 1476. By 1500, indulgences for the dead were connected to the jubilee years. SA III, 3, 25, 26, 27.

justified (German: *gerecht/recht*). In SA, and more generally in both medieval and modern German, *Recht(en)*, as adjective, noun, and adverb, has a variety of meanings. Other possible translations are "right, correctness, righteousness, privilege, power, reason, dominance, justice, law, claim, title, truth, legitimacy, authority, administration of justice," etc. SA, Preface 2, 10, 12; II, 1, 3.

law(s) (German: *Recht/recht*). In SA, and more generally in both medieval and modern German, *Recht(en)*, as adjective, noun, and adverb, has a variety of meanings. Other possible translations are "right, correctness, righteousness, privilege, power, reason, dominance, justice, justify, law, claim, title, truth, authority, administration of justice," etc. SA, Preface, 2, 10, 12.

legitimacy (German: *Recht/recht*). In SA, and more generally in both medieval and modern German, *Recht(en)*, as adjective, noun, and adverb, has a variety of meanings. Other possible translations are "right, correctness, righteousness, privilege, power, reason, dominance, justice, justify, law, claim, title, truth, authority, administration of justice," etc. SA, Preface, 2, 10, 12.

magic (German: *Gaukelei/Gäukelei*). A term used by Luther to mock various pious practices of the sixteenth-century Roman Catholic Church, which he considered rather superstitious. Other possible translations include "hocus-pocus," "tricks," and "sleight-of-hand." SA, Preface, 14; SA III, 12, 3; SA III, 15, 4, 5. *WATR* 5:634$_{11ff.}$; *WATR* 5:636$_{26ff.}$; *On the Councils and the Church,* 1539 (*LW* 41:17).

Massling (German: *Messeknecht*). Literally translated "mass-slave/servant." Cochläus says that the reformer invented this pejorative word to lampoon the theology of the priestly role in the celebration of the Mass (*CC,* 17). SA II, 2, 7, 10.

Melanchthon, Philip (d. 1560). An influential and important coworker with Luther in the Reformation. Master Philip (he never attained the doctorate) came to the University of Wittenberg in 1518 as an instructor in Greek. He wrote the first Lutheran dogmatics, the *Loci communes,* in 1521, which was revised and reprinted some eighty times in his lifetime. Melanchthon's participation in the establishment or reorganization of the Universities of Marburg, Königsberg, Jena, and Leipzig earned him the title *Praeceptor Germaniae* ("The Teacher of Germany").

Mohammed. The Muslim prophet (A.D. 570?–632). Luther's 1542 introduction to *Verlegung des Alcoran Bruder Richardi,* 1542 (*WA* 53:272$_{16-24}$). SA III, 8, 9.

Münzer, Thomas (d. 1525). Leader of a sixteenth-century revolutionary movement that sought to establish the reign of God on earth. Münzer was an early follower of Luther who broke with the reformer over differences regarding the relationship between politics and the gospel. Münzer, who occasionally referred to himself as "Martin's competitor for the affection of the Lord," became, in Luther's mind, the symbolic representation of all the radical or left-wing Reformation movements. Münzer was executed when his theocracy at Frankenhausen was overthrown in May 1525. Carter Lindberg, "Müntzeriana," *LQ* 4, 2 (Summer 1990): 195–214.

one form of the sacrament. This refers to the practice of distributing just the bread, and not the wine, to the congregation during the celebration of Mass. SA III, 6, 2.

opportunity (German: *Stätt und Raum haben*). Literally, this idiom could be translated "to have place and room." SA III, 2, 2.

orders (of creation) (German: *Ständ(en)*). Luther mentions three such created orders (or "estates") in SA: church, government, and home/economy. These created orders connote for the reformer the spheres of life in which one lives out one's vocation or calling. Although Luther numbered and labeled these "orders of creation" variously throughout his career, in SA the reformer tends to identify three basic categories: the church, the home (marriage/family and the economy), and the state (government). Christian participation in the *Ständen* is how the church influences the social arena, as Christians live out their vocation or calling. See the Latin epigram the reformer penned on the cover of his original monograph of SA; SA, Preface, 12, 13 14; II 3, 2; II, 4, 7; III, 11, 1.

papist (German: *Papist(en)*). A pejorative word used by Luther to describe someone who submits to papal authority (i.e., a Roman Catholic). Luther often described the church of Rome as "papal" (*papistische*) rather than "catholic" (*katholische*). SA III, 12, 3. *Sermons on the Gospel of John*, 1538 (*LW* 24:310), and Friedrich Heiler, *Urkirche und Ostkirche* (Munich: Verlag von Ernst Reinhardt, 1937), 9.

Paul III, Pope (d. 1549). Published the council bull *Ad dominici gregis curam*, on June 2, 1536 (*UuA*, 15). Pentecost in 1537 was on May 23. After numerous postponements and delays, the council met at Trent, from 1545 to 1565. See H. Jedin, *A History of the Council of Trent* (London: Thomas Nelson & Sons, 1957), 1:288ff. SA, Preface, 15, and the note in that place.

penance (German: *Busse*). *Busse* can also be translated "repentance." At some points in SA, Luther has in mind repentance as a faithful response to the recognition of one's sin. At other points, he has in mind penance as a liturgical, sacramental act. See Bernhard Lohse, "Beichte und Busse in der lutherischen Reformation," in *Lehrverurteilungen—kirchentrennend?* vol. 2: *Materialien zu den Lehrverurteilungen und zur Theologie der Rechtfertigung*, ed. Karl Lehmann (Göttingen: Vandenhoeck & Ruprecht, 1989), 283–95.

In its verbal forms, both the German (*Busse tun* or *büssen*) and the Latin (*poententiam agite*) can be translated into English as "repent" or "do penance." Luther had interpreted this phrase in the first thesis of *The Disputation on the Power and Efficacy of Indulgences* (the Ninety-five Theses), 1517 (*WA* 1:233–38; *LW* 31:19–33) as a call for the entire Christian life to be a life of repentance. This ambiguity is evident in the 1959 *Book of Concord:* Theodore Tappert translated the title of AC 12 as "Repentance," whereas Jaroslav Pelikan translated the title of ACAp 12 as "Penitence." SA III, 3.

pests, noxious (German: *Unziefers*). Should be seen in relation to Luther's well-known designation of the "enthusiasts" of the Reformation period as a "swarm" (*Schwärmerei*). SA II, 2, 11; SA III, 3, 42; III, 8, 4; and *Sermons on the Gospel of St. John* (*LW* 22:68).

Pomeranius, John. *See* Bugenhagen, John.

rascal/rascality (German: *Buben/Buberei*). SA II, 2, 1, 7, 16, 22; SA II, 4, 3; SA III, 3, 20; Letter from Justus Jonas to Luther, June 1530 (*WABr* 5:431); *A*

Treatise on the New Testament, that is the Holy Mass, 1520 (*LW* 35:102); *The Babylonian Captivity of the Church*, 1520 (*LW* 36:55, 56); and Thomas Aquinas (d. 1275), *Summa theologiae*, III, Question 64, Articles 5 and 9.

real(ly) (German: *gerecht/recht*). In SA, and more generally in both medieval and modern German, *Recht(en)*, as adjective, noun, and adverb, has a variety of meanings. Other possible translations are "authority, right, administration of justice, righteousness, correctness, privilege, power, reason, dominance, justice, justify, law, claim, title, truth, legitimacy," etc. SA, Preface, 2, 10, 12.

remorse (German: *Reu*). Luther uses this word to translate the Latin word *contritio* ("contrition" or "remorse") into German. This was seen by the medieval church as the first step in "penance" (the second being "confession" and the third being "satisfaction"). Luther, however, thought that repentance had two parts: remorse and faith in the gospel of the forgiveness of sin. SA III, 3, 2, 12, 15–18, 27, 29, 36; SA III 3, 4.

repentance (German: *Busse*). *Busse* can also be translated "penance." At some points in SA, Luther has in mind repentance as a faithful response to the recognition of one's sin. At other points, he has in mind penance as a liturgical, sacramental act. See Bernhard Lohse, "Beichte und Busse in der lutherischen Reformation," in *Lehrverurteilungen—kirchentrennend?* vol. 2: *Materialien zu den Lehrverurteilungen und zur Theologie der Rechtfertigung*, ed. Karl Lehmann (Göttingen: Vandenhoeck & Ruprecht, 1989), 283–95. In its verbal forms, both the German (*Busse tun* or *büssen*) and the Latin (*poententiam agite*) can be translated into English as "repent" or "do penance." Luther had interpreted this phrase in the first thesis of *The Disputation on the Power and Efficacy of Indulgences* (the Ninety-five Theses), 1517 (*WA* 1:233–38; *LW* 31:19–33) as a call for the entire Christian life to be a life of repentance. This ambiguity is evident in the 1959 *Book of Concord:* Theodore Tappert translated the title of AC 12 as "Repentance," whereas Jaroslav Pelikan translated the title of ACAp 12 as "Penitence." SA III, 3.

right/righteous/righteousness (German: *gerecht/recht*). In SA, and more generally in both medieval and modern German, *Recht(en)*, as adjective, noun, and adverb, has a variety of meanings. Other possible translations are "correctness, privilege, power, reason, dominance, justice, jusitify, law, claim, title, truth, legitimacy, authority, administration of justice," etc. SA, Preface 2, 10, 12.

saved (German: *selig/seligerweise*). The root word *selig* is often related to the concept of salvation. Various forms of *selig* occur in SA and can be translated "save," "saved," "salvation," "salvific," etc. SA II, 4, 4, 12.

scholastic theologians (German: *Schultheologen*). Literally translated "school theologians." This word generally describes the Roman Catholic, university-based theologians of the late medieval church. Prominent among the school theologians were Albertus Magnus, Thomas Aquinas (d. 1275), and, later, John Duns Scotus (d. 1308). SA III, 1, 3; ACAp 2, 15; FCSD 2, 76.

sleight-of-hand (German: *Gaukelei/Gäukelei*). A term used by Luther to mock various pious practices of the sixteenth-century Roman Catholic Church, which he considered rather superstitious. Other possible translations include "hocus-pocus," "magic," and "tricks." SA, Preface, 14; SA III, 12, 3; SA III, 15, 4, 5. *WATR* 5:634$_{11\text{ff}}$; *WATR* 5:636$_{26\text{ff}}$; *On the Councils and the Church*, 1539 (*LW* 41:17).

sophist (German: *Sophist(en)*). A pejorative word, used by late medieval humanists to vilify scholastic theologians and their theological programs. Friedrich Lepp, *Schlagwörter des Reformationszeitalters* (Leipzig: M. Heinsius, 1908), 78–82. SA III, 3, 9; SA III, 6, 2, 5.

soul baths. Patrons founded free, public baths for the poor in order to demonstrate and enhance their (i.e., the donors') blessedness. *WA* 30^{II}:252, 260 n. 39; *Exhortation to All Clergy Assembled at Augsburg*, 1530 (*WA* 30^{II}:348$_{21}$; *LW* 34:54); *The Private Mass and the Consecration of Priests*, 1533 (*WA* 38:217$_{18}$; *LW* 38:173); *Matth. 18–24 in Predigten ausgelegt: Das dreiundzwanzigste Kapitel*, 1537–40 (*WA* 47:497$_{14}$). Gerhard Uhlhorn, *Die christliche Liebestätigkeit im Mittelalter* (Stuttgart, 1884), 2:310–13. SA II, 2, 12.

Spalatin, George (d. 1545). Luther's friend, court chaplain and private secretary to Fredrick the Wise and boyhood tutor of Elector John Fredrick. Spalatin served as secretary of a small meeting of evangelical theologians that had gathered to discuss what was to become SA in December of 1536. Spalatin made a copy of SA and delivered it to Elector John Fredrick in early January of 1537. Spalatin exercised great influence on behalf of the Reformation in the Saxon court.

spirituality (German: *Geisterei*). This word is related to Luther's rejection of what he calls "fanatical spirits" (German: *Rottengeister*). SA 8, 5.

superabundant works (German: *die ubrigen Verdienste*; Latin: *opera superabundantia* or *supererogationis*). The merits of the saints, or works of supererogation, were seen in the medieval period as those works that were performed by saints even after they had accumulated enough merit for themselves to gain entrance into heaven. The church, preeminently the pope, had the power to dispense these saints' "extra grace" or "extra merit," which were understood to accumulate in the church's "treasury of merit," to penitent sinners. SA II, 2, 24.

supererogation, works of. *See* superabundant works.

thunderclap (German: *Donneraxt*). Literally translated "thunder-axe." Luther uses this term to describe how the law, in its theological sense, works in a person's life. SA III, 2, 2.

transubstantiation (Latin: *transubstantio*). A theological explanation of how the sacrament works was established as dogma by Pope Innocent III at the Fourth Lateran Council in 1215. According to this theory, the "essence" or "substance" of the bread and the wine was changed into the real body and blood of Christ through the liturgical consecration of the priest. The outward, physical characteristics of the bread and the wine (the "nonsubstantial" or "nonessential" aspects of the elements—e.g., looks, taste, color), however, remained the same. SC VI. *The Blessed Sacrament of the Holy and True Body of Christ, and the Brotherhoods*, 1519 (*WA* 2:749; *LW* 35:59f.); *To the Christian Nobility of the German Nation concerning the Reform of the Christian Estate*, 1520 (*WA* 6:456; *LW* 44:198f.); *The Babylonian Captivity of the Church*, 1520 (*WA* 6:508–12; *LW* 36:28–35); *Contra Henricum Regem Angliae*, 1522 (*WA* 10^{II}:202–8); *Antwort deutsch auf König Heinrichs Buch*, 1522 (*WA* 10^{II}:245–49); *The Adoration of the Sacrament*, 1523 (*WA* 11:441; 36:287f.); *Confession concerning Christ's Supper*, 1528 (*WA* 26:437–45; *LW* 37:294–303); Letter from Luther to Prince George of Anhalt, May 25, 1541 (*WABr* 9:419); Letter from Luther to Prince John and Prince George of Anhalt, June 11 and 12, 1541 (*WABr* 9:443–45).

tricks (German: *Gaukelei/Gäukelei*). A term used by Luther to mock various pious practices of the sixteenth-century Roman Catholic Church, which he considered rather superstitious. Other possible translations include "hocus-pocus," "magic," and "sleight-of-hand." SA, Preface, 13, 14; SA III, 12, 3; SA III, 15, 4, 5. *WATR* 5:634$_{11ff.}$; *WATR* 5:636$_{26ff.}$; *On the Councils and the Church*, 1539 (*LW* 41:17).

true(ly) (German: *gerecht/recht*). In SA, and more generally in both medieval and modern German, *Recht(en)*, as adjective, noun, and adverb, has a variety of meanings. Other possible translations are "right, righteousness, correctness, privilege, power, reason, dominance, justice, justify, law, claim, title, legitimacy, authority, administration of justice," etc. SA, Preface, 2, 10, 12; II, 4, 10.

vicar (German: *Vikarist*). Low-ranking clergy who were attached to parish churches and served as representatives of the pastor. Vicars were also known as "chaplains" (German: *"Altarist"*). Cf. Georg Matthaei, *Die Vikariestiftungen der Lüneburger Stadtkirchen im Mittelalter und im Zeitalter der Reformation* (Göttingen, 1928). SA II, 2, 21.

Waim (or Wain), Gervasius of Memmingen. An ambassador of French King

Francis I, was in Saxony in 1531. Melanchthon once referred to him as "a most hostile enemy to our cause" (*CR* 2:517). *WABr* 2:31 n. 4; *WABr* 6:130 n. 1; Letter from Luther to Elector John Fredrick, February 9, 1537 (*WABr* 8:36$_{34-37}$); Letter from Luther to Justus Jonas, February 9, 1537 (*WABr* 8:39); *WATR* 6:4383. SA, Preface, 8.

Appendix C

Topical Index to Luther's Works and Lutheran Confessional Writings

ban, the. *See* **excommunication.**

baptism. AC 9; ACAp 9; SA III, 5; SC IV; LC IV; FCEp 12, 11–13. *A Sermon on the Estate of Marriage,* 1519 (*WA* 2:168; *LW* 44:9f.); *Eyn Sermon von dem heyligen Hochwirdigen Sacrament der Tauffe,* 1519 (*WA* 2:727–37); *The Babylonian Captivity of the Church,* 1520 (*WA* 6:526–38; *LW* 36:57–81); *The Order of Baptism,* 1523 (*WA* 12:42–48; *LW* 53:95–103); *Register über sämtliche Predigten* (*WA* 22:lxxxvif.); *Confession concerning Christ's Supper,* 1528 (*WA* 26:506; *LW* 37:367f.); *The Schwabach Articles,* 1529 (*WA* 30^{III}:89; trans. in Michael Reu, ed., *The Augsburg Confession: A Collection of Sources with Historical Introduction* [Chicago: Wartburg Publishing House, 1930], 2:44f.); *Predigt am 2. Sonntag nach Epiphaniä,* January 18, 1534 (*WA* 37:258–67); *Predigt am Sonntag Septuagesimä,* February 1, 1534 (*WA* 37:270–75); *Predigten des Jahres 1534* (*WA* 37:627–72); *On the Councils and the Church,* 1539 (*WA* 50:630f.; *LW* 41:150f.); *Against Hanswurst,* 1541 (*WA* 51:487, 502; *LW* 41:199, 206f.).

baptism of children. LC IV, 47–57. *Lectures on Galatians,* 1519 (*WA* 2:507ff.; *LW* 27:246ff.); *The Babylonian Captivity of the Church,* 1520 (*WA* 6:538; *LW* 36:74f.); *WA* 11:301; *WA* 11:452; *WA* 17^{II}:78–88; *WA* 26:137f., 144–74; *The Schwabach Articles,* 1529 (*WA* 30^{III}:89; trans. in Reu, *The Augsburg Confession,* 2:44f.); *The Marburg Articles,* 1529 (*WA* 30^{III}:168f.; *LW* 38:88); Letter from Luther to Melanchthon, January 13, 1522 (*WABr* 2:425–27; *LW* 48:365–71); Letter from Luther to Spalatin, May 29, 1522 (*WABr* 2:546). Theodor Kolde, *Analecta Lutherana* (Gotha: Friedrich Andreas Perthes, 1883), 219f. The section "On Baptism" in WC.

bishops. SA II, 4, 1; Tr 13–17. *Disputatio I. Eccii et M. Lutheri Lipsiae habita,* 1519 (*WA* 2:261); *Contra malignum I. Eccii iudicium M. Lutheri defensio,* 1519 (*WA* 2:641f.); *Against the Roman Papacy, an Institution of the Devil,* 1545 (*WA* 54:243; *LW* 41:307f.); *On the Councils and the Church,* 1539 (*WA* 50:538f., 550, 576, 581; *LW* 41:41f., 56f., 88f., 93f.). SA III, 10, 1; *Exhortation to All Clergy Assembled at Augsburg,* 1530 (*WA* 30^{II}:340–43; *LW* 34:50–52); *The Private Mass and the Consecration of Priests,* 1533 (*WA* 38:195$_{17f.}$,

236$_{23ff}$; *LW* 38:147, 194); *Predigt am Sonntag Exaudi*, May 9, 1535 (*WA* 41:241$_1$); *WATR* 4:4595.

blasphemy. AC 27, 11–14; ACAp 27, 20; SA II, 3, 2; SA II, 4, 3; SA III, 3, 43; SA III, 14, 3.

both forms, Communion in. AC 22; ACAp 22; SA III, 6 2–4. *The Blessed Sacrament of the Holy and True Body of Christ, and the Brotherhoods*, 1519 (*WA* 2:742f.; *LW* 35:49f.); *Verklärung etlicher Artikel in dem Sermon von dem heiligen Sakrament*, 1520 (*WA* 6:79–81); *Antwort auf die Zettel, so unter des Officials zu Stolpen Siegel ausgegangen*, 1520 (*WA* 6:137–40); *Ad schedulam inhibitionis sub nomine episc. Misnensis editam responsio*, 1520 (*WA* 6:144–51); *A Treatise on the New Testament, that is the Holy Mass*, 1520 (*WA* 6:374; *LW* 35:106f.); *To the Christian Nobility of the German Nation concerning the Reform of the Christian Estate*, 1520 (*WA* 6:456; *LW* 44:197f.); *The Babylonian Captivity of the Church*, 1520 (*WA* 6:498–500, 502–7; *LW* 36:12–16, 19–27); *Assertio omnium articulorum M. Lutheri per bullam Leonis X*, 1520 (*WA* 7:122–24); *Defense and Explanation of All Articles*, 1521 (*WA* 7:389–99; *LW* 32:55–62); *Receiving Both Kinds in the Sacrament*, 1522 (*WA* 10^{II}:20f., 24–29; *LW* 36:245f., 255); *Contra Henricum Regem Angliae*, 1522 (*WA* 10^{II}:201); *Antwort deutsch auf König Heinrichs Buch*, 1522 (*WA* 10^{II}:242); The Fifth Sermon, March 13, 1522, Friday after Inovcavit (*WA* 10^{III}:45f.; *LW* 51:90–91); *An Order of Mass and Communion for the Church at Wittenberg*, 1523 (*WA* 12:217; *LW* 53:34); *A Letter of Consolation to the Christians at Halle*, 1527 (*WA* 23:413–17; *LW* 43:151–56); *Ein Bericht an einen guten Freund*, 1528 (*WA* 26:564f., 590–614); *Exhortation to All Clergy Assembled at Augsburg*, 1530 (*WA* 30^{II}:320–23; *LW* 34:38–40); *Commentary on the Alleged Imperial Edict*, 1521 (*WA* 30^{III}:348–52; *LW* 34:80–82); *The Private Mass and the Consecration of Priests*, 1533 (*WA* 38:244–48; *LW* 38:204–9); *Sprüche wider das Konstanzer Konzil*, 1535 (*WA* 39^I:13–38); *Against Hanswurst*, 1541 (*WA* 51:490; *LW* 41:201); *Against the Thirty-Five Articles of the Louvain Theologians*, 1545 (*WA* 54:426, 432; *LW* 34:348–50, 355); Letter from Luther to Philip Melanchthon, August 1, 1521 (*WABr* 2:371f.; *LW* 48:277–82); Letter from Luther to John Hess in Oels, March 25, 1522 (*WABr* 2:482); Letter from Luther to George Spalatin, April 4, 1524 (*WABr* 3:265); Letter from Justus Jonas to Luther, June 30, 1530 (*WABr* 5:430; Letter from Luther to Justus Jonas, August 28, 1530 (*WABr* 5:593); Letter from Luther to Elector John, August 26, 1530 (*WABr* 5:572f.; *LW* 49:406–10); Letter from Luther to Lazarus Spengler, August 28, 1530 (*WABr* 5:590f.); Letter from Melanchthon to Luther, June 26, 1530 (*WABr* 5:397); Letter from Luther to George Spalatin, July 27, 1530 (*WABr* 5:502, 504f., 573f.; *CR* 2:208–14, 304, 349f., 354f.; *CR* 4:991–93, 1009–11.

church, the. AC 7; AC 8; ACAp 7 and 8; SA III, 12; Tr 66–76; LC II, 40–59. *Sermo de virtute excommunicationis,* 1518 (*WA* 1:642); *Ad dialogum Silvestri Prieratis de potestate papae responsio,* 1518 (*WA* 1:656f., 685; *Proceedings at Augsburg,* 1518 (*WA* 2:20; *LW* 31:282f.); *Resolutio Lutheriana super propositione XIII. de potestate papae,* 1519 (*WA* 2:190, 208 239); *Disputatio I. Eccii et M. Lutheri Lipsiae habita,* 1519 (*WA* 2:279, 287); *Resolutiones Lutherianae super propositionibus suis Lipsiae disputatis,* 1519 (*WA* 2:430); *On the Papacy in Rome, Against the Most Celebrated Romanist in Leipzig,* 1520 (*WA* 6:292–97; *LW* 39:65–71); *The Babylonian Captivity of the Church,* 1520 (*WA* 6:560f.; *LW* 36:106–17); *Answer to the Hyperchristian, Hyperspiritual and Hyperlearned Book by Goat Emser in Leipzig—Including Some Thoughts regarding His Companion, the Fool Murner,* 1521 (*WA* 7:684f.: *LW* 39:220f.); *Ad librum eximii Magistri Nostri Magistri Ambrosii Catharini, defensoris Silvestri Prieratis acerrimi, responsio,* 1521 (*WA* 7:719–22); *Luther at the Diet of Worms,* 1521 (*WA* 7:846; *LW* 32:118); *The Bondage of the Will,* 1525 (*WA* 18:650f.; *LW* 33:85f.); *Confession concerning Christ's Supper,* 1528 (*WA* 26:506f.; *LW* 37:367f.); *Artikel wider die ganze Satanschule und alle Pforten der Hölle,* 1530 (*WA* 30^{II}:421, 425); *The Schwabach Articles,* 1529 (*WA* 30^{III}:89f.; trans. in Reu, *The Augsburg Confession,* 2:43); *The Private Mass and the Consecration of Priests,* 1533 (*WA* 38:221; *LW* 38:176f.); *Vorrede zu Antonius Covinus, Quatenus expedit aeditam, etc.,* 1534 (*WA* 38:277f.); *Sermon Preached in Castle Pleissenburg on the Occasion of the Inauguration of the Reformation in Leipzig,* May 24, 1539 (*WA* 47:772–79; *LW* 51:301–12); *The Three Symbols or Creeds of the Christian Faith,* 1538 (*WA* 50:283; *LW* 34:229); *On the Councils and the Church,* 1539 (*WA* 50:624–53; *LW* 41:143–78); *Against Hanswurst,* 1541 (*WA* 51:476–531; *LW* 41:193–224).

Communion by oneself. SA II, 2, 8, 13. Luther's Sermon on November 21, 1537 (*WA* 45:287$_{26}$).

Communion, Holy. *See* **Sacrament of the Altar.**

confession. AC 11; AC 25; ACAp 11; ACAp 12, 98–178; SA III, 3, 19; SA III, 8; SC V, LC V, "A Brief Exhortation to Confession"; FCEp 7, 16–20. *Sermone aus den Jahren 1514–17* (*WA* 1:98f.); *Sermo de poenitentia,* 1518 (*WA* 1:322–24); *Decem praecepta Wittenbergensi praedicata populo,* 1518 (*WA* 1:509, 516f.); *Eine kurze Unterweisung, wie man beichten soll,* 1519 (*WA* 2:59f.); *Contra malignum I. Eccii iudicium M. Lutheri defensio,* 1519 (*WA* 2:645f.); *A Discussion on How Confession Should Be Made,* 1520 (*WA* 6:158–69; *LW* 39:23–47); *The Babylonian Captivity of the Church,* 1520 (*WA* 6:546–48; *LW* 36:81–90); *Assertio omnium articulorum M. Lutheri per bullam Leonis X,* 1520 (*WA* 7:117–19); *An Instruction to Penitents concern-*

ing the Forbidden Books of Dr. Martin Luther, 1521 (*WA* 7:297f.; *LW* 44:228f.); *Defense and Explanation of All Articles*, 1521 (*WA* 7:367–71; *LW* 32:42–47); *Von der Beicht, ob die der Babst macht habe zu gepieten*, 1521 (*WA* 8:138–85); *Receiving Both Kinds in the Sacrament*, 1522 (*WA* 10^{II}:32f.; *LW* 36:257f.); The Eighth Sermon, March 16, 1522 (*WA* 10^{III}:58–64; *LW* 51:97–100); *Predigt am Sonntag Lätare Nachmittags*, March 15, 1523 (*WA* 11:65); *An Order of Mass and Communion for the Church at Wittenberg*, 1523 (*WA* 12:216f.; *LW* 53:34f.); *Eyn Sermon am grunen donnerstag*, 1523 (*WA* 12:491–93); *Predigt am Palmsonntage*, March 20, 1524 (*WA* 15:481–89); *Predigt am Palmsonntag*, April 9, 1525 (*WA* 17^{I}:170f.); *Sermon von dem Sakrament*, 1526 (*WA* 19:513–23); *Confession concerning Christ's Supper*, 1528 (*WA* 26:507; *LW* 37:368f.); *Predigt am Gründonnerstag*, April 9, 1528 (*WA* 27:95–97); *Predigt am Palmsonntag*, March 21, 1529 (*WA* 29:136–46); *Exhortation to All Clergy Assembled at Augsburg*, 1530 (*WA* 30^{II}:287f.; *LW* 34:19f.); *The Schwabach Articles*, 1529 (*WA* 30^{III}:89; trans. in Reu, *The Augsburg Confession*, 2:43); *The Marburg Articles*, 1529 (*WA* 30^{III}:166f.; *LW* 38:87); *Sendschreiben an die zu Frankfurt a.M.*, 1533 (*WA* 30^{III}:565–70); Letter from Andreas Osiander to Luther, June 30, 1530 (*WABr* 5:433); Letter from Luther and Melanchthon to the Council of Nürnberg (*WABr* 6:454f.; *LW* 50:76f.; WC (*WABr* 12:21168–73). Kolde, *Analecta Lutherana*, 219.

creation. TCS I, 1; TCS II, 2; TCS III, 3, 4; AC 1, 1–4; SA I, 1; SC II; LC II, 9–24.

creeds. *See* **Holy Trinity.**

discipline. *See* **excommunication.**

ecclesiology. *See* **church, the.**

education. AC 27, 15–17; ACAp 27, 4–8; SA II, 3, 1. *To the Christian Nobility of the German Nation concerning the Reform of the Christian Estate*, 1520 (*WA* 6:439f., 452, 461; *LW* 44:173f., 191f., 205f.); *To the Councilmen of All Cities in Germany: That They Establish and Maintain Schools*, 1524 (*WA* 15:47; *LW* 45:370f.); *Confession concerning Christ's Supper*, 1528 (*WA* 26:504; *LW* 37:364); *Exhortation to All Clergy Assembled at Augsburg*, 1530 (*WA* 30^{II}:315–17; *LW* 34:36–38); *Einer aus den hohen Artikeln des päpstlichen Glaubens*, 1537 (*WA* 50:77f.); *On the Councils and the Church*, 1539 (*WA* 50:617, 651; *LW* 41:135, 176f.; WATR 4:675). See Martin Brecht's discussion of Luther's efforts in behalf of public education in the middle 1520s in *Martin Luther, vol. 2: Shaping and Defining the Reformation 1521–1532* (Minneapolis: Fortress Press, 1990), 141.

emperor, Holy Roman. SA II, 4, 16; Luther had referred to the emperor as "pious Charles, who is a sheep among wolves" (Letter from Luther to

Kaspar von Teutleben, June 19, 1530 [*WABr* 5:37330]); *Auf das Schreien etlicher Papisten über die siebenzehn Artikel,* 1530 (*WA* 30[III]:196f.); *Dr. Martin Luther's Warning to His Dear German People,* 1531 (*WA* 30[III]:291–98; *LW* 47:29–35); *Commentary on the Alleged Imperial Edict,* 1531 (*WA* 30[III]:331f., 362, 388; *LW* 34:67f., 88, 104); Letter from Luther to Nikolaus Hausmann, July 6, 1530 (*WABr* 5:440; *LW* 49:348–52); *WATR* 2:1687, 2695.

empty effort/ritual. In 1520, Luther called the church of Rome a *Beth-aven,* a word borrowed from the Hebrew prophets (e.g., Hosea 4:15 and 10:5) that literally means "house of emptiness" (*The Babylonian Captivity of the Church* [*WA* 6:547; *LW* 36:88]). In his 1521 treatise, *The Misuse of the Mass,* Luther called the Wittenberg Castle Church (which housed the Elector's large and famous collection of relics) a *Beth-aven* (*WA* 8:561$_{21}$; *LW* 36:227). See also Isaiah 42:29; Zechariah 10:2; Habakkuk 1:3; *De abroganda missa privata Martini Lutheri sententia,* 1521 (*WA* 8:475$_{20}$); *The Misuse of the Mass,* 1521 (*WA* 8:556$_{22}$; *LW* 36:227); and Letter from Luther to George Spalatin, November 22, 1521 (*WABr* 2:405$_{14}$; *LW* 48:338). SA II, 3, 2.

Eucharist. *See* **Sacrament of the Altar.**

evil. *See* **sin.**

excommunication. AC 28, 8–21; ACAp 11, 4; ACAp 28, 13–14; SA III, 9; Tr 60, 74; FCEp 12, 26; FCSD 11, 89ff. *Explanations of the Disputation concerning the Value of Indulgences,* 1518 (*WA* 1:615–16; *LW* 31:228–30); *Sermo de virtute excommunicationis,* 1518 (*WA* 1:638–43); *A Sermon on the Ban,* 1520 (*WA* 6:63–75; *LW* 39:3–22); *Assertio omnium articulorum M. Lutheri per bullam Leonis X,* 1520 (*WA* 7:126f.); *Defense and Explanation of All Articles,* 1521 (*WA* 7:405–7; *LW* 32:65–67); *Matth. 18–24 in Predigten ausgelegt,* 1537–40 (*WA* 47:279ff. [esp. *WA* 47:282$_{23f.}$, and 284$_{22–26}$]); *Predigt am Sonntag Invokavit, nachmittags,* February 23, 1539 (*WA* 47:669–71); *WATR* 4, Nr. 4381. *Instructions for the Visitors of Parish Pastors in Electoral Saxony,* 1528 (*WA* 26:233–35; *LW* 40:311–13); *Predigt am 13. Sonntag nach Trinitatis, nachmittags,* August 22, 1529 (*WA* 29:539$_{1–3}$); Letter from Dionisius Binne to Luther, September 17, 1532 (*WABr* 6:360); Letter from Luther to Tilemann Schnabel and the other Hessen Clergy gathered at Homberg, June 26, 1533 (*WABr* 6:498$_{23f.}$); *WATR* 4:4073; *WATR* 5:5477. James Spalding, "Discipline as a Mark of the True Church in Its Sixteenth Century Lutheran Context," in *Piety, Politics, and Ethics: Reformation Studies in Honor of George Wolfgang Forell,* ed. Carter Lindberg (Kirksville, Mo.: Sixteenth Century Journal Publishers, 1984), 132.

filioque. TCS II, 3; TCS III, 22; SA I, 2.

good works. AC 6; AC 20; ACAp 4, 5–121; ACAp 20; SA III, 13; FCEp 3; FCSD 3. *Sermo de poenitentia,* 1518 (*WA* 1:324); *Heidelberg Disputation,*

1518 (*WA* 1:353, 356–59; *LW* 31:39f., 43–48); *Explanations of the Disputation concerning the Value of Indulgences,* 1518 (*WA* 1:593, 616; *LW* 31:189f., 230f.); *Luthers Unterricht auf etliche Artikel,* 1519 (*WA* 2:71f.); Lectures on Galatians 1–6, 1519 (*WA* 2:443–618; *LW* 27:151–410); *Disputatio de fide infusa et acquisita,* 1520 (*WA* 6:85f.); *Von den guten Werken,* 1520 (*WA* 6:202–76); *The Freedom of a Christian,* 1520 (*WA* 7:21–38, 50–73; *LW* 31:343–77); *Adversus armatum virum Cokleum,* 1523 (*WA* 11:298–302); *The Adoration of the Sacrament,* 1523 (*WA* 11:453; *LW* 36:300f.); *De loco Iustificationis,* 1530 (*WA* 30^{II}:657–76); *The Schwabach Articles,* 1529 (*WA* 30^{III}:88; trans. in Reu, *The Augsburg Confession,* 2:43f.); *The Marburg Colloquy and the Marburg Articles,* 1529 (*WA* 30^{III}:162–64, 166; *LW* 38:86–88); *The Disputation concerning Justification,* 1536 (*WA* 39^{I}:78–126; *LW* 34:145–96); *Die Promotionsdisputation von Palladius und Tilemann,* 1537 (*WA* 39^{I}:205 [see also XII and *WA* 39^{II}:426]); Lectures on Galatians, 1535 (*WA* 40^{I}:33—*WA* 40^{II}:184; *LW* 26:1–461—*LW* 27:1–144); *On the Councils and the Church,* 1539 (*WA* 50:597f.; *LW* 41:596ff.); Preface to the Epistle of St. Paul to the Romans, *WADB* 7:10$_{28ff.}$, 16$_{30ff.}$; *LW* 35:371, 374f.); Letter from Luther and Bugenhagen to Elector John Fredrick, May 10 or 11, 1541 (*WABr* 9:406–8); *Luther, Antwort auf schriftliche Fragen Melanchthons,* 1536 (*WABr* 12:189–95); *WATR* 6:6727.

gospel. AC 4; AC 5; ACAp 4; SA III, 4; FCEp 5; FCEp 6; FCSD 5; FCSD 6. *Sermo Dominica II. Adventus,* ca. 1514–17 (*WA* 1:105); *The Disputation on the Power and Efficacy of Indulgences* (the Ninety-five Theses), 1517 (*WA* 1:236$_{22f.}$; *LW* 31:31); *Explanations of the Ninety-Five Theses,* 1518 (*WA* 1:616f.; *LW* 31:230f.); *Ad librum eximii Magistri Nostri Magistri Amrosii Catharini, defensoris Silvestri Prieratis acerrimi, responsio,* 1521 (*WA* 7:720f.); *Adventspostille: Evangelium am 3. Adventssonntag,* 1522 (*WA* 10^{I,2}:158ff.); Sermons on the First Epistle of St. Peter, 1523 (*WA* 12:260; *LW* 30:3f.); *Ein Sendbrief des Herrn Wolfen von Salhausen an Doctor Martinus und Antwort Martin Luthers,* 1524 (*WA* 15:228); *Against the Heavenly Prophets in the Matter of Images and Sacraments,* 1525 (*WA* 18:65; *LW* 40:82); *Confession concerning Christ's Supper,* 1528 (*WA* 26:506; *LW* 37:366f.); *WA* 30^{III}:164f.; *The Schwabach Articles,* 1529 (*WA* 30^{III}:88; trans. in Reu, *The Augsburg Confession,* 2:44f.); *Preface to the New Testament,* 1546 (*WADB* 6:2–10; *LW* 35:357–62).

Holy Trinity. TCS I; TCS II; TCS III; AC 1; AC 3; ACAp 1; AC 3; SA I; SC II; LC I, 1; II; FCEp 8; FCSD 8. Cf. also *The Adoration of the Sacrament,* 1523 (*WA* 11:450$_{28–32}$; *LW* 36:298); *Confession concerning Christ's Supper,* 1528 (*WA* 26:500–502, 505; *LW* 37:361–63, 365f.); *The Schwabach Articles,* 1529 (*WA* 30^{III}:86f.; trans. in Reu, *The Augsburg Confession,* 2:40–44); *The Mar-*

burg Articles, 1529 (*WA* 30III:160–62; *LW* 38:85f.); *Ein Bekenntnis christlicher Lehre und christlichen Glaubens*, 1530 (*WA* 30III:178f.); *The Three Symbols or Creeds of the Christian Faith*, 1538 (*WA* 50:273–82; *LW* 34:215–29).

human regulations. AC 15; AC 26; AC 28, 29–78; ACAp 4, 233–43, 261–85; ACAp 4, 143–56; ACAp 7, 30–46; ACAp 15; ACAp 27, 14–37; SA III, 15; SC, Preface, 4–6; FCEp 10; FCSD 10. Cf. also *Confession concerning Christ's Supper*, 1528 (*WA* 26:509; *LW* 37:371f.); *The Schwabach Articles*, 1529 (*WA* 30III:91; trans. in Reu, *The Augsburg Confession*, 2:45); *The Marburg Colloquy and the Marburg Articles*, 1529 (*WA* 30III:168; *LW* 38:88).

incarnation. TCS I, 2; TCS II, 2; TCS III, 27; AC 3, 1–2; ACAp 3; SC II, 3–4; LC II; FCEp 8, 5, 11, 14, 15, 33; FCSD 8, 6, 24, 37, 71–73, 85.

indulgences. AC 25, 5; AC, Conclusion, 2; ACAp 12, 15, 98–105, 133–37, 175; ACAp 21, 23; SA II, 2, 24; SA III, 3, 24–27; Tr 45–48. Letter from Luther to Cardinal Albrecht, October 31, 1517 (*WABr* 1:111₂₁f.; *LW* 48:46). *Ex Sermone habito Domin. X. post Trinit.*, 1516 (*WA* 1:65–69); *Sermo de indulgentiis pridie Dedicationis* (*WA* 1:98f.); *Sermon on St. Matthew's Day*, February 24, 1517 (*WA* 1:141; *LW* 30f.); *The Disputation on the Power and Efficacy of Indulgences* (the Ninety-five Theses), 1517 (*WA* 1:233–38; *LW* 31:19–33); *Eynn Sermon von dem Ablasz unnd gnade durch den wirdigenn doctornn Martinum Luther Augustiner zu Wittenbergk*, 1517 (*WA* 1:243–46); *Eine Freiheit des Sermons päpstlichen Ablass und Gnade belangend*, 1518 (*WA* 1:383–93); Letter from Luther to John von Staupitz, May 30, 1518 (*WA* 1:525–27; *LW* 48:64–70); *Explanations of the Ninety-Five Theses*, 1518 (*WA* 1:527–628; *LW* 31:77–252); *Proceedings at Augsburg*, 1518 (*WA* 2:6–26; *LW* 31:253–92); *Appellatio a Caietano ad Papam*, 1518 (*WA* 2:28–30); *Luthers Unterricht auf etliche Artikel*, 1519 (*WA* 2:70); *Disputatio I. Eccii et M. Lutheri Lipsiae habita*, 1519 (*WA* 2:344–58); *The Babylonian Captivity of the Church*, 1520 (*WA* 6:497f.; *LW* 36:11f.); *Assertio omnium articulorum M. Lutheri per bullam Leonis X*, 1520 (*WA* 7:125f.); *Defense and Explanation of All Articles*, 1521 (*WA* 7:399–405; *LW* 32:62–66); *Papst Clemens VII zwei Bullen zum Jubeljahr*, 1525 (*WA* 18:255–69); *Confession concerning Christ's Supper*, 1528 (*WA* 26:507; *LW* 37:369); *Exhortation to All Clergy Assembled at Augsburg*, 1530 (*WA* 30II:281–86; *LW* 34:16–18); *Bulla papae Pauli tertii de indulgentiis contra Turcam, etc.*, 1537 (*WA* 50:113–16); *Nachwort zu Johann Agricolas Übersetzung*, 1537 (*WA* 50:35₁₃f.); *Against Hanswurst*, 1541 (*WA* 51:488f.; *LW* 41:200); *WATR* 4:4153; *WABr* 1:111f.

Cochläus (cf. SA, Preface, 1 and the note in that place) responds to Luther: "Even though the guilt is forgiven by means of remorse and confession, sin must be punished through some works of penance: praying, fasting, vigils, pilgrimages, hard beds, hair-shirts, alms, etc., as has been done in the church for many hundreds of years" (*CC,* 27).

jubilee year(s). *To the Christian Nobility of the German Nation concerning the Reform of the Christian Estate,* 1520 (*WA* 6:437; *LW* 44:169f.); *Papst Clemens VII zwei Bullen zum Jubeljahr,* 1525 (*WA* 18:255–69); *Vermahnung an die Geistlichen, versammelt auf dem Reichstag zu Augsburg,* 1530 (*WA* 30[II]:253); *Exhortation to All Clergy Assembled at Augsburg,* 1530 (*WA* 30[II]:283; *LW* 34:16); *Einer aus den hohen Artikeln des päpstlichen Glaubens,* 1537 (*WA* 50:75f.); *Against the Roman Papacy, an Institution of the Devil,* 1545 (*WA* 54:268; *LW* 41:338f.); *Luthers Vorrede über den Propheten Daniel,* 1545 (*WADB* 11[II]:86). Jubilee years were held in 1300, 1350, 1390, 1423, 1450, 1475, 1500, 1525.

justification. AC 2; AC 4; AC 6; 20; ACAp 4; SA II, 1; SA III, 4; SA III, 13; FCEp 3; FCEp 5; FCSD 3; FCSD 5.

keys, the. AC 25, 3–5; AC 28, 5–8; SA III, 7; ACAp 11, 2. Cf. also *Sermo in die Purificationis Mariae,* ca. 1514–17 (*WA* 1:131); *The Disputation on the Power and Efficacy of Indulgences* (the Ninety-five Theses), 1517 (*WA* 1:236[18f.]; *LW* 31:31); *Explanations of the Disputation concerning the Value of Indulgences,* 1518 (*WA* 1:594–96, 615; *LW* 31:193–96, 228f.); *Proceedings at Augsburg,* 1518 (*WA* 2:11; *LW* 31:266f.); *Resolutio Lutheriana super propositione XIII. de potestate papae,* 1519 (*WA* 2:187–94); *Sermon Preached in the Castle at Leipzig on the Day of St. Peter and St. Paul,* June 29, 1519 (*WA* 2:248f.; *LW* 51:59f.); *The Sacrament of Penance,* 1519 (*WA* 2:722f.; *LW* 35:21); *On the Papacy in Rome, Against the Most Celebrated Romanist in Leipzig,* 1520 (*WA* 6:309; *LW* 39:86); *Concerning the Ministry,* 1523 (*WA* 12:183–85; *LW* 40:25f.); *The Keys,* 1530 (*WA* 30[II]:435–507; *LW* 40:321–77); *Matth. 18–24 in Predigten ausgelegt,* 1537–40 (*WA* 47:288–97); *On the Councils and the Church,* 1539 (*WA* 50:631f.; *LW* 41:152f.); *Against the Roman Papacy, an Institution of the Devil,* 1545 (*WA* 54:249–52; *LW* 41:315–19).

law. ACAp 4; ACAp 5; ACAp 6; ACAp 12, 88–90; SA III, 2; FCEp 5; FCEp 6; FCSD 5; FCSD 6. Cf. also *WA* 1:398; *WA* 7:23f., 52f., 63f.; *WA* 8:609; *Kirchenpostille, Epistel am Neujahrstage,* Galatians 3:2-29, 1522 (*WA* 10[I,1]:450–66); *Adventspostille: Evangelium am 3. Adventssonntag,* Matthew 11:2-20, 1522 (*WA* 10[I,2]:155–58); *Ein Sendbrief des Herrn Wolfen von Salhausen an Doctor Martinus und Antwort Martin Luthers,* 1524 (*WA* 15:228f.); *Against the Heavenly Prophets in the Matter of Images and Sacraments,* 1525 (*WA* 18:65; *LW* 40:82f.); *Theses concerning Faith and Law,* 1535 (*WA* 39[I]:50f.; *LW* 34:114ff.); *Die Tesen gegen die Antinomer,* 1537–40 (*WA* 39[I]:347); *Die zweite Disputation gegen die Antinomer,* 1538 (*WA* 39[I]:423–25); *Preface to the Epistle of St. Paul to the Romans,* 1546 (*WADB* 7:2–6,

12ff.; *LW* 35:365–69, 371ff.); Prefaces to the Old Testament, 1545 (*WADB* 8:16ff.; *LW* 35:238ff.).

marriage of priests. AC 23; ACAp 23; SA III, 11; Tr 78; LC I, 213–16. Cf. also *Contra malignum I. Ecci iudicium M. Lutheri defensio,* 1519 (*WA* 2:644); *Ad schedulam inhibitionis sub nomine episc. Misnensis editam responsio,* 1520 (*WA* 6:146); *On the Papacy in Rome, Against the Most Celebrated Romanist in Leipzig,* 1520 (*WA* 6:307f.; *LW* 39:83f.); *To the Christian Nobility of the German Nation concerning the Reform of the Christian Estate,* 1520 (*WA* 6:440–43; *LW* 44:175–79); *The Babylonian Captivity of the Church,* 1520 (*WA* 6:565; *LW* 36:114f.); *Answer to the Hyperchristian, Hyperspiritual and Hyperlearned Book by Goat Emser in Leipzig—Including Some Thoughts regarding His Companion, the Fool Murner,* 1521 (*WA* 7:674–78; *LW* 39:206–12); *Am dritten sontage ym Advent Epistell S. Pauli. I. Corinth. 4,* 1522 (*WA* 10^{1,2}:144f.); *Against the Spiritual Estate of the Pope and the Bishops Falsely So Called,* 1522 (*WA* 10^{II}:126–30, 149–53, 156f.; *LW* 39:266–68, 289–94, 297f.); *The Estate of Marriage,* 1522 (*WA* 10^{II}:279f.; *LW* 45:21f.); The Third Sermon, Tuesday after Invocavit, March 11, 1522 (*WA* 10^{III}:23–26; *LW* 51:79–81); *The Adoration of the Sacrament,* 1523 (*WA* 11:455; *LW* 36:303); 1 Corinthians 7 (*WA* 12:92–142; *LW* 28:1–56); *Exhortation to All Clergy Assembled at Augsburg,* 1530 (*WA* 30^{II}:323–40; *LW* 34:40–52); *Artikel wider die ganze Satanschule und alle Pforten der Hölle,* 1530 (*WA* 30^{II}:423, 426f.); *The Schwabach Articles,* 1529 (*WA* 30^{III}:90; trans. in Reu, *The Augsburg Confession,* 2:44); *Vorrede zu Confessio fidei ac religionis, etc.,* 1538 (*WA* 50:380); *On the Councils and the Church,* 1539 (*WA* 50:634–41; *LW* 41:156–64); Letter from Luther to Melanchthon, August 1, 1521 (*WABr* 2:370f.; *LW* 48:277f.); Letter from Luther to Melanchthon, August 3, 1521 (*WABr* 2:373f.; *LW* 48:283f.); Letter from Luther to Cardinal Albrecht, Archbishop of Mainz, December 1, 1521 (*WABr* 2:408; *LW* 48:342f.); Letter from Luther to Wenzeslaus Link, July 4, 1522 (*WABr* 2:575); Letter from Luther to Justus Jonas, June 30, 1530? (*WABr* 5:431); Letter from Luther to Lazarus Spengler, August 28, 1530 (*WABr* 5:593); Letter from Luther to the Brotherchurch in Mähren, November 5, 1536 (*WABr* 7:586).

Mass, the. AC 13; AC 21; AC 24; ACAp 13; ACAp 21; ACAp 24; SA II, 2; FCEp 7, 21ff.; FCSD 7, 108ff. Cf. also *A Treatise on the New Testament, that is the Holy Mass,* 1520 (*WA* 6:353–78; *LW* 35:75–111); *To the Christian Nobility of the German Nation concerning the Reform of the Christian Estate,* 1520 (*LW* 44:191f.; *WA* 6:451f.); *The Babylonian Captivity of the Church,* 1520 (*WA* 6:512–26; *LW* 36:35–57); *De abroganda missa privata Martini Lutheri sententia,* 1521 (*WA* 8:411–76); *The Misuse of the Mass,* 1521 (*WA* 8:482–563; *LW* 36:127–230); *Receiving Both Kinds in the Sacrament,* 1522 (*WA*

10^{II}:29; *LW* 36:254); *Contra Henricum Regem Angliae,* 1522 (*WA* 10^{II}:208–20; *Antwort deutsch auf König Heinrichs Buch,* 1522 (*WA* 10^{II}:249–58); The Second Sermon, Monday after Invocavit, March 10, 1522 (*WA* 10^{III}:14–18; *LW* 51:75–78); *The Adoration of the Sacrament,* 1523 (*WA* 11:441f.; *LW* 36:287f.*); The Abomination of the Secret Mass,* 1525 (*WA* 18:22–36; *LW* 36:307–28); *WA* 26:508; *WA* 30^{II}:293–309, 610–15; *WA* 30^{III}:90f., 310f.; *WA* 38:195ff., 262–72; *WA* 39^I:139–73; Letter from Luther to Melanchthon, August 1, 1521 (*WABr* 2:37273; *LW* 48:281); *Luther an Propst, Dekan und kanoniker des Allerheiligenstifts zu Wittenberg,* August 19, 1523 (*WABr* 3:130–32); *An Order of the Mass and Communion for the Church at Wittenberg,* 1523 (*WA* 12:205–20; *LW* 53:15–40) and *The German Mass and Order of Service,* 1526 (*WA* 19:72–113; *LW* 53:51–90); *Confession concerning Christ's Supper,* 1528 (*LW* 37:316f.); Letter from Luther to Spalatin, July 27, 1530 (*WABr* 5:504f.); *Exhortation to All Clergy Assembled at Augsburg,* 1530 (*LW* 34:22f.); *Dr. Martin Luther's Warning to His Dear German People,* 1531 (*LW* 47:43f.). Luther referred to the Mass and celibacy as "the two pillars upon which the papacy rests": *A Letter of Dr. Martin Luther concerning His Book on the Private Mass,* 1534 (*WA* 38:271$_{37}$; *LW* 38:233); *Contra Henricum Regem Angliae,* 1522 (*WA* 10^{II}:220$_{13-16}$); *WATR* 1:113, 662, 1141; *WATR* 3:2852, 3319; *WATR* 5:6046.

masses, abuses of. *The Disputation on the Power and Efficacy of Indulgences* (the Ninety-five Theses), 1517 (*WA* 1:234$_{33f.}$; *LW* 31:28); *The Babylonian Captivity of the Church,* 1520 (*LW* 36:35f.); *De abroganda missa privata Martini Lutheri sententia,* 1521 (*WA* 8:452–54); *The Misuse of the Mass,* 1521 (*WA* 8:531–33; *LW* 35:190–98); *Kirchenpostille: Evangelium am Tage der Heiligen drei Könige, Matth. 2:1-12,* 1522 (*WA* 10^{I,II}:585–87); *Against the Spiritual Estate of the Pope and the Bishops Falsely So Called,* 1522 (*WA* 10^{II}:153$_{8-10}$; *LW* 39:293f.); *Vorrede zu Menius, Der Wiedertäufer Lehre,* 1530 (*WA* 30^{II}:211); *Excurs* to *Exhortation to All Clergy Assembled at Augsburg* (*WA* 30^{II}:254); *Exhortation to All Clergy Assembled at Augsburg,* 1530 (*WA* 30^{II}:347$_{28}$; *LW* 34:54f.); *Widerruf vom Fegefeuer,* 1530 (*WA* 30^{II}:385); *Dr. Martin Luther's Warning to His Dear German People,* 1531 (*WA* 30^{III}:310f.; *LW* 47:43f.); *Predigten des Jahres 1531,* Nr. 58, June 18 (*WA* 34^I:534$_f$); *Predigten des Jahres 1539,* Nr. 35, September 29 (*WA* 47:857$_{8-15}$); *WATR* 3:3695.

masses for the dead. SA II, 2, 12. Commemorations held a year after a person's death are noted by the early church fathers: Tertullian (d. A.D. 220) in chapter 3 of *De corona* (MSL 2, 79). Ambrose of Milan (d. 397) mentions commemorations on the week and month after death in chapter 3 of *De obitu Theodosii oratio* (MSL 16, 1386). *Eine Freiheit des Sermons päpstlichen Ablass und Gnade belangend,* 1518 (*WA* 1:389$_{35}$); *A Treatise on the New Tes-*

tament, that is the Holy Mass, 1520 (*WA* 6:370₃₅; *LW* 35:101f.); *To the Christian Nobility of the German Nation concerning the Reform of the Christian Estate,* 1520 (*WA* 6:444₂₂; *LW* 44:180f.); *De abroganda missa privata Martini Lutheri sententia,* 1521 (*WA* 8:452ff.); *The Misuse of the Mass,* 1521 (*WA* 8:531; *LW* 36:190f.); *To the Councilmen of All Cities in Germany that They Establish and Maintain Christian Schools,* 1524 (*WA* 15:3022; *LW* 45:350f.); *Ein senndbrief Martini Lutheri an den Wolgebornen herren Bartholomeum von Staremberg aussganngen,* 1524 (*WA* 18:6); *Confession concerning Christ's Supper,* 1528 (*WA* 26:5085; *LW* 37:369); *Exhortation to All Clergy Assembled at Augsburg,* 1530 (*WA* 30ᴵᴵ:297₂₇, 347₃₀, 348₁₈₋₂₀; *LW* 34:26, 54); *Widerruf vom Fegefeuer,* 1530 (*WA* 30ᴵᴵ:375₂₉); *Admonition concerning the Sacrament of the Body and Blood of Our Lord,* 1530 (*WA* 30ᴵᴵ:611₁₀; *LW* 38:118); Preface to Psalm 117, 1530 (*WA* 31ᴵ:226₁₁; *LW* 14:6); *Predigten des Jahres 1531,* Nr. 58, June 18 (*WA* 34ᴵ:536₂₄); Letter from Luther to George Spalatin, May 7, 1525 (*WABr* 3:48815); *WATR* 4:3984; *WATR* 5:6200.

orders of creation. SA, Preface, 12, 14; SA III, 14, 3; SC V, 3; *Confession concerning Christ's Supper,* 1528 (*WA* 26:504; *LW* 37:364); *On the Councils and the Church,* 1539 (*WA* 50:652; *LW* 41:177); and Luther's Exposition of Psalm 111:3, 1530 (*WA* 31ᴵ:409; *LW* 13:368). Two helpful explications of Luther's ethics of vocation are George Forell, *Faith Active in Love* (Minneapolis: Augsburg Publishing House, 1959), 112ff., and Gustaf Wingren, *Luther on Vocation* (Philadelphia: Muhlenberg Press, 1957), 63ff.

ordination. AC 5; AC 14; ACAp 13, 7–17; ACAp 14; SA III, 10; Tr 23–29; Tr 60–77. Cf. also *The Babylonian Captivity of the Church,* 1520 (*WA* 6:560–67; *LW* 36:106–17; *Contra Henricum Regem Angliae,* 1522 (*WA* 10ᴵᴵ:220f.); *Concerning the Ministry,* 1523 (*WA* 12:169–96; *LW* 40:3–44); *Instructions for the Visitors of Parish Pastors in Electoral Saxony,* 1528 (*WA* 26:235; *LW* 40:313); *The Private Mass and the Consecration of Priests,* 1533 (*WA* 38:236–56; *LW* 38:194–214); *On the Councils and the Church,* 1539 (*WA* 50:632–34; *LW* 41:154–56); Letter from Capito to Luther, June 13, 1536 (*WABr* 7:432); *The Ordination of Ministers of the Word,* 1539 (*LW* 43:187–211); *The Private Mass and the Consecration of Priests,* 1533 (*WA* 38:220f.); *Predigt am Sonntag Exaudi,* May 9, 1535 (*WA* 41:240–42); *Predigt am Mittwoch nach Lucä,* October 20, 1535 (*WA* 41:457f.).

papacy. AC 28; ACAp 7, 23–31; ACAp 15, 18–42; ACAp 28, 12–27; SA II, 4; SA III, 3, 24–27; SA III, 10; SA III, 12; Tr. Cf. also *Explanations of the 95 Theses,* 1518 (*WA* 1:571; *LW* 31:152f.); Letter from Luther to George Spalatin, November 25, 1518 (*WABRr* 1:253; *LW* 48:93–94); *Proceedings at Augsburg,* 1518 (*WA* 2:20; *LW* 31:280f.); *The Leipzig Debate,* 1519 (*WA* 2:161; *LW* 31:318); *Resolutio Lutheriana super propositione XIII. de potestate* *papae,* 1519 (*WA* 2:183, 225, 236); *Sermon Preached in the Castle at Leipzig on the Day of St. Peter and St. Paul,* Matthew 16:13-19, June 29, 1519 (*WA* 2:248; *LW* 51:59); Letter from Luther to Hieronymus Dungersheim, December 1519 (*WABr* 1:567); Letter from Luther to Hieronymus Dungersheim, December 1519 (*WABr* 1:601–3); Letter from Justus Jonas to Luther (*WABr* 5:432); *Disputatio I. Eccii et M. Lutheri Lipsiae habita,* 1519 (*WA* 2:255, 258, 264); *Resolutiones Lutherianae super propositionibus suis Lipsiae disputatis,* 1519 (*WA* 2:397f., 432–35); *Contra malignum I. Eccii iudicium M. Lutheri defensio,* 1519 (*WA* 2:628–42); *On the Papacy in Rome, Against the Most Celebrated Romanist in Leipzig,* 1520 (*WA* 6:285, 287; *LW* 39:49, 57f.); *Epitoma responsionis ad Martin Luther,* 1520 (*WA* 6:328–48); *To the Christian Nobility of the German Nation concerning the Reform of the Christian Estate,* 1520 (*WA* 6:425f., 435; *LW* 44:152f., 166); *The Babylonian Captivity of the Church,* 1520 (*WA* 6:497f.; *LW* 36:11f.); *Assertio omnium articulorum M. Lutheri per bullam Leonis X,* 1520 (*WA* 7:127–31); *Warum des Papstes und seiner Jünger Bücher von D. Martin Luther verbrannt sind,* 1520 (*WA* 7:176); *Answer to the Hyperchristian, Hyperspiritual and Hyperlearned Book by Goat Emser in Leipzig—Including Some Thoughts regarding His Companion, the Fool Murner,* 1521 (*WA* 7:630$_{34}$–631$_3$; *LW* 39:153–55); *Passional Christi und Antichristi,* 1521 (*WA* 9:703); *Defense and Explanation of All Articles,* 1521 (*WA* 7:409, 411; *LW* 32:68f.); *Ad librum eximii Magistri Nostri Magistri Ambrosii Catharini, defensoris Silvestri Prieratis acerrimi, responsio,* 1521 (*WA* 7:705–78); *Contra Henricum Regem Angliae,* 1522 (*WA* 10^{II}:197); *Antwort deutsch auf König Heinrichs Buch,* 1522 (*WA* 10^{II}:241); *Confession concerning Christ's Supper,* 1528 (*WA* 26:506; *LW* 37:366f.); *Concerning Rebaptism,* 1528 (*WA* 26:152f.; *LW* 40:237f.); Letter from Justus Jonas to Luther, June, 1530 (*WABr* 5:432); *The Keys,* 1530 (*WA* 30^{II}: 488; *LW* 40:353f.); *Vorrede zu R. Barns, Vitae Romanorum pontificum,* 1536 (*WA* 50:4); *Einer aus den hohen Artikeln des päpstlichen Glaubens,* 1537 (*WA* 50:78, 83, 84, 86$_{15–22}$, 87); *Epistola Sancti Hieronymi ad Evagrium de potestate papae,* 1538 (*WA* 50:341–43); *The Three Symbols or Creeds of the Christian Faith,* 1538 (*WA* 50:269; *LW* 34:210f.); *On the Councils and the Church,* 1539 (*WA* 50:578; *LW* 41:90); *Luthers Vorrede über den Propheten Daniel,* 1545 (*WADB* 11^{II}:528f.); *Against the Roman Papacy, an Institution of the Devil,* 1545 (*WA* 54:209, 227, 229f., 235, 236, 243; *LW* 41:266, 288, 291f., 298, 307f.).

penance. Peter Lombard (d. 1160) taught a threefold understanding of penance (*contritio cordis, confessio oris, satisfactio operis*). *Sermo de indulgentiis pridie Dedicationis,* ca. 1514–17 (*WA* 1:98); Lectures on Romans, 1515 (*WA* 56:311–13; *LW* 25:298–300); Lectures on Romans, 1515 (*WA* 56:1; *WA*

57:5, *LW* 25:3; Wilhelm Pauck, ed., *Luther: Lectures on Romans* [Philadelphia: Westminster Press, 1961], 3); *Ein Sermon von Ablass und Gnade*, 1517 (*WA* 1:243); *Sermo de poenitentia*, 1518 (*WA* 1:319); *Adversus execrabilem Antichristi bullam*, 1520 (*WA* 6:610); *Wider die Bulle des Endechrists*, 1520 (*WA* 6:624f.); *Assertio omnium articulorum M. Lutheri per bullam Leonis X*, 1520 (*WA* 7:112f.); *Defense and Explanation of All Articles*, 1521 (*WA* 7:351–55; *LW* 32:32–38); *Predigten des Jahres 1531*, Nr. 31, April 11 (*WA* 34¹:301–10); *Against the Thirty-Two Articles of the Louvain Theologians*, 1545 (*WA* 54:427, 436; *LW* 34:355–57). See **repentance.**

pilgrimages. AC 20, 3; AC 25, 6; ACAp 12, 13–16, 145–47; ACAp 20, 8; ACAp 21, 16, 37; SA II, 2, 18. Cf. also *Decem praecepta Wittenbergensi praedicata populo*, 1518 (*WA* 1:422–24); *To the Christian Nobility of the German Nation concerning the Reform of the Christian Estate*, 1520 (*WA* 6:437f., 447f.; *LW* 44:269ff., 185f.); *Crucigers Sommerpostille, Epistel am 22 Sonntag nach Trinitatis (Philippians 1:3-11)*, 1537 (*WA* 22:36023); *Excurs* to *Exhortation to All Clergy Assembled at Augsburg* (*WA* 30ᴵᴵ:253f.; *Exhortation to All Clergy Assembled at Augsburg* (*WA* 30ᴵᴵ:296f; *LW* 34:25f.); *Against Hanswurst*, 1541 (*WA* 51:489₂₅ff.; *LW* 41:200); *WATR* 1:1157.

prayer to saints. AC 21; ACAp 7, 22–28; ACAp 21; ACAp 27, 50–57; SA II, 2, 24; Tr 47, LC I, 11–15; LC I, 91, 92. Cf. also *Decem praecepta Wittenbergensi praedicata populo*, 1518 (*WA* 1:411–26); *Doctor Martinus Luther Augustiners Unterricht auff etlich Artickell, die im von seynen abgunnern auff gelegt und zu gemessen Wuerden*, 1519 (*WA* 2:69f.); *A Sermon on Preparing to Die*, 1519 (*WA* 2:696f.; *LW* 42:113f.); Lecture on Psalm 84, 1513–16 (*WA* 3:647; *LW* 11:142f.); *Adventspostille: Epistel am 2. Adventssonntag*, 1522 (*WA* 10¹,²:82–84); *Epistel oder unterricht von den heiligen*, 1522 (*WA* 10ᴵᴵ:165f.); *The Adoration of the Sacrament*, 1523 (*WA* 11:451f.; *LW* 36:299f.); *Wider den neuen Abgott und alten Teufel, der zu Meissen soll erhoben werden*, 1524 (*WA* 15:192–98); *Confession concerning Christ's Supper*, 1528 (*WA* 26:508₁₃₋₁₆; *LW* 37:370); *On Translating, An Open Letter*, 1530 (*WA* 30ᴵᴵ:643–45; *LW* 35:198–201); Luther an Propst, Dekan und Kanoniker des Allerheiligenstifts zu Wittenberg, August 19, 1523 (*WABr* 3:131f.); *WATR* 3:3695; *WATR* 4:4153, 4779; *WATR* 5:5267f.

purgatory. ACAp 12, 13, 118, 134–39, 156, 167, 174–75; 24, 89–90; SA II, 2, 7, 12, 13, 14; SA III, 3, 21, 22, 26, 27. *Sermone habito Domin. X post Trinit.*, 1517 (*WA* 1:65); *The Disputation on the Power and Efficacy of Indulgences* (the Ninety-five Theses), 1517 (*WA* 1:233; *LW* 31:26); *Ein Sermon von Ablass und Gnade*, 1517 (*WA* 1:246); *Explanations of the Ninety-Five Theses*, 1518 (*WA* 1:555, 586; *LW* 31:125ff., 178); *Doctor Martinus Luther Augustiners Unterricht auff etlich Artickell, die im von seynen abgunnern auff gelegt* *und zu gemessen Wuerden* (*WA* 2:70); *Disputatio I. Eccii et M. Lutheri Lipsiae habita*, 1519 (*WA* 2:322–44); *Defense and Explanation of All Articles*, 1521 (*WA* 7:451–55; *LW* 32:95–97); *De abroganda missa privata Martini Lutheri sententia*, 1521 (*WA* 8:452ff.); *The Misuse of the Mass*, 1521 (*WA* 8:531, *LW* 36:190f.); *Kirchenpostille: Evangelium am Tage der heiligen drei Könige (Matth. 2:1-12)*, 1522 (*WA* 10^{II}:588f.); *The Adoration of the Sacrament* (*WA* 11:451; *LW* 36:299; *Sermon auf das Evangelium Luc. 16. Von dem reichen Manne und dem armen Lazarus*, June 7, 1523 (*WA* 12:596); *Confession concerning Christ's Supper*, 1528 (*WA* 26:508; *LW* 37:369f.); *Widerruf vom Fegefeuer*, 1530 (*WA* 30^{II}:367–90); *Dr. Martin Luther's Warning to His Dear German People*, 1531 (*WA* 30^{III}:309; *LW* 47:41f.); Letter from Luther to George Spalatin, November 7, 1519 (*WABr* 1:553); Letter from Luther to Nicholas von Amsdorf, January 13, 1522 (*WABr* 2:422; *LW* 48:362f.); *WATR* 3, Nr. 3695.

real presence. AC 10, 12; ACAp 10, 12; SA II, 2; SA III, 6; SC V; LC IV, 54–55; LC V; FCEp 7; FCSD 7. *Against the Heavenly Prophets in the Matter of Images and Sacraments*, 1525 (*WA* 18:170–75; *LW* 40:180–85); *That These Words of Christ, "This is My Body" Still Stand Firm against the Fanatics*, 1527 (*WA* 23:251; *LW* 37:130); *Confession concerning Christ's Supper*, 1528 (*WA* 26:506; *LW* 37:367f.); Letter from Luther to Martin Bucer, January 22, 1531 (*WABr* 6:25; *LW* 50:6f.); Letter from Luther to the Evangelicals in Venice, Vicenza, Treviso, June 13, 1543 (*WABr* 10:331).

rebaptism. *Concerning Rebaptism*, 1528 (*WA* 26:154–66; *LW* 40:239–54).

relics. SA II, 2, 22; LC I, 91; *Excurs* to *Exhortation to All Clergy Assembled at Augsburg*, 1530 (*WA* 30^{II}:254, 265f.); *Exhortation to All Clergy Assembled at Augsburg*, 1530 (*WA* 30^{II}:297$_{18}$, 298$_{17ff.}$, 348$_{29}$; *LW* 47:25, 27, 54); *Dr. Martin Luther's Warning to His Dear German People*, 1531 (*WA* 30^{III}:315$_{24ff.}$; *LW* 47:50); *The Last Sermon, Preached in Eisleben*, February 15, 1546 (*WA* 51:193$_{15f.}$; *LW* 51:390f.); *Neue Zeitung vom Rhein*, 1542 (*WA* 53:404f.); *WATR* 2:1272, 2399, 2638; *WATR* 3:3637b, 3785, 3867; *WATR* 4:4391, 4721, 4921, 4925; *WATR* 5:5484, 5844, 5853, 6466, 6469.

remorse, penitential. *Sermo de poenitentia*, 1518 (*WA* 1:319–22); *Decem praecepta Wittenbergensi praedicata populo*, 1518 (*WA* 1:446); *The Babylonian Captivity of the Church*, 1520 (*WA* 6:544f.; *LW* 36:84); *Assertio omnium articulorum M. Lutheri per bullam Leonis X*, 1520 (*WA* 7:113–17); *Defense and Explanation of All Articles*, 1521 (*WA* 7:355–67; *LW* 32:34–38).

repentance. AC 12; ACAp 12; SA III, 3; LC IV, 77–88; FCSD 5, 7ff. *Lectures on Romans*, 1515 (*WA* 56:311–13; *LW* 25:298–300); *Lectures on Romans*, 1515 (*WA* 56:1; *WA* 57:5; *LW* 25:3); Pauck, *Luther: Lectures on Romans*, 3; *Sermo de indulgentiis pridie Dedicationis*, ca. 1514–17 (*WA* 1:98f.); *The Disputa-*

tion on the Power and Efficacy of Indulgences (the Ninety-five Theses), 1517 (*WA* 1:233; *LW* 31:25f.); *Ein Sermon von Ablass und Gnade*, 1517 (*WA* 1:243–46); *Sermo de poenitentia*, 1518 (*WA* 1:319–24); Letter from Luther to John von Staupitz, May 30, 1518 (*WA* 1:525f.; *LW* 48:65f.); *Explanations of the Disputation concerning the Value of Indulgences*, 1518 (*WA* 1:530f.: *LW* 31:84f.); *Ad dialogum Silvestri Prieratis de potestate papae responsio*, 1518 (*WA* 1:648ff.); *The Leipzig Debate*, 1519 (*WA* 2:160; *LW* 31:317); *Disputatio I. Eccii et M. Lutheri Lipsiae habita*, 1519 (*WA* 2:359–83); *The Sacrament of Penance*, 1519 (*WA* 2:713–23; *LW* 35:3–22); *The Babylonian Captivity of the Church*, 1520 (*WA* 6:543–49; *LW* 36:81–91); *Against the Heavenly Prophets in the Matter of Images and Sacraments*, 1525 (*WA* 18:65; *LW* 40:82f.); *WA* 24:448$_{5f.}$; *WA* 30^{II}:288–92; *Sommerpostille am 1. Sonntag nach Ostern*, 1526 (*WA* 10^{1,2}:233$_{15–18}$); Lectures on Zechariah, 1526 (*WA* 13:662$_{5–7}$; *LW* 20:142); *Predigten des Jahres 1531*, Nr. 31, April 11 (*WA* 34^{I}:301–10); Lectures on Galatians, 1535 (*WA* 40^{II}:86$_{12}$–87$_{3}$; *LW* 27:68f.); *Matth. 18–24 in Predigten ausgelegt*, 1537–40 (*WA* 47:326$_{16–19}$); Sermons on the Gospel of St. John, Chapters 1–4, 1537 (*WA* 46:781$_{8–25}$; *LW* 22:266f.); *Die Thesen gegen die Antinomer*, 1538 (*WA* 39^{I}:345–47, 350); *WATR* 1:121; *WATR* 3:3777. See **penance.**

right hand of God. TCS I, 2; SA I, 4.

Sacrament of the Altar. AC 10, 12; ACAp 10, 12; SA II, 2; SA III, 6; SC V; LC IV, 54–55; LC V; FCEp 7; FCSD 7. *The Blessed Sacrament of the Holy and True Body of Christ, and the Brotherhoods*, 1519 (*WA* 2:742–54; *LW* 35:49–67); *The Babylonian Captivity of the Church*, 1520 (*WA* 6:508, 511; *LW* 36:28f., 34); The Sixth Sermon, Friday after Invocavit, March 14, 1522 (*WA* 10^{III}:48–54; *LW* 51:92–95); The Seventh Sermon, Saturday before Reminiscere, March 15, 1522 (*WA* 10^{III}:55–58; *LW* 51:95–96); *The Adoration of the Sacrament*, 1523 (*WA* 11:432–43; *LW* 36:275–89); *Letter to the Christians at Strassburg in Opposition to the Fanatic Spirit*, 1524 (*WA* 15:394f.; *LW* 40:65f.); *Predigt am Palmsonntage*, March 20, 1524 (*WA* 15:490–97); *Against the Heavenly Prophets in the Matter of Images and Sacraments*, 1525 (*WA* 18:101–25, 134–200; *LW* 40:118–43, 144–209); *Erste Vorrede zum Schwäbischen Syngramm*, 1526 (*WA* 19:457–61); *The Sacrament of the Body and Blood of Christ against the Fanatics*, 1526 (*WA* 19:482–512; *LW* 36:329–61); *Register über sämtliche Predigten* (*WA* 22:lxxxviif.); *That These Words of Christ, "This is My Body" Still Stand Firm against the Fanatics*, 1527 (*WA* 23:64–283; *LW* 37:3–150); *Confession concerning Christ's Supper*, 1528 (*WA* 26:261–498, 506; *LW* 37: 161–360, 366f.); *Admonition concerning the Sacrament of the Body and Blood of Our Lord*, 1530 (*WA* 30^{II}:595–626; *LW* 38:91–137; *The Schwabach Articles*, 1529 (*WA* 30^{III}:89; trans. in Reu, *The Augsburg*

Confession, 2:44f.); *The Marburg Colloquy and the Marburg Articles*, 1529 (*WA* 30ᴵᴵᴵ:110–59, 169f.; *LW* 38:15–85, 88f.); *Sendschreiben an die zu Frankfurt a.M.*, 1533 (*WA* 30ᴵᴵᴵ:558–65); *Glossae D. Martini Lutheri super sententias patrum*, 1534 (*WA* 38:298f.); *On the Councils and the Church*, 1539 (*WA* 50:631; *LW* 41:152); *Brief Confession concerning the Holy Sacrament*, 1544 (*WA* 54:161–67; *LW* 38:311); *Against the Thirty-Two Articles of the Louvain Theologians*, 1545 (*WA* 54:426; *LW* 34:354f.); *Letzte Streitschrift (contra asinos Parisienses Lovaniensesque)*, 1545/46 (*WA* 54:452).

saints. ACAp 22, 32–34; SA II, 2, 25–28; LC I, 11. Luther's *Fourteen Consolations*, 1519–20, which was revised by Luther and reissued in 1536 (*WA* 6:99–134; *LW* 42:117–66); *Quaestio de viribus et voluntate hominis sine gratia disputata*, 1516 (*WA* 1:150); *Decem praecepta Wittenbergensi praedicata populo*, 1518 (*WA* 1:412–16); Letter from Luther to George Spalatin, December 31, 1516 (*WABr* 1, 82f.).

satisfaction, penitential. ACAp 12, 13–16, 24. Cf. also *Ex Sermone habito Domin. X. post Trinit.*, 1516 (*WA* 1:65–69); *Sermo de indulgentiis pridie Dedicationis*, ca. 1514–17 (*WA* 1:98); *The Disputation on the Power and Efficacy of Indulgences* (the Ninety-five Theses), 1517 (*WA* 1:233; *LW* 31:25f.); *Ein Sermon von Ablass und Gnade*, 1517 (*WA* 1:243f.); *Sermon de poenitentia*, 1518 (*WA* 1:324); *Eine Freiheit des Sermons päpstlichen Ablass und Gnade belangend*, 1518 (*WA* 1:383–86); *The Babylonian Captivity of the Church*, 1520 (*WA* 6:548f.; *LW* 36:89f.); *Adversus execrabilem Antichristi bullam*, 1520 (*WA* 6:610); *Wider die Bulle des Endechrists*, 1520 (*WA* 6:624f.); *Against Hanswurst*, 1541 (*WA* 51:487f.; *LW* 41:199f.).

schools. *See* **education.**

sin. AC 2; AC 18; AC 19; ACAp 2; ACAp 18; SA III, 1; FCEp 1; FCEp 2; FCSD 1. *Lectures on Romans*, 1515 (*WA* 56:51ff., 309f.; 311–13; *LW* 25:44ff., 298–300); Lectures on Romans, 1515 (*WA* 56:1; *WA* 57:5; *LW* 25:3; Pauck, *Luther: Lectures on Romans*, 3). *Sermo in Die sancti Matthaei*, ca. 1514–17 (*WA* 1:86); *Sermo Die Circumcisionis*, ca. 1514–17 (*WA* 1:121); *Quaestio de viribus et voluntate homininis sine gratia disputata*, 1516 (*WA* 1:145ff.); *Disputation against Scholastic Theology*, 1517 (*WA* 1:224; *LW* 31:9f.); *Sermo de poenitentia*, 1518 (*WA* 1:324); *Explanations of the Disputation concerning the Value of Indulgences*, 1518 (*WA* 1:544; *LW* 31:105f.); *Heidelberg Disputation*, 1518 (*WA* 1:354; 359f.; *LW* 31:40f., 47ff.); *The Leipzig Debate*, 1519 (*WA* 2:161; *LW* 31:318); *Sermon Preached in the Castle at Leipzig on the Day of St. Peter and St. Paul*, Matthew 16:13-19, June 29, 1519 (*WA* 2:246f.; *LW* 51:56f.); *Ein Sermon gepredigt zu Leipzig auf dem Schloss am Tage Petri und Pauli*, 1519 (*WA* 2:424–26); *Assertio omnium articulorum M. Lutheri per bullam Leonis X*, 1520 (*WA* 7:142–49); *Adversus execrabilem Antichristi bul-*

lam, 1520 (*WA* 6:608); *Wider die Bulle des Endechrists*, 1520 (*WA* 6:622); *Defense and Explanation of All Articles*, 1521 (*WA* 7:445–51; *LW* 32:92–94); *Adventspostille*, 1522 (*WA* $10^{1,2}$:$28_{20–26}$; *Fastenpostille*, 1525 (*WA* 17^{II}:80); *The Bondage of the Will*, 1525 (*WA* 18:600–787; *LW* 33:3–295); *Confession concerning Christ's Supper*, 1528 (*WA* 26:502f.; *LW* 37:362f.); *The Schwabach Articles*, 1529 (*WA* 30^{III}:87f.; *The Marburg Articles*, 1529 (*WA* 30^{III}:162f.; *LW* 38:85f.); *Commentary on the Alleged Imperial Edict*, 1531 (*WA* 30^{III}:359–64; *LW* 34:87–89); *Commentary on Psalm 50*, 1532 (1538) (*WA* 40^{II}:383f.: *LW* 12:350f.); *The Disputation concerning Justification*, 1536 (*WA* 39^{I}:84, 110–18; *LW* 34:153f., 179–87); *Commentary on Psalm 51*, 1538 (*WA* 40^{II}:322–25; *LW* 12:308–10); Thomas Aquinas, *Summa theologiae*, II, 1, Question 82, Article 3.

tradition. *See* **human regulations.**

vocation. *See* **ordination.**

vows, monastic. AC 27, ACAp 27; SA II, 3; SA III, 3, 28; SA III, 14. Cf. also *WA* 2:735f.; *WA* 6:440, 538–42; *WA* 7:625; *WA* 8:323–35; *Judgment of Martin Luther on Monastic Vows*, 1521 (*WA* 8:577–669; *LW* 44:243–400); *Kirchenpostille 1522, Gal. 3:23-29*, New Year's Day (*WA* $10^{1,1}$:481–98); *The Gospel for the Festival of the Epiphany, Matthew 2:1-12*, 1522 (*WA* $10^{1,1}$:681–709; *LW* 52:250–74); *An Answer to Several Questions on Monastic Vows*, 1526 (*WA* 19:287–93; *LW* 46:139–54); Letter from Luther to Philip Melanchthon, August 1, 1521 (*WABr* 2:370f.; *LW* 48:277–82); Letter from Luther to Philip Melanchthon, August 3, 1521 (*WABr* 2:374f.; *LW* 48:284f.); Letter from Luther to Philip Melanchthon, September 9, 1521 (*WABr* 2:382–85; *LW* 48:296–304); *To the Christian Nobility of the German Nation concerning the Reform of the Christian Estate*, 1520 (*WA* 6:440$_{5f}$; *LW* 44:174); *The Babylonian Captivity of the Church*, 1520 (*WA* 6:539$_{16–19}$; *LW* 36:75f.); Lectures on Deuteronomy, 1525 (*WA* 14:624–26; *LW* 9:83f.); Lectures on Isaiah, 1527–29 (*WA* 25:186$_{22–25}$; *LW* 16:227f.); *Exhortation to All Clergy Assembled at Augsburg*, 1530 (*WA* 30^{II}:300$_{26–28}$; *LW* 34:27f.); *Predigt am 2. Sonntag nach Epiphaniä*, January 15, 1531 (*WA* 34^{I}:92$_{4f}$); *Kleine Antwort*, 1533 (*WA* 38:148–58); *The Private Mass and the Consecration of Priests*, 1533 (*WA* 38:226$_{11}$f.; *LW* 38:183); *WA* 45:524$_{10}$f.; *LW* 24:); *Predigt in Halle gehalten*, January 6, 1546 (*WA* 51:113$_{5f}$); *Against Hanswurst*, 1541 (*WA* 51:487$_{24–28}$; *LW* 41:199); *Against the Roman Papacy, an Institution of the Devil*, 1545 (*WA* 54:266$_{18–22}$; *LW* 41:336); Thomas Aquinas, *Summa theologiae*, II, 2, Question 189, Article 3.

Wittenberg Concord. A compromise statement on Protestant understandings of the sacraments. Representatives of both the southern and the northern German Protestants signed WC at Wittenberg in May of 1536.

WC played an important role in the historical context surrounding the formulation of SA.

Word of God. Galatians 1:8. FCEp, Introduction, 1. *Ein Sermon gepredigt zu Leipzig auf dem Schloss am Tage Petri und Pauli,* 1519 (*WA* 2:427₈ff.); *Assertio omnium articulorum M. Lutheri per bullam Leonis X,* 1520 (*WA* 7:131–33); and *Defense and Explanation of All Articles,* 1521 (*WA* 7:423–27; *LW* 32:76–79); Sermons on the Gospel of John, Chapters 1–4, 1537 (*WA* 46:781; *LW* 22:266).

Bibliography

Ahlstrom, Sydney E. *A Religious History of the American People.* Vol. 1. Garden City, N.Y.: Image Books, 1975.

Aland, Kurt. *Hilfsbuch zum Lutherstudium.* Witten: Luther-Verlag, 1970.

Allbeck, Willard D. *Studies in the Lutheran Confessions.* Philadelphia: Muhlenberg Press, 1952.

Althaus, Paul. *The Theology of Martin Luther.* Translated by Robert C. Schultz. Philadelphia: Fortress Press, 1966.

Badcock, Francis J. *The History of the Creeds.* 2nd ed. London: SPCK, 1938.

Bainton, Roland H. *Here I Stand: A Life of Martin Luther.* Nashville: Abingdon-Cokesbury Press, 1950.

Barraclough, Geoffrey. *The Medieval Papacy.* New York: W. W. Norton, 1968.

Bente, Friedrich, ed. *Concordia Triglotta.* St. Louis: Concordia Publishing House, 1921.

———. *Historical Introductions to the Book of Concord.* St. Louis: Concordia Publishing House, 1965.

———. *The Smalcald Articles: A Reprint from the "Concordia Triglotta" in Commemoration of the Four-Hundredth Anniversary of the Presentation of This Confession of the Lutheran Church at Schmalkalden, Germany, in 1537.* St. Louis: Concordia Publishing House, 1937.

Bizer, Ernst. "Zum geschichtlichen Verständnis von Luthers Schmalkaldischen Artikeln." *ZKG* 67 (1955–56).

———. "Noch einmal: Die Schmalkaldischen Artikel." *ZKG* 68 (1957): 287–94.

———. "Die Wittenberger Theologen und das Konzil 1537." *Archiv für Reformationsgeschichte* 47 (1956): 77–101.

Boehmer, Heinrich. *Martin Luther: Road to Reformation.* Cleveland: World Publishing Co., 1967.

Bouman, Walter. "The Gospel and the Smalcald Articles." *Concordia Theological Quarterly* 40 (Summer 1969): 87–98.

Brecht, Martin. *Martin Luther: His Road to Reformation, 1483–1521.* Philadelphia: Fortress Press, 1985.

———. *Martin Luther: Shaping and Defining the Reformation, 1521–1532.* Minneapolis: Fortress Press, 1990.

————. *Martin Luther: The Preservation of the Church, 1532–1546.* Minneapolis: Fortress Press, 1992.

Brecht, Martin, and Reinhard Schwarz, eds. *Bekenntnis und Einheit der Kirche.* Stuttgart: Calwer Verlag, 1980.

Briggs, C. A. *Theological Symbolics.* New York: Charles Scribner's Sons, 1914.

Brunstäd, Friedrich. *Theologie der Lutherischen Bekenntnisschriften.* Gütersloh: C. Bertelsmann Verlag, 1951.

Buchwald, Georg. "Luther-kalendarium." *Schriften des Vereins für Reformationsgeschichte* 47, Heft 2 (Nr. 147), 1929.

Carpzov, Johann Benedict. *Isagoge in libros ecclesiarum lutheranarum symbolicos.* Leipzig, 1665.

Cipolla, Carlo M. *The Economic History of World Population.* Baltimore: Penguin Books, 1962.

Clarkson, John, et al. *The Church Teaches.* St. Louis: Herder Book Co., 1955.

Clemen, Otto C. *Georg Helts Briefwechsel.* Leipzig, 1907.

Ebeling, Gerhard. *Luther: An Introduction to His Thought.* Translated by R. A. Wilson. Philadelphia: Fortress Press, 1972.

————. "Hundert Jahre Weimarer Lutherausgabe." *Lutherjahrbuch* 52 (1985).

Ebstein, Wilhelm. *Dr. Martin Luthers Krankheiten.* Stuttgart: Verlag von Ferdinand Enke, 1908.

Edwards, Mark U. *Luther's Last Battles.* Ithaca, N.Y.: Cornell University Press, 1983.

Fast, Heinold. *Der linke Flügel der Reformation.* Bremen: C. Schünemann, 1962.

Forell, George. *Faith Active in Love.* Minneapolis: Augsburg Publishing House, 1959.

Forell, George, and James McCue, eds. *Confessing One Faith.* Minneapolis: Augsburg Publishing House, 1981.

Gieschen, Gerhard. "The Smalcald Articles." In *The Encyclopedia of the American Lutheran Church.* Minneapolis: Augsburg Publishing House, 1967.

Gilbert, Creighton. "When Did a Man in the Renaissance Grow Old?" *Studies in the Renaissance* 14 (1967).

Gritsch, Eric W., and Robert W. Jenson. *Lutheranism: The Theological Movement and Its Confessional Writings.* Philadelphia: Fortress Press, 1976.

Haile, H. G. *Luther: An Experiment in Biography.* Princeton: Princeton University Press, 1980.

Harrisville, Roy. *Ministry in Crisis.* Minneapolis: Augsburg Publishing House, 1987.

Hendrix, Scott. "Urbanus Rhegius and the Augsburg Confession." *SCJ* 11, no. 3 (1980): 62–74.

Hillerbrand, Hans, ed. *Radical Tendencies in the Reformation: Divergent Per-*

spectives. Sixteenth Century Essays and Studies, vol. 9. Kirksville, Mo.: Sixteenth Century Journal Publications, 1986.

Jacobs, Henry E., ed. *The Book of Concord*. 2 vols. Philadelphia: United Lutheran Publication House, 1888.

Kittelson, James M. *Luther the Reformer*. Minneapolis: Augsburg Publishing House, 1986.

Klotsche, E. H. *Christian Symbolics*. Burlington, Iowa: Lutheran Literary Board, 1929.

Kolde, Theodor. *Historische Einleitung in die symbolischen Bücher der evangelisch-lutherischen Kirche, deutsch und lateinisch*. Besorgt von J. T. Müller. Gütersloh: C. Bertelsmann Verlag, 1912.

————, ed. *Analecta Lutherana*. Gotha: Friedrich Andreas Perthes, 1883.

Köstlin, Julius T. and Gustav Kawerau. *Martin Luther: Sein Leben und seine Schriften*. 2 vols. Berlin: Verlag von Alexander Duncker, 1903.

Krauth, C. P. *The Conservative Reformation and Its Theology*. Reprint, Minneapolis: Augsburg Publishing House, 1963.

Küchenmeister, F. *Dr. Martin Luthers Krankengeschichte*. Leipzig, 1881.

Lau, Franz. "Luthers Schmalkaldische Artikel als eine Einführung in seine Theologie." *ZTK* 18 (December 1937).

Lindberg, Carter. *Martin Luther: Justified by Grace*. Nashville: Graded Press, 1988.

————, ed. *Piety, Politics, and Ethics: Reformation Studies in Honor of George Wolfgang Forell*. Kirksville, Mo.: Sixteenth Century Journal Publishers, 1984.

Lohff, Wenzel, and Lewis W. Spitz, eds. *Widerspruch, Dialog und Einigung*. Stuttgart: Calwer Verlag, 1977.

Lohse, Bernhard. *Martin Luther: An Introduction to His Life and Work*. Translated by Robert C. Schultz. Philadelphia: Fortress Press, 1986.

Manns, Peter, and Harding Meyer, eds. *Luther's Ecumenical Significance*. Philadelphia: Fortress Press, 1984.

Maurer, Wilhelm. *Historical Commentary on the Augsburg Confession*. Translated by H. George Anderson. Philadelphia: Fortress Press, 1986.

McDonough, Thomas. *The Law and the Gospel in Luther*. London: Oxford University Press, 1963.

Meuser, Fredrick, ed. *Interpreting Luther's Legacy*. Minneapolis: Augsburg Publishing House, 1969.

Müller, Gerhard. "Luthers theologisches Testament." *Lutherische Monatshefte* 26 (1987).

Müller, Johann Tobias, ed. *Die symbolischen Bücher der evangelisch-lutherischen Kirche*. Gütersloh: C. Bertelsmann Verlag, 1912.

Nestingen, James. *Roots of Our Faith*. Minneapolis: Augsburg Publishing House, 1976.

Neve, Jürgen L. *Introduction to the Symbolical Books of the Lutheran Church*. 2nd rev. ed. Columbus, Ohio: Lutheran Book Concern, 1926.

Oberman, Heiko. *Luther: Mensch zwischen Gott und Teufel*. Berlin: Severin & Siedler, 1982.

―――. "*Teufelsdreck*: Eschatology and Scatology in the 'Old' Luther." *SCJ* 19, no. 3 (Fall 1988).

Pinomaa, Lennart. *Der existentielle Charakter der Theologie Luthers*. Helsinki: Finnische Akademie der Wissenschaften, 1940.

Pipping, Heinrich. *Historisch-theologische Einleitung zu denen sämtlichen gewöhnlichsten symbolischen Schrifften der Evangelisch-Lutherischen Kirchen*. Leipzig, 1703.

Plass, E., ed. *What Luther Says*. St. Louis: Concordia Publishing House, 1986.

Preus, Robert. *Getting into the Theology of Concord*. St. Louis: Concordia Publishing House, 1977.

Reiter, Paul J. *Martin Luthers Umwelt, Charakter und Psychose*. Vol. 2. Copenhagen: Ejnar Munksgaard, 1941.

Reu, Michael. *The Augsburg Confession*. Chicago: Wartburg Publishing House, 1930.

―――. *Luther's Small Catechism*. Chicago: Wartburg Publishing House, 1929.

Reumann, John. *Ministry Examined*. Minneapolis: Augsburg Publishing House, 1987.

Ritschl, Albrecht. *A Critical History of the Christian Doctrine of Justification and Reconciliation*. Edinburgh: Edmonston and Douglas, 1874.

Rupp, Gordon E. *Luther's Progress to the Diet of Worms*. New York: Harper & Row, 1964.

Sander, F. "Geschichtliche Einleitung zu den Schmalkaldischen Artikeln." *Jahrbücher für deutsche Theologie* 20 (1875).

Scaer, David. *Getting into the Story of Concord*. St. Louis: Concordia Publishing House, 1977.

Schaff, Philip. *The Creeds of Christendom*. Vol. 1. New York: Harper & Brothers, 1919.

Schirrmacher, Friedrich Wilhelm. *Briefe und Acten zu der Geschichte des Religionsgespräches zu Marburg 1529 und des Reichtages zu Augsburg 1530*. Amsterdam: Verlag B. R. Grüner, 1968.

Schlink, Edmund. *Theology of the Lutheran Confessions*. Philadelphia: Fortress Press, 1961.

Schott, Erdmann. "Christus und die Rechtfertigung allein durch den Glauben in Luthers Schmalkaldischen Artikeln." *ZST* 22 (1953).

Schwiebert, Ernest G. *Luther and His Times.* St. Louis: Concordia Publishing House, 1950.

Spitz, Lewis W., and Wenzel Lohff, eds. *Discord, Dialogue, and Concord.* Philadelphia: Fortress Press, 1977.

Tappert, Theodore, ed. *Lutheran Confessional Theology in America 1840–1880.* New York: Oxford University Press, 1972.

Thieme, Karl. *Augsburgische Konfession.* Giessen, 1930.

———. *Luthers Testament wider Rom in seinen Schmalkaldischen Artikeln.* Leipzig: A. Deichert, 1900.

Todd, John M. *Luther: A Life.* New York: Crossroad, 1982.

van Dülmen, Andrea. *Luther-Chronik.* Munich: DTV, 1983.

Virck, Hans. "Zu den Beratungen der Protestanten über die Konzilsbulle vom 4. Juni 1536." *ZKG* 13 (1892).

Volz, Hans. *Luthers Schmalkaldische Artikel und Melanchthons Tractatus de potestate papae.* Gotha: Leopold Klotz Verlag, 1931.

———. *Urkunden und Aktenstücke zur Geschichte von Martin Luthers Schmalkaldischen Artikeln, 1536–1574.* Berlin: Walter de Gruyter, 1957.

———. "Zur Entstehungsgeschichte von Luthers Schmalkaldischen Artikeln." *ZKG* 73, no. 3–4 (1963).

———. "Luthers Schmalkaldischen Artikel." *ZKG* 68 (1957).

von Loewenich, Walther. *Martin Luther: The Man and His Work.* Translated by Lawrence W. Denef. Minneapolis: Augsburg Publishing House, 1986.

Walch, Johann Georg. *Christliches Concordienbuch.* Jena, 1750.

———, ed. *Dr. Martin Luthers sämtliche Schriften.* 23 vols. St. Louis: Concordia Publishing House, 1907.

Williams, George H. *The Radical Reformation.* Philadelphia: Westminster Press, 1962.

Willkomm, Martin. *Ein Vermächtnis Luthers an die Kirche.* Zwickau: Verlag von Johannes Herrmann, 1936.

Zangemeister, K. *Die Schmalkaldischen Artikel vom Jahre 1537.* Heidelberg: Carl Winter Universitätsbuchhandlung, 1886.

Index